D0221470

14 DAY BOOK
This book
th

WITHDRAWN

WITHDRAWN

3 0700 10852 0544

In Calmer Times

In Calmer Times

The Supreme Court
and Red Monday

Arthur J. Sabin

University of Pennsylvania Press

Philadelphia

Copyright © 1999 University of Pennsylvania Press
All rights reserved
Printed in the United States of America on acid-free paper

10 9 8 7 6 5 4 3 2 1

Published by
University of Pennsylvania Press
Philadelphia, Pennsylvania 19104-4011

Library of Congress Cataloging-in-Publication Data
Sabin, Arthur J., 1930–
In calmer times : the Supreme Court and Red Monday / Arthur J. Sabin.
p.   cm.
Includes bibliographical references and index.
ISBN 0-8122-3507-X (alk. paper)
1. Communist trials—United States.   2. Subversive activities—United
States—History.   3. Communism—United States—History.   I. Title.
KF221.C55S22   1999
364.1'31—dc21   99-27312
                                                                    CIP

Frontispiece. *The Smith Act.* Lithograph by Rockwell Kent. Artist and
political activist Rockwell Kent portrayed his reaction to the Supreme
Court decision in the *Dennis* case, which affirmed the conviction of
eleven national leaders of the Communist Party-USA for violation
of the Smith Act. Liberty is being burned at the stake. Books are being
burned and the dove of peace is being consumed. Reproduction courtesy
of the Rockwell Kent Legacies.

To Neal F. Sabin, Karen A. Gitles, and Alan E. Gitles,
and to Rachel, Benjamin, and Elaine Gitles,
with the hope that this book will help you understand
the importance of law in our lives and
in the life of our country.

In Memoriam

To my John Marshall Law School colleagues
Edward B. Arnolds, Melvin B. Lewis, and Robert Kratovil,
who were wonderful attorneys and who excelled
at professing the law.

Contents

Illustrations

Preface

The United States was victorious in the two world wars of the twentieth century; after each it was more powerful, more dominant, and more prosperous than before. Neither conflagration significantly touched the country's mainland; both were fought in distant lands where enemies or allies sustained the greatest combat losses. Death and destruction came only to American fighting personnel and war materiel, not to the civilian population or America's farms, towns, and cities. In all these respects, the American experience was unique.

Despite the nation's stunning victories, each world war left in its wake a significant Red Scare. Twice, national paranoia infected the one major warring power that had experienced the least disruption of its political, social, and economic foundations.

Among the institutions that continued to function during these wars —and to which the task of resolving major Red Scare issues fell—were the state and federal courts. Indeed, the decisions of the Supreme Court of the United States were to be of utmost importance in addressing those issues and in signaling to government prosecutors and lower courts whether the climate was favorable for punishing "subversive" individuals and organizations.

The origins of the Red Scares were manifold and the manifestations variegated. Many factors have been blamed, many causes unearthed, and many rationalizations given for the hunt for "Reds" following both world wars. One explanation is particularly noteworthy: the United States was the only nation that could afford to indulge in a Red Scare. Losing nations were forced, at least temporarily, to relinquish control of their destinies. The other victorious nations had to deal with healing their land and people, as well as establishing their peacetime political and economic structures. The irony is that the victor least affected by either war was the only one that engaged in a wide-ranging quest to expose internal enemies that were portrayed as a real threat to the survival of the country and its way of life.

This study concentrates on the second Red Scare era. Particularly, it addresses the federal government's attempt to prosecute political dissenters because of their alleged membership in the Communist Party or in other left-wing organizations or causes following World War II.

The Red Scare era after World War II affected most Americans in some way. The hunt for subversives made the front page of newspapers and was beamed into American homes via radio and through the new medium of television. More directly, millions of citizens had more intimate contact through loyalty oaths or security checks. Many were caught up in controversies concerning school board policies or in their church or temple's positions on Red Scare issues and personalities. Veterans' organizations and other groups took positions on the Red Scare from 1947 through the 1950s. "How do you stand on Senator McCarthy — for him — against him?" became an everyday issue before the American public from 1950 until his death in 1957. Even Hollywood idols and behind-the-scenes writers and directors were vulnerable to the demands of the House Un-American Activities Committee, a major venue for Red Scare action.

Just how deeply the Red Scare era has been etched in the public mind can be glimpsed by reading obituaries of the 1990s. Invariably, when the deceased was in some way (even peripherally) involved in some event, in some trial or with some controversial person of those times, that fact is highlighted. For example, an entire death notice published in the *Chicago Tribune* on August 3, 1997, reads:

Robert Warren Barnett, 85, U.S. diplomat; he was accused by Sen. Joseph McCarthy (R-Wis.) of being a communist sympathizer during the Red Scare of the 1950s but beat the charges; July 25 in Washington of cancer and pneumonia.

When a former president of the American Bar Association died on June 1, 1990, his obituary in the *American Bar Association Journal* published in August 1997 included this statement:

As chancellor of the Philadelphia Bar Association in 1953, [Bernard G.] Segal organized the legal defense for nine Philadelphians denounced as communists during the height of McCarthyism.

When a man described by William F. Buckley, Jr., as one who "may have been more McCarthyesque than the Senator himself" died, the obituary headline in the *New York Times* of January 2, 1997, read, "Robert J. Morris is Dead at 82; Crusader Against Communists." Morris was chief counsel to the Senate Judiciary Subcommittee on Internal Security from 1951 to 1953 and from 1956 to 1958.

The Red Scare was pervasive then and, more than forty years later, remains a highly controversial, pivotal, and defining era for this nation.

The specific focus of this book is why and how the Supreme Court began to substantially dismantle Red Scare prosecutions. The crucial point is June 17, 1957, dubbed "Red Monday," when four decisions were announced that significantly altered the course of legal history and the Red Scare. My aim is to examine what motivated a majority of the Court to move from routinely confirming guilty verdicts, and thus endorsing government prosecutions of leftists and other dissidents, to raising substantial legal barriers to further prosecutions.

More than a change in Court personnel was involved; the nation itself had changed by 1957. The Zeitgeist had shifted from an atmosphere that drove Congress, state legislatures, the federal executive branch, law enforcement, and even the media to seek signs of Red influence and subversion, to a calmer, more rational approach. Law and the courts mirror society, and when American culture shifted away from the intense Red Scare days of 1947 to 1954, so, too, did the Court.

More than Senator Joseph R. McCarthy, a leading player in Red Scare times was J. Edgar Hoover. McCarthy's power lasted some four years and was highly dependent on Hoover's guidance and assistance; when McCarthy fell out of favor with Hoover, the senator's fall was certain. Furthermore, Hoover was the link between the two major Red Scares of the century; he played a key role in both, and it may well be questioned whether the Red Scare following World War II would have taken place but for his crusading zeal, power, and tenacity. Thus, the involvement of Hoover and the FBI is a constant theme in this work. Looking at Hoover's personal reaction to Red Monday decisions and their precursors, it becomes evident that his was a most important response and one of enduring influence.

The story follows the history of the clash between the power of government and the right to dissent, commencing with the early days of the Republic. Moving through American legal history, I examine the first Red Scare following World War I and Supreme Court cases that were its progeny. The result was a body of precedent that would influence courts faced with similar prosecutions following World War II. The march through leading cases of the times brings the reader back to the Red Monday cases themselves and explains what the decisions meant for America and why the Court rendered them.

Supreme Court history, and legal history in general, are not just for the legal professional or academic. Just as the Red Scare era touched millions of lives and was a major focus for the nation, the decisions of the high court pragmatically affected (and reflected) the changing national attitude toward allegations of disloyalty. The legitimacy of denying the right to engage in forms of dissent and of punishing those accused of subversion or disloyalty was tested in the American legal system, ultimately by the Supreme Court. If the Court agreed with the actions of Congress as it legislated, investigated and punished for contempt; if the Court agreed that loyalty oaths could be enforced as a prerequisite for employment or practicing a profession; if the Court agreed that the FBI and others need not present witnesses or reports for cross-examination; if, overall, the Supreme Court agreed that government had the right to punish dissent when, where, and how it felt a threat existed, then such government action would have the sanctifying seal of the Supreme Court's approval. Once that seal was broken, once the prosecutions and hearings were challenged, the foundation—perhaps the keystone—for continuing the Red Scare began to crumble.

The Court's actions during the 1950s are relevant to all who would understand the era and the potential for recurrence of the same events in the future. Any understanding of why the Court condoned or condemned the acts of government on issues brought to its door is, at best, subjective. Yet, it is evident that the Court has never operated in a vacuum and that the justices have always been participants in the same events as the rest of the nation, perhaps even more so, located as they are at the apex of the federal judicial system. Their personalities, proclivities, and prejudices are vital in assessing their positions on cases. They, too, are exposed to the media and affected by the Zeitgeist, as well as by their socio-economic origins and status.

Benjamin N. Cardozo, in *The Nature of the Judicial Process*, emphasized this point, adding, "the spirit of the age, as it is revealed to each of us, is too often only the spirit of the group in which the accidents of birth or education or occupation or fellowship have given us a place." He quotes James H. Robinson: "We [judges as well as others] are abjectly credulous by nature and instinctively accept the verdicts of the group. We are suggestible not merely when under the spell of an excited mob or a fervent revival, but we are ever and always listening to the still small voice of the herd, and are even ready to defend and justify its instructions and warnings, and accept them as the mature results of our own reasoning" (in Sara Robbins, ed., "Law," in *A Treasury of Art and Literature* (New York: Hugh Lauter Levin Assoc., 1990, pp. 305–8).

Significantly, the Supreme Court placed no major legal obstacles in the path of government prosecutions following World War I and its Red Scare. In every major case involving government prosecution of dissent resulting in conviction that was then appealed, the Supreme Court confirmed the guilt of the accused. That the Supreme Court reacted differently after years of condoning convictions generated by the second Red Scare warrants an examination of what happened and why.

In 1951, at the height of the second Red Scare, the Supreme Court affirmed the convictions of the top American Communist Party officials in *Dennis v. United States.* In this leading decision of the era, Justice Hugo L. Black dissented. In doing so, he made a prediction: that in "calmer times" another view defining the right of political dissent would prevail. He was correct. Why it took place six years later is the story that unfolds in this book.

Chapter 1
Red Monday and J. Edgar Hoover

June 17, 1957 was an unusually hot day in Washington, D.C. The thermometer soared to 95 degrees, matching the highest temperature recorded for that date and sending eighteen people suffering from heat fatigue to area hospitals.[1]

One man, J. Edgar Hoover, longtime director of the Federal Bureau of Investigation (FBI), was livid, but not because of the heat: that day the United States Supreme Court had announced decisions in four cases that substantially diminished the government's potential for continued success in Red Scare prosecutions.[2]

In 1919, Hoover had joined the attorney general's office, and since 1924, when he became acting director of the agency that was to become the FBI, he and the Bureau he was to rule for almost fifty years had crusaded against communists, their American party, and a variety of other political dissenters. To be the object of Hoover's crusade required only that he believe the person or group was politically suspect. Until the mid-1950s Hoover was overwhelmingly successful in court decisions, which for the most part sustained his views. Then came June 17, 1957, a day he called "Red Monday"—not because of the red-hot weather, but because, as he saw it, that day the United States Supreme Court handed down four decisions favoring the "Reds."[3]

Nine days later, Hoover sent a memorandum to President Dwight D. Eisenhower's cabinet and to other top government officials. It was entitled "Reaction of Communist Party, USA to Recent Supreme Court Decisions," and it stated that the "Party as a whole is jubilant over these decisions." The reaction of the Party, as he recited it, was his justification for calling June 17, 1957, Red Monday.[4] He further predicted that the Red Monday decisions would rejuvenate the Party. Quoting a Communist who said it was good to have an "extreme leftist" on the Court, Hoover refrained from naming which justice he meant.

Hoover was probably the single most knowledgeable person in government with respect to political trends in all three branches of the national government. He maintained a diverse and highly efficient network of informants and contacts in Congress, the executive branch, and even the judiciary. Across his desk flowed an incredible volume of information gleaned from these sources. Also at hand were reports from his nationwide network of FBI agents, articles from newspapers and magazines, speeches given at public and private gatherings, correspondence (whether intended for publication or private), and the products of wiretaps, surveillance, and a host of electronic devices. The result was to make Hoover exceptionally well informed. His phenomenal files were especially detailed and exhaustive on the sex lives and appetites of just about anyone of consequence, as well as many who were not, but could be.

To underestimate what Hoover knew and when he knew it, and his ability to use the information, could be a serious act of stupidity; Hoover was both extremely knowledgeable and as astute and powerful a bureaucrat as the nation has seen.

While Hoover was angry with the decisions of June 17, 1957, he was not surprised by them. He was well aware, as early as a year or more before, that his most cherished crusade—the continued war on communists, their party, and others who met his broad definition of disloyalty—was in trouble because of the Supreme Court. Throughout the 1950s, when most of the important Red Scare cases were before the Court, Hoover not only had personal and ideological supporters on the Court, he had informants, including Supreme Court clerks, marshals, and Court police.

To Hoover, a justice's "loyalty" was defined by his willingness to affirm convictions in Red Scare prosecutions. Alexander Charns put it most succinctly: "Anyone who opposed the director of the FBI was considered subversive."[5]

It has been well documented that Hoover's FBI collected extensive information on each Supreme Court justice and even gathered information on law clerks. The extent to which Hoover's agents would gather material on the activities, private lives, and friends of justices, particularly those whom he considered suspect, is astounding. Twenty thousand pages of FBI records on the Supreme and federal judiciary are now available; still more is withheld from public review, hidden to this day behind a claim of "must be kept secret." FBI wiretaps recorded the conversations of twelve Supreme Court justices as they spoke with targets of Bureau surveillance; transcripts of what they said were made and used by Hoover. The most famous use (which was certainly an abuse) is said to have dissuaded President Harry S Truman in 1946 from nominating Justice William O. Douglas as chief justice; he chose Fred M. Vinson instead.[6]

Chief among those who were in disfavor with Hoover at the time of Red Monday were Justices Felix Frankfurter, William O. Douglas, and Hugo Black. Given Douglas's and Black's views on Red Scare cases and First Amendment rights, Hoover's wrath was understandable. His suspicions of Frankfurter, however, were far less supported by the legal positions Frankfurter actually took on Red Scare issues. Indeed, it is evident that Hoover paid little attention to fine points of the law. His concern was with one criterion: did the justice's vote favor communists or subversives? Thus, apparently more important than Frankfurter's legal arguments were the words of General Douglas MacArthur, who told the FBI director that his "best bet for the real brains of subversive leadership in the country is justice Felix Frankfurter."[7]

Douglas, however, had enjoyed regular and friendly contacts with Hoover and FBI agents from the late 1930s to the late 1940s; Hoover even invited him to address the graduating class at the FBI National Academy in 1944. The relationship deteriorated to one of hostility after Douglas's dissent in the 1951 *Dennis v. United States* case, where he and Justice Hugo Black opposed the Court's majority decision to sustain the conviction of the top leadership of the Communist Party for violating the Smith Act, a 1940 federal statute that prohibited advocating the overthrow of the U.S. government.

Named for its initial sponsor, Representative Howard W. Smith of Virginia, the Smith Act was a reaction to the prewar anxieties of this country as it watched Europe go up in flames. Part of the act, the Alien Registration Act, required all aliens to register with the government; if they were found to have ties to "subversive" organizations, deportation could follow. But Title 1 of the Smith Act dealt with citizens as well. It was the nation's first peacetime sedition law since the Alien and Sedition Acts of 1798. It stated, in part:

Whoever knowingly or willfully advocates, . . . or teaches the duty, necessity, desirability, or propriety of overthrowing or destroying the government of the United States . . . ; or

Whoever, with intent to cause the overthrow or destruction of any such government, prints, publishes, . . . or teaches the duty, necessity, desirability, or propriety of overthrowing or destroying any government in the United States by force or violence, or attempts to do so; or

Whoever organizes . . . any . . . group, or assembly of persons who teach, advocate, or encourage the overthrow or destruction of any such government by force or violence; or becomes or is a member of . . . any such group,

Shall be fined not more than $20,000 or imprisoned not more than twenty years, or both . . . .

If two or more persons conspire to commit any offense named in this section, each shall be fined not more than $20,000 or imprisoned not more than twenty years, or both.[8]

The key words are "advocates," "publishes," "organizes," and "or is a member." It was J. Edgar Hoover who urged and cajoled the use of the Smith Act to prosecute leaders of the Communist Party after World War II. Thus any justice who opposed the use of the Smith Act was, to Hoover, a communist sympathizer and an enemy.

Any rational reading of what Douglas had stated, both in his written opinions and in his views, which he openly expressed outside the Court, provided ample evidence of his anti-communist stand, but that was beside the point for Hoover. The *Dennis* case and those that followed, where Douglas was on the "wrong side" of Red Scare legal issues, were enough to end their cordial relations. There were other reasons Hoover grew to detest Douglas, including Douglas's personal life (four marriages and three divorces), his outspoken position on environmental issues, and his frequent engagement in political commentary.

The culmination of this rift was Hoover's and the FBI's involvement in a 1970 movement to impeach Douglas, a move apparently initiated by President Richard M. Nixon. Nixon assigned then-Representative Gerald R. Ford to the task, and Ford and his collaborators relied heavily on the FBI for information on Douglas. The Bureau came through, delivering thousands of pages of documents that went back forty years. Douglas was forced to mount a feverish defense; eight months later a House judiciary subcommittee vindicated his position.[9]

For years Justice Hugo L. Black was another target of Hoover's attention, again because of his positions on Red Scare and First Amendment cases. At the instigation, or at least with the tacit approval, of Chief Justice Fred M. Vinson, during the crucial days of the final pleas to the Supreme Court in the *Rosenberg* atomic bomb spy case (1951–53), the FBI not only maintained close surveillance of certain justices but also, at Hoover's direction, wiretapped Black's home. Though Black was contemptuous of Hoover and spoke of him as a menace, he also feared Hoover's proven ability to ruin people's reputations. Friends of Black contacted Morris Ernst, a well-known liberal prominent in the American Civil Liberties Union, to put in a good word at the Bureau for Black; what was not known at the time was that Ernst was also an FBI informant.[10]

Hoover's power—one that the FBI still exerts over the Supreme and all other federal courts—included that of preparing reports on nominees or potential nominees for judicial appointment. Ironically, it began with President Eisenhower's 1953 nomination of Earl Warren as chief justice. The irony with respect to Warren is that the report on him was prepared hurriedly and was biased in favor of the chief justice-designate because Warren was then in favor with Hoover. After the Warren Court's "left turn," as Hoover saw it, he (as well as Eisenhower) came to regret the earlier pro-Warren bias; thereafter Hoover maneuvered to see that justices that were more to his liking were placed on the Court.[11]

Disappointment in the rulings of justices on the Supreme Court, in effect their failure to behave as predicted (and desired), is part of Supreme Court lore. Presidents from Thomas Jefferson on have been cited to prove the point that their nominees, once serving as justices, disappointed them. President Eisenhower had this experience in the 1950s. In a memo, Arthur Krock, columnist for the *New York Times*, wrote in 1960 after a meeting with Eisenhower, "It was clear that the President has been disappointed in a far leftist trend of Chief Justice Warren, and has been equally astounded at the conformity to this of Justice Brennan." Five years later, in an interview given to his biographer Stephen E. Ambrose, Eisenhower heatedly replied to the question of his biggest mistake: "The appointment of that S.O.B. Earl Warren."[12]

Justice Charles E. Whittaker, who gained a seat in 1957, was an example of a candidate Hoover favored. Whittaker was reported to be on the "right" side of issues, as well as being friendly to the FBI. By 1958, Hoover had an "all-star list" of pro-FBI judges that he could use to identify those who were "appropriate" for promotion to the high court. Another candidate who enjoyed high ratings from Hoover was Potter Stewart; it helped when an agent who knew Stewart said that the judge "frequently commented . . . that the FBI and John Edgar Hoover were doing a grand job."[13] Anticipating Justice Harold Burton's retirement in 1958, Hoover ordered his Bureau people to compile a list of qualified candidates. Specifically, he wanted to know whether Stewart was conservative and favorably disposed to strict law enforcement and the efforts of the Bureau. On October 13, 1958 reports favoring Judge Stewart were forwarded to Attorney General William Rogers; the next day President Eisenhower, who had by then grown unhappy with what he saw as the "liberal" rulings of Chief Justice Earl Warren and Justice William Brennan, nominated Stewart.[14]

In ways large and small, J. Edgar Hoover attempted to influence the Supreme Court and the federal judiciary in terms of its personnel (including law clerk applicants, whom the FBI scrutinized for liberal, leftist, or subversive links) and in turn, the decisions that would emanate from the courts. While his goals included protecting his criminal prosecutions from those he considered "soft" on criminal defendants, his major passion over his almost fifty-year reign as FBI director was his crusade against Reds, leftists, and subversives, as he called these persons or groups. In the heyday of the Red Scare in the 1940s and 1950s, New Deal liberals and intellectuals joined the groups that Hoover felt were enemies.

Because Hoover used illegal methods, including electronic bugs, wiretapping, mail tampering, blackmailing, and illegal break-ins ("black bag" jobs), which violated basic constitutional rights, his goals included protecting these clandestine operations from public knowledge or judicial scrutiny. He and his FBI were circumspect in conduct and put on a public face as being above politics.

In fact, Hoover and his Bureau were deeply political: Hoover was used by and thereby came to use presidents from Franklin D. Roosevelt to Richard Nixon. Hoover manipulated senators, representatives, and committees. He used his extensive file resources, as well as Bureau facilities and contacts, to reward as well as to threaten. Hoover's assiduous protection of the Bureau through expert public relations efforts, backed by careful manipulation of the media, left him and his FBI effectively above the control of its nominal superior, the United States attorney general, and, ultimately, above the law.

It is clear that Hoover perceived the Warren Court as an enemy well before Red Monday. His perception, which was not wrong, was that the Court could no longer be counted on to uphold convictions under the Smith Act, nor would the Court be amenable to further upholding contempt-of-Congress decisions, prosecutions of union leaders for refusing to disclose their associations as required by the Taft-Hartley Act, or a myriad of other Red Scare-type prosecutions. Hoover then had to take matters into his own hands.

He did so through a series of Counter-Intelligence Programs (COINTELPROs). The COINTELPROs were not a product of an in-depth study of the Court's Red Monday opinions. Realistically, those decisions did not fully dismantle the legal bases for prosecutions; the Court did not hold (and never has held) the Smith Act unconstitutional. Rather, Hoover acted based on a pragmatic perception that the Court had changed its views sufficiently to lead him to want to do more, and with a freer hand, than the decisions would allow. One author succinctly described Hoover's new methodology: "The COINTELPROs were nationally targeted formal programs specifically designed to circumvent the constitutional constraints of the U.S. justice system thereby denying targeted groups and individuals the capacity to directly challenge the legality of the coercive actions taken against them."[15]

Eleven months before Red Monday, in August 1956, Hoover launched the first COINTELPRO, aimed at the destruction of the Communist Party of the United States of America (CPUSA); there were to be at least eleven more COINTELPROs lasting to 1971. In fact, the CPUSA was,

Figure 1. J. Edgar Hoover as he appeared at a Senate Internal Security Subcommittee hearing on November 17, 1953. UPI Corbis-Bettmann photograph.

by the end of 1955, practically nonexistent. It was reduced to 22,000 members, was loaded with FBI agents, and was certainly discredited and ineffective. Within two years, damaged not only by COINTELPRO activities but by Nikita Khrushchev's revelations about Stalin, the Party was down to fewer than 4000 members.

The stated aim of the COINTELPROs was to "expose, disrupt, misdirect, discredit, disorganize or otherwise neutralize" specifically targeted dissident individuals and political organizations Hoover considered enemies.[16] The only reason the program was closed down prior to Hoover's death in 1972 was that in 1971 the first concrete evidence publicly disclosed its existence, when a group broke into FBI offices in Media, Pennsylvania and escaped with documents bearing the COINTELPRO code word.[17]

A few years later the matter of COINTELPRO operations came under scrutiny by a U.S. Senate committee chaired by Senator Frank Church (D.-Idaho). The results of its investigation were published in a final report in April 1976. What the Church Committee, as it became commonly known, found was that COINTELPROs were domestic covert action programs, unique in American history. Under the heading *COINTELPRO: The FBI's Covert Action Programs Against American Citizens*, the report detailed how the Bureau "went beyond the collection of intelligence to [engage in] secret action designed to 'disrupt' and 'neutralize' target groups and individuals."[18]

The report described how techniques of covert action ranged from the trivial to the degrading to the dangerous as the FBI waged personal wars against defined enemies. Perhaps because Hoover died in 1972, the 1976 final report did not point to him as the instigator and ultimate decision maker, even though he was. The report stated that the programs ended in 1971; however, this assertion has been vehemently denied by others who believe that COINTELPRO operations and activities continued and in fact were in evidence in 1976, the year of the final report.[19] Litigation by the Socialist Workers Party (SWP) against the attorney general for compensation and injunctive relief because of the COIN-TELPRO directed against it supports the argument that COINTELPRO actions continued until at least September 1976, when the attorney general ended them.[20]

The Church Committee's report quoted William C. Sullivan, who, under Hoover, was in charge of the programs. Sullivan described the techniques used as "rough, tough and dirty"; these included violation of criminal statutes, acts involving risk of serious bodily injury or death to targets (deaths did take place), and other actions the committee agreed were abhorrent in a free society. Indeed, the report contained an incredible listing of dirty tricks, falsifications, deceptions, disinformation, and operations using techniques of an openly criminal nature.[21]

The report concluded that the first COINTELPRO against the Communist Party was the result of the Supreme Court's reversal of the Smith Act convictions of the second-string Party leadership in *Yates v. United States*, the most prominent of the four major Red Monday decisions. Quoting the FBI unit chief's testimony:

Supreme Court rulings had rendered the Smith Act technically unenforceable. . . . It made it ineffective to prosecute Communist Party members, made it impossible to prosecute Communist Party members at the time.[22]

The report noted that the Red Monday cases to which the statement refers came in 1957, while COINTELPRO was initiated in 1956. Though the report suggested that the reference may have been a mistake—and was referring to another case that was not a Smith Act decision[23]—in fact, it was not an error.

Hoover's network of intelligence gathering, both inside and outside the Court, together with his acute assessment of the times, people and issues involved, anticipated by a year what was to happen on Red Monday. Hoover's major clue came when, in late 1955, the Supreme Court granted certiorari in the *Yates* case; that meant that, instead of affirming further convictions of Party members under the Smith Act by refusing review, the Court would take the case, opening up the chance—if not the likelihood—that it would damage Hoover's crusade by changing its position on Red Scare issues. Four votes are necessary for certiorari. Thus at least four justices in late 1955 wanted to reexamine the 1951 *Dennis* decision and, perhaps, redefine the use of the Smith Act as the major tool in the prosecution of communists. All that was necessary was five votes to overturn the convictions in *Yates*. The vote of at least four justices calling for this review, assuming they then voted to make substantial changes, meant that the Court needed just one more justice to reach a new majority position. Hoover could assess this situation, and he certainly could count.

Furthermore, early the next year, on March 15, 1956, the Justice Department, as the government's prosecuting agency, notified the FBI, its investigative arm, that future Smith Act prosecutions would have to include evidence of "an actual plan for a violent revolution," or the department would not prosecute. That meant that the more vague standard used in the *Dennis* case as evidence of violation of the Smith Act would no longer suffice. Hoover reacted, and by July or August 1956, COINTELPRO-CPUSA was operational.[24]

Before commencing this first COINTELPRO, Hoover was apparently careful enough to get authorization for this move. On March 8, 1956 Hoover presented his case to the National Security Council. His aim was broad authority to mount intensified operations against the Communist Party. What he wanted was permission to expand his operations against the Party from investigation to hard-hitting—and quite illegal—actions, many of which the FBI had already been conducting well prior to this meeting. Hoover's concept of "permission" was informing his superiors of some, but never all, of what he intended to do; if no one forbade his conduct, that was sufficient justification.

Instead of presenting an honest appraisal of the Communist Party as practically moribund—which it clearly was—Hoover told his audience that the Party remained a very serious threat. Under the title "The Present Menace of Communist Espionage and Subversion," Hoover detailed his assessment to President Eisenhower, to the vice president, and to the secretaries of state and defense and other heads of the highest government agencies.[25]

No longer could the courts, and particularly the Supreme Court, be counted on to confirm guilt in a variety of Red Scare prosecutions.

No longer was the Justice Department likely to use the Smith Act for prosecutions as it had in the past. Therefore Hoover had to use these new methods—methods not dependent on the Justice Department, the courts, or statutes, but extralegal and at his command. What the senators didn't know when they took testimony and when they wrote their report was that this initial COINTELPRO had been authorized by the National Security Council.

Hoover wanted action to destroy his enemies at a time when the courts were apparently rethinking the legal issues involved. His answer to the changes portended by the Court in accepting review of the *Yates* case, and to the Justice Department directive, was the first COINTEL-PRO. He neither needed nor wanted to wait for court cases where, as he anticipated, results would run counter to his crusade. Besides, he knew he could not meet the *Yates* standard; his informants and agents, many of whom were actually in positions of leadership and trust in the Communist Party, could not provide him with a plan for revolution or overt acts beyond generalized, conditional advocacy.[26]

Hoover's eye was not on the fine points of the law; he knew the Smith Act was not declared unconstitutional by the *Yates* case on Red Monday, nor was the 1951 *Dennis* case flatly reversed. He also knew, however, that as a pragmatic result of the Red Monday and certain earlier cases there would be substantially fewer prosecutions for violations of the Smith Act or other antisubversive laws. Thus, for Hoover, extralegal means were necessary. His judgment was both anticipatory and correct: of the fourteen Communist Party defendants in the *Yates* case, five were entirely discharged by the Court's decision, and the Justice Department chose not to reprosecute the remaining nine.

In fact, there were no new Smith Act prosecutions initiated after Red Monday except for the prosecution under the "membership" provision of the Smith Act of a few officers of the Party from the Boston area. These final prosecutions were made in response to a plank in the Republican Party platform for 1956 promising vigorous enforcement of subversion laws.[27] Hoover was also correct in the sense that the COINTEL-PRO against CPUSA was a success; by 1957 the Party was nothing but a shell. Herbert Brownell retired as attorney general at the end of 1957, content that he had accomplished one of his goals: crushing the Communist Party. Notwithstanding that reality, Hoover continued and even expanded the COINTELPRO against the Party, rejecting all evidence and refusing to relent, even though so much had changed in the courts, the country, and the world. His success led to new COINTELPROs against his designated enemies, such as one to discredit Dr. Martin Luther King, Jr., and another against student protest organizations of the 1960s.[28]

Not everyone considered COINTELPRO a success, however. The hallmark of these programs was, to the detriment of the American justice system, a refusal to abide by the rule of law. The Church Committee cogently argued at the conclusion of its report that "the Department [of Justice] will have [to] acknowledge—finally—that COINTELPRO was wrong." The report continued by stating:

The American people need to be assured that never again will an agency of the government be permitted to conduct a secret war against those citizens it considers threats to the established order. Only a combination of legislative prohibition and Departmental control can guarantee that COINTELPRO will not happen again.[29]

In sum, the Justice Department and the FBI recognized the Red Monday decisions of June 17, 1957 as confirmation of a changed majority position on the Supreme Court on Red Scare issues. The *Yates* decision of Red Monday meant that further Smith Act prosecutions of communists would be a waste of time, money, and effort. As noted, a few more Smith Act indictments involving the use of the "membership" clause and fulfilling a Republican Party platform promise in 1956 were pursued; two eventually made their way to the Court and were decided in 1961. But even on that "membership" basis, where it won one case in the Supreme Court, the Justice Department recognized the futility of further prosecutions. What had begun in 1948 with the indictment of the top eleven Communist Party members pragmatically ended in 1957. The Supreme Court gave a green light to criminal charges under the Smith Act with the *Dennis* case in 1951; in 1957, the light turned red.

Following the *Dennis* decision in 1951, fifteen groups of multiple defendants (second-string state Party leaders) were indicted and prosecuted between 1951 and 1953; the lower courts, using *Dennis* as precedent, affirmed convictions in all but one Smith Act case. After Red Monday, and particularly after the *Yates* case, no federal appellate court ever again affirmed a conviction based on the "advocacy" clause of the Smith Act. It was nothing less than a judicial revolution.[30]

The focus on J. Edgar Hoover in this review of Red Monday is warranted because he was the primary mover in the use of the Smith Act to prosecute CPUSA members and because his reaction to the changed position of the Supreme Court is the best indication of the serious impact of the Red Monday decisions. Tom Clark, then attorney general of the United States, stated that Hoover personally pressed for the initial indictments of the top Communist Party members in 1948. At the time there was substantial doubt whether the Smith Act would provide a sound legal basis for the indictments and subsequent prosecutions. But Hoover's FBI mounted a multifaceted campaign to press indictments under the Act. His influence extended to Congress, where his allies introduced the Mundt-Nixon Subversive Activities Control Act in order to pressure the executive branch into a choice: use the Smith Act or accept proposed new legislation, which the Truman administration opposed. The Justice Department began prosecuting under the Smith Act.[31]

Clark later stated, "Mr. Hoover recommended strongly that we have the prosecutions" and, "I usually followed the recommendations." He added that Hoover "had spent so much of his money on communist prosecutions, I guess he wanted to see some fruits." Hoover "handed [the *Dennis* case] to us on a silver platter." [32]

One scholar of the events has concluded that the Smith Act indictments "were based on an FBI effort to enlarge its powers and cripple a movement [CPUSA] its Director had been fighting for thirty years. The results of the FBI war would change the internal atmosphere in the United States dramatically and contribute to a deepening Cold War climate, consequences which the FBI must have anticipated eagerly." [33]

Once again, Hoover was right. The Smith Act was sufficient not only to obtain indictments, but also to provide an exceptional record of convictions. Between 1948 and 1957, 129 indictments were obtained against alleged CPUSA members.[34] Convictions were secured and sustained by federal appellate courts, including the Supreme Court, in almost every case until June 17, 1957.[35] Thereafter, new prosecutions virtually ended. Hoover moved on with his crusade through his COINTELPRO, pragmatically responding to the shift in the Supreme Court's position on Smith Act prosecutions. Hoover thus changed the battlefield but not the war. In reality, however, Hoover did not leave the battlefield of the Supreme Court in the sense that he continued his careful watch on the Court, gathered inside information on its doings, and attempted to shape the Court by his use of the FBI responsibility to report on candidates or nominees. His successes in this regard were significant.

A Mississippi representative, John Bell Williams, called May 17, 1954, the day the Supreme Court announced its unanimous decision in the *Brown v. Board of Education* desegregation decision, "Black Monday" to characterize the civil rights victory as a time of darkness and woe for the nation.[36] Hoover and many others would feel similarly about Red Monday just three years later.

After *Brown*, segments of Southern society responded with techniques to delay, if not destroy, the mandate of *Brown* and its progeny by waging war against racial integration in schools. Similarly, Hoover was in the unique position of being able to wage his own personal war on a number of fronts against Red Monday and its implications. The appellations Black Monday and Red Monday, given by critics of the Supreme Court decisions, reflected the undeniable truth that in 1954 and 1957 the Supreme Court dealt with politically charged issues as rarely before in its history. In both cases, the Court's enemies struck back.

The memories of COINTELPRO were resurrected in the aftermath of the 1995 Oklahoma City bombing with the Clinton administration's proposed Omnibus Counterterrorism Act. Critics feared that portions of the act would put the FBI back into the business of investigating political groups, remembering vividly how this led to all the extralegal acts of the Hoover years.[37]

Chapter 2
Historical Antecedents of the Second Red Scare

This country was born in revolution and held itself out as an exemplar of the right of free political expression. Yet it was but a short twenty-two years after the Declaration of Independence was signed that an initial attempt to curb political freedom occurred. The Alien and Sedition Acts, passed in 1798 during the presidency of John Adams, were the Federalist Party's response to the perceived threat that the radical ideas of the French Revolution would infect the new nation's populace.[1] War with revolutionary France seemed imminent. Rumors of French plots and espionage created an atmosphere of fear and hostility. Congress reacted with an attempt to rid the country of aliens the president judged "dangerous to the peace and safety" and an attempt to allow criminal prosecution of anyone voicing opposition to the government, the president, or Congress.

The Adams administration never used the Alien Act, and the act expired in 1800, although some aliens left the country or went into hiding as a result of the threat it posed. But there were at least twenty-five arrests and fifteen indictments under the Sedition Act. Fines and jail sentences resulted. All the defendants were members of the opposition Republican Party.

While none of these Sedition Act cases reached the United States Supreme Court, lower appeals courts sustained every conviction. This is all the more startling given that the prosecutions were virtually contemporaneous with the incorporation of the Bill of Rights into the Constitution; yet these courts found that the sedition and seditious libel convictions did not violate the protections of the First Amendment.

There was, however, vocal opposition to those 1798 Sedition Act prosecutions, most notably in the Kentucky and Virginia Resolutions, which reflected the views of Thomas Jefferson and James Madison. The country's reaction to the Alien and Sedition Acts helped determine the Republican victory in the elections of 1800. Jefferson, once in office, pardoned all those convicted. A year after the Alien Act ended, the Sedition Act expired in 1801.[2]

Thus the new nation, under the Constitution, experienced its first serious brush with an attempt to legislate and prosecute political opposition. The next peacetime attempt at a national sedition law was the Smith Act in 1940; in the interim there was a wartime sedition act enacted during American participation in World War I.

Despite the eighteenth-century attempt to suppress political dissent and thus limit the overriding commands contained in the First Amendment, the Supreme Court was not directly confronted with issues of political dissent, subversion, and the right of political association and First Amendment interpretation until 1919.[3] While the terrible advent of the Civil War led military officials to restrict individual rights and political expression, again, as in the case of the Alien and Sedition Acts, the issues involved did not become the subject of Supreme Court review. The closest the Court got to such issues was in 1866 in *Ex parte Milligan*, when, after the Civil War had ended, the Supreme Court asserted its right to review the actions of a military commission and to nullify them if they were unlawful under the Constitution. In *Milligan*, the Court further declared that the constitutional protection of civil liberties operated during wartime as well as peacetime.[4]

American involvement in World War I brought this first direct confrontation between government authority and political civil liberties to the doors of the Supreme Court. After remaining out of the European conflagration that had been raging since 1914, Congress responded to President Woodrow Wilson's call for war in April 1917. The country in turn exhibited a zeal that included not only a mighty military response but also fanatical opposition to persons or groups that questioned or in any way opposed an all-out war effort.

Two months after the United States entered the war, Congress passed and the president signed the Espionage Act of 1917. One year later, and only six months before the end of the war, the Sedition Act became law as an amendment to the Espionage Act.[5] The Sedition Act defined as criminal any "disloyal, profane, scurrilous, or abusive language, or language intended to cause contempt, scorn, contumely or disrepute as regards the form of government of the United States; or the Constitution; or the flag."[6]

The acts made interference with recruitment into military service a felony; they also allowed post office bureaucrats, without any prior hearing or challenge, to ban from the mails any material deemed treasonable or seditious. Among the numerous publications so banned from time to time were the *Saturday Evening Post* and the *New York Times*, as well as a variety of radical and dissident publications.

In terms of popular culture, the nation responded with often irrational demands for conformity to the war effort: schools ceased teaching the German language; persons with German-sounding names were treated with scorn, suspicion, and even physical abuse. In terms of court proceedings, the government prosecuted almost 2200 people under the newly passed acts; more than 1000 were convicted. But it was not until 1919, after the war was over, that cases challenging the constitutionality of these statutes came to the Supreme Court.[7]

Though the fighting had ended, 1919 was a tumultuous year in the nation as well as in war-devastated Europe. Anarchists blew up banks and sent bombs to dozens of public figures, including the U.S. attorney general. Seventy Blacks were lynched that year as race riots in Chicago, Washington, D.C., and other cities rocked the postwar peace. Major strikes renewed labor troubles. But that which seemed most ominous was the new Soviet dictatorship in Russia. The Soviet regime was apparently bent on exporting revolution to Europe and elsewhere with the aim of overthrowing capitalist governments.

Immediately after 1919, the mood was one of ultranationalism ("we won the war, single-handedly") and anxiety. Anti-alien sentiment hastened the end of a liberal immigration policy; there was fear of race war and fear of labor battles and mass revolution. The latter was inspired by Russia's successes in promoting some revolutions in Europe and fear generated by the organization of a new communist party in the United States. The overall result of these tumultuous times was the first major Red Scare of the twentieth century—a reaction to fear of aliens, radicals, political dissent, and all ideas and movements considered foreign to a conforming image of America. There was also anger and disappointment with America's altruistic (as it was portrayed) involvement in the Great War.[8]

World War I had focused authority in the federal government and encouraged the aggressive nationalism that was to grow in the 1920s. State governments diminished in power, as did Congress relative to the presidency. The voice of the Supreme Court, however, became more authoritative, and, overall, it enhanced the forces of nationalism and the accretion of centralized federal power.

Just what were the limits on dissent? Was the Constitution truly there in wartime as well as in peacetime? What could Congress and the states criminalize in terms of speech, writing, or association with others, and still allow to pass constitutional muster? The Supreme Court's answers, beginning in 1919, reflected the times in which the Court was operating and the views and proclivities of the justices, as well as the evolution of law on the subject of dissent.

The major doctrine governing the clash between the First Amendment and the power of government to control dissenting speech or association was derived from English law as it applied to seditious libel. Known as the "bad tendency test," it measured the legality of expression by its tendency to cause an illegal action. Though criticized as an unworthy vestige of English law in view of the First Amendment, it was nevertheless employed by the Supreme Court in the early twentieth century. Thus Justice Oliver Wendell Holmes, speaking for a majority of the Supreme Court in 1907, held that newspaper criticism of judicial behavior concerning pending cases tended to obstruct the administration of justice and therefore could be punished as unlawful.[9] Eight years later, the Court again spoke through Holmes, holding that an article encouraging a boycott against anyone interfering with nude bathing tended to encourage or incite a crime, breach of the peace, or acts of violence by encouraging violations of a law against indecent exposure.[10]

It was, however, in signal cases decided in 1919 that the Court began to place important curbs on civil liberties. These cases arising out of American participation in World War I and the Espionage and Sedition Acts generated by that war raised serious issues concerning dissent. The impact of those decisions was to be felt in the aftermath of another world war and another Red Scare.

The most significant of these cases involved Charles Schenck, the general secretary of the Socialist Party, who was convicted of conspiring to violate the Espionage Act of 1917 by participating in the printing and circulating of some fifteen thousand leaflets urging noncompliance with the draft. Schenck claimed that the law he was accused of violating ran afoul of the First Amendment. His case eventually reached the U.S. Supreme Court. Justice Oliver W. Holmes, writing for a unanimous Court, disagreed.[11]

Holmes had no problem recognizing the leaflet's "bad tendency" to influence opposition to the draft. The Court thus found that the First Amendment did not protect Schenck from criminal conviction under the Espionage Act. Holmes went on to enter some of the most memorable phrases on the right of government to limit dissent in any form:

We admit that in many places and in ordinary times the defendants in saying all that was said in the circular would have been within their constitutional rights. But the character of every act depends upon the circumstances in which it is done. . . . The most stringent protection of free speech would not protect a man in falsely shouting fire in a theatre and causing a panic. . . . The question in every case is whether the words used are used in such circumstances and are of such a nature as to create a *clear and present danger* that they will bring about the substantive evils that Congress has a right to prevent. It is a question of proximity and degree. When a nation is at war many things that might be said in time of peace are such a hindrance to its effort that their utterance will not be endured so long as men fight and that no Court could regard them as protected by any constitutional right.[12]

To the concept of bad tendency was now added to the "clear and present danger" test, tying what was said to the circumstances of actual war. Thirty-two years later, in 1951, the Supreme Court majority in the *Dennis* case (the prosecution of the leaders of the American Communist Party) applied a similar standard as a result of another Red Scare prosecution.

Holmes did not, however, deem First Amendment guarantees superseded by the Espionage Act. The language he used called for a proximate causal relationship between the deed (writing, speaking) and a clear and present danger. In *Schenck* Holmes found such a relationship. But a few months later, in *Abrams v. United States*,[13] a case based on a conviction for violation of the Sedition Act, Holmes began a line of dissents, joined by Justice Louis D. Brandeis, from what he believed was an abuse and misuse of the clear and present danger test by the Court.

After the *Schenck* decision but before *Abrams*, Holmes led the Court in two other cases affirming Espionage Act convictions. In March 1919, the Court upheld the conviction of the labor leader Eugene V. Debs, who was also the presidential candidate of the Socialist Party.[14] A speech by Debs was found to justify his conviction and imprisonment based on the jury's finding that "one purpose of the speech . . . was to oppose not only war in general but this war, and that the opposition was so expressed that its natural and intended effect would be to obstruct recruiting."[15] Debs went to jail with a ten-year sentence; he was pardoned by President Warren G. Harding.

On the same day as the *Schenck* decision, *Frohwerk v. United States* affirmed the conviction and ten-year sentence of an editor of a German-language paper who was found guilty of publishing statements against United States involvement in the war. With Holmes again writing the Court's opinion, the Court conceded, "it may be that all this [that had been published] might be said or written even in time of war in circumstances that would not make it a crime. We do not lose our right to condemn either measures or men because the country is at war." Holmes then added, "but we must take the case on the record as it is, and on that record it is impossible to say that it might not have been found that the circulation of the paper was in quarters [German readers] where a little breath would be enough to kindle a flame."[16]

What had commenced with *Schenck*, in the elaboration of a bad tendency standard into an expression of clear and present danger, the Supreme Court applied in *Debs* and *Frohwerk*, resulting in grounds for affirming the convictions in each. Why, then, the change in Holmes just a few months later? Why his dissent with Brandeis in *Abrams*?

Jacob Abrams was a Russian immigrant and an anarchist who, along with four others, was prosecuted under the Sedition Act for publishing leaflets condemning President Wilson for sending American troops to intervene in Russia. The leaflets called for a general strike to protest the intervention. All five defendants were found guilty and sentenced to lengthy prison terms. Using Holmes's reasoning, the Court majority found that a clear and present danger existed and that the language of the leaflets fit into categories that Congress had outlawed.

Holmes was moved to dissent in *Abrams*, and in doing so he crucially refined the bad tendency and clear and present danger standards. He apparently was disturbed by the antiradical hysteria of the times and was won over by a group of friends who pressed a more libertarian interpretation of the conflict between the right to dissent and laws designed to limit nonconformity. Among those influencing him were Professor Zechariah Chaffee, Federal District Judge Learned Hand, Harold J. Laski, and Justice Brandeis.[17]

The importance of the Holmes dissent in *Abrams*—which Brandeis joined—lies in the fact that two lines of thought emerged from the clash between the government's right to limit speech and the guarantees of the First Amendment; both lines emanated from Holmes. The clear and present danger test of *Schenck* retained the core of the bad tendency concept and became a guidepost for those defending the legal bases for restricting expression. On the other hand, the *Abrams* dissent became the liberal watchword for those supporting the primacy of First Amendment protection.

Holmes's shift between *Schenck* and *Abrams* was of great significance. Under his later view, there must be an imminent danger produced or intended: in effect, acts or threats of action, not just expressions or advocacy unrelated to a significant threat of immediate interference with the law.

Scholars continue to argue over the Holmes switch in the *Abrams* case. Plainly put, it appears that his goal was to put a stop to government prosecution of dissent that he believed had gone too far. As such, his limiting language—the new standard—if applied, would have resulted in overturning the earlier convictions in *Schenck*, *Frohwerk*, and *Debs*. It would have turned "clear and present danger" into a shield protecting speech instead of a sword in the hands of government to punish dissent.[18] The line from these two views extends from the 1920s to the 1950s, when another Red Scare and another series of congressional acts placed these same vital issues before the Court.

In *Abrams*, as in every single Espionage and Sedition Act case appealed to the Supreme Court, the government neither proved nor even alleged a single instance of actual defiance of the war effort as a result of any defendant's activity. That was not necessary under these laws criminalizing expression rather than results. When the Court decided *Abrams*, the Holmes/Brandeis dissent asserted that the standard for conviction for expression should at least be limited to threats of immediate interference with the law where necessary to save the country. Using that standard, it was clear that the *Abrams* defendants and their leaflets were indeed "puny." In opposing bail for the defendants during the appeal of their convictions, the government, on the other hand, argued that they were prominent and influential propagandists who had deliberately attempted to weaken the country by an attack on the purity of its motives.

In December 1920 Congress repealed the Sedition Act, the law that was the basis for their prosecution, leaving the Espionage Act of 1917 in place.[19] In essence, the Sedition Act took aim at wartime dissent, and since the Armistice of November 11, 1918, the underlying rationale for prosecuting seditious utterances during wartime was gone.

The Red Scare that followed in the wake of World War I had produced ominous ramifications in the executive branch of the federal government. A Bureau of Investigation had existed in the federal government since 1908, when it was created to help the Justice Department enforce antitrust laws. Even before the war, the Bureau had expanded its activities and begun surveillance of radical groups. After the bomb scares in early 1919, Congress began appropriating money to fight radicalism.

Attorney General Palmer and his associates decided to create a General Intelligence Division within the Bureau to be headed by J. Edgar Hoover, a twenty-four-year-old who had impressed his seniors. Hoover organized and ran this division until his appointment as head of the Bureau of Investigation (later changed to the Federal Bureau of Investigation) in 1924. Hoover was a zealot who despised radicals. As early as 1920, he stated that "civilization faces its most terrible menace of danger since the barbarian hordes overran west Europe and opened the dark ages. . . . [These radicals] threaten the happiness of the community, the safety of every individual. . . . They would destroy the peace of the country and thrust it into a condition of anarchy and lawlessness and immorality that pass imagination."[20]

Unfortunately for Hoover, the armistice and the revocation of the Sedition Act left his division without any statutory basis for prosecuting radicals and dissidents. His fervor, however, was not quelled. He began to create an extensive file system on left-wing individuals and organizations and continued to conduct wide-ranging surveillance of individuals and groups he considered dangerous or wrong thinking. It was not until

1940 and the Smith Act that he had a peacetime sedition statute that renewed the opportunity for prosecutions. However, by 1920, he had already developed two traits that would be part of his modus operandi: a disregard for legal niceties, such as search warrants, and an obsession with the sexual activities of those whom he targeted.[21]

But by the end of 1920 the nation's first Red Scare was significantly diminished as a major public concern. The threat of world-engulfing communism seemed less serious. With the decrease of the external threat, the concept of a serious internal danger from radicalism abated as a major American concern, replaced by the 1919 Chicago Black Sox scandal, hedonism, jazz, Prohibition, gangsters, returning prosperity, and the rising stock market. Like the war itself and the rejection of the League of Nations, the threat of radicals was felt to be best put out of mind. Even the new president, Warren G. Harding, stated that "too much has been said about Bolshevism in America."[22] The exception was Hoover, for whom crusading against Reds, radicals, and dissenters was never out of style.

There were, however, significant legacies of World War I and its aftermath. Institutional changes persisted beyond the immediate rise and fall of the public's general interest. Courts had to deal with the many hundreds of cases brought under wartime legislation; as has been seen, major legal developments came from the Supreme Court well after the war had ended. The bias against all things, people, and involvement considered foreign resulted in a period of isolationism that bode ill for a shrinking, increasingly unstable world. The armistice of 1918 was, unfortunately, short-lived; just twenty-one years later the world was again at war.

In some respects the contrast to events after World War II is great: wishing to avoid the errors of isolationism, this country sponsored and even physically housed the new world organization, the United Nations, accepting, albeit reluctantly for many, a mandatory role in world affairs. Once again, however, the disappointment with the aftermath of victory, highlighted by the schism between the Soviet Union and the West that created the Cold War, led to a renewed paranoia directed against supposed internal enemies that once again were seen as threatening this victorious nation. The result was a second major Red Scare.

As this Red Scare unfolded, the high court once again confronted the clash between the right to dissent and the power of government to criminalize dissenting views and acts. Given our common law system with its use of binding precedent, the Court naturally turned to the judicial voices of the post-World War I Court. But which path would it choose? By the 1950s Holmes and Brandeis were dead, as were the justices who had penned the majority opinions of the 1920s. The words reflecting the tug of priorities in this clash were, however, very much alive and available.

Two personalities were also alive and active in the second Red Scare era: Judge Learned Hand, who had influenced Holmes in moving to his *Abrams* position and who would play a crucial role in the continuing story, and J. Edgar Hoover, whose power grew over the intervening years and whose great opportunity was to come, breathing new life into his crusade against dissenters, radicals, communists, liberals, intellectuals, and all those whose views were encompassed within his personal definition of "un-American."

There was a period of relative quiet during the interwar years on the matter of First Amendment rights. The United States was so deeply immersed in the Great Depression that dissent in various forms was generally tolerated in a nation that seemed to have lost its confidence. There were, however, three important cases that came to the U.S. Supreme Court during the interwar years, each based on convictions for violating state laws designed to curb dissent.

New York had a criminal anarchy statute that later became the model for the federal Smith Act. Under that law, in the early 1920s, Benjamin Gitlow and three others were convicted because they published a manifesto of the left wing of the Socialist Party. It called for overthrow of the government and mass strikes as a method of promoting revolution. The Supreme Court upheld the convictions as a reasonable exercise of the state's police power.[23] Holmes and his colleague Louis D. Brandeis dissented, arguing that freedom of speech is so important that there must be more than an idea or theory put forth. "Every idea," they said, "is an incitement."[24] They argued that there was no "present danger" involved, and thus, free speech should have been given reign, but to no avail.

Gitlow and his associates went to prison but were later pardoned by Governor Alfred E. Smith of New York. The *Gitlow* case has been recognized for an important and overriding aspect of constitutional law interpretation: that the First Amendment is in effect incorporated into the Fourteenth and is applicable to the states. This enduring legacy (albeit sometimes challenged) has imposed the limitations of the First Amendment on all states.

In another such case between the wars, a woman, Anita Whitney, was convicted of violating the California Criminal Syndicalism Act of 1919. Her offense was that she joined and participated in the split of the Socialist Party that took place in 1919 and then followed the breakaway Communist Labor Party. Though she testified that she sought change through the ballot box, the mere fact that she was a knowing, active member of this party was apparently enough to convince a California jury of her guilt; on appeal in 1927, that verdict was affirmed by the U.S. Supreme Court. The majority held that the California law did not violate the due process clause of the Fourteenth Amendment, so no relief was allowed.[25]

Brandeis, with Holmes joining him, found himself having to concur with the majority, but only because Whitney did not appropriately raise the proper issues in the correct forum so as to challenge the denial of her freedom of speech and assembly by the state.

Brandeis chose powerful words:

Those who won our independence by revolution were not cowards. They did not fear political change. They did not exalt order at the cost of liberty. To courageous, self-reliant men, with confidence in the power of free and fearless reasoning applied through the process of popular government, no danger flowing from speech can be deemed clear and present, unless the incidence of the evil apprehended is so imminent that it may befall before there is opportunity for full discussion.[26]

But these sentiments could not prevail over the failure properly to raise the free speech and assembly issues; on the other hand, given the times and the makeup of the Court, the probability seems to have favored confirming California's action, technical violations aside. Whitney never went to prison; Governor Young of California pardoned her.

The most significant case of the Depression era to reach the Supreme Court came from Oregon and was decided in 1937.[27] In this case, Dirk De Jonge was charged with committing a crime for having assisted in conducting a meeting called by the Communist Party. De Jonge's contentions that no unlawful conduct took place or was even advocated at the meeting were brushed aside; he was found guilty and sentenced to a seven-year prison term. The Supreme Court, distinguishing the acts leading to conviction in *Gitlow* and other cases from the facts in *De Jonge* and applying the protections of the First Amendment through the Fourteenth, reversed the conviction based on the defendant's right of free speech and assembly. What the Court was saying was that Party membership alone was not enough, and that those who attended the meeting could have discussed any number of innocuous subjects. Without using either the original concept of clear and present danger or the narrowed Holmes-Brandeis view of speech, the Court was plainly saying that the states had to allege and prove a good deal more to establish criminal behavior. Certainly more than the mere fact that a meeting took place would be needed before a state could convict and imprison the attendees.

For the most part, while the Great Depression revived interest in prosecuting dissenters and radicals because of the perceived threat contained in their answers to the economic collapse, this revival was balanced by the New Deal liberalism of 1933 and later. Federal laws of the World War I era were left dormant as a new liberal outlook focused on freeing the country from its economic woes. As a result, there was a broad tolerance for varieties of expression, perhaps broader than at any previous time in American history.[28]

This tolerant attitude began to change as darkening clouds portended another world war in Europe and Asia. Isolationists played on the fear of another war, portraying this country as being drawn into new battles on foreign soil, which would serve only foreign interests. Because Franklin D. Roosevelt was perceived to be in the Wilsonian internationalist camp, this isolationist stance also fit into efforts to diminish the power of the New Dealers and the liberal wing of the Democratic Party, with its tolerant attitudes toward dissent.

Enter Representative Howard Smith, ultraconservative segregationist Democrat from Virginia and recipient of J. Edgar Hoover's special favors and information. Smith introduced a bill in 1939 modeled on the New York Anarchy Act of 1902, which was used in the *Gitlow* case in the first Red Scare. The crucial portions of this legislation were finally approved by Congress and signed by the president on June 29, 1940.[29]

Advocacy of revolution and organizing (becoming a member of a revolutionary group) and conspiring to overthrow the government were made federal crimes; one need not have acted, but merely have advocated. Teaching, writing, or meeting was sufficient to establish guilt. The Smith Act was what Attorney General Palmer and Hoover had wanted, but did not have, as a weapon in the first Red Scare.

Smith himself went on to have his own investigative committee in 1943, the Special House Committee to Investigate Executive Agencies, with the implicit purpose of discrediting the New Deal.[30]

The Smith Act was prompted by fear of another world war and disappointment with the aftermath of World War I, combined with an opportunity to attack New Deal liberalism. It was directed against enemies from within who might urge war or revolution through speech, writing, or organization. The Smith Act became national law during those troubled months between the outbreak of the war in Europe on September 1, 1939, and the Japanese attack on Pearl Harbor on December 7, 1941. During these twenty-seven months, the nation was torn between wanting to stay out of the war and yet also wanting to deal with the threat to national and world stability posed by the Axis nations. That President Roosevelt signed the Smith Act into law is itself a reflection of these troubled times and political realities.

After the Soviet Union was attacked in June 1941, communists everywhere wholeheartedly supported the Allied war effort, joining almost every other segment of the American population. Indeed, when Hitler invaded Russia, the Communist Party did a flip-flop, reversing its prior pro-neutrality position and demanding that the United States enter the war on the side of England and the Soviet Union. The combination of Japanese aggression of December 7, 1941, the subsequent declaration of war against the United States by Germany and Italy, and the partnership with the Soviet Union temporarily put the Smith Act on the shelf; it was only used twice for criminal prosecutions prior to the commencement of the second Red Scare era.

Political radicalism and dissent were thus dormant during the war years 1941–45; for a short time even the American Communist Party dissolved itself into a "political association," stating that it would promote its program through existing political parties. Thus, in significant contrast to the circumstances of World War I, there was practically no dissent or overt opposition to America's war effort. Furthermore, other than the very questionable decision of interning Japanese-Americans from the West Coast (sanctioned by the Supreme Court in *Hirabayashi v. United States*[31] and *Korematsu v. United States*[32]), there was little hysteria during the war of the type exhibited by segments of the population after April 6, 1917. It is ironic that so much more was at stake in World War II, including questions of national existence, yet war fever and patriotism did not require suspending the teaching of the German, Italian, or Japanese languages or the playing of music from composers associated with Axis countries. It was only *after* the war that other forms of national paranoia pervaded the land.

When the major Allied powers joined with the Soviet Union, they created a shotgun marriage, a unity of convenience in the face of Axis aggression and attempt at world domination. Hitler made few errors. One was to attack another totalitarian power, the Soviet Union, before defeating England, forcing England and later the United States into alliance with Russia. War exigencies changed overt hostility by Western governments and their citizens toward Russia to a policy of embracing that nation, its leaders, and its people as vital allies against a common enemy. The Soviet Union's continued presence in the war was crucial to Allied victory. There was also the appreciation that most of the land fighting and casualties in battle, as well as physical devastation, were suffered by the Soviet Union. The hope of the Allied leaders, particularly President Roosevelt, was that the postwar world would yield continued cooperation and friendly engagement between Russia and the West.

That such cooperation was not meant to be strengthened the arguments of those who contended that alliance with the Soviet Union was a mistake, but almost all historians have disputed this revisionist view. What is left in the light of the reality of that wartime alliance (a necessity for both the Soviet Union and the West) is the issue of who is to blame for the Cold War that followed hard on the heels of the destruction of Nazi Germany, Fascist Italy, and Imperial Japan. Regardless of where and why blame is assessed, the concern here is the unfolding of the domestic counterpart of the Cold War.

Entering the arena of the second Red Scare, one is met with a number of vital questions. One often posed question is: when did the second Red Scare begin? The usual answer is when the Truman administration instituted its loyalty program in 1947, reacting to attacks on the administration as "soft on communism" or to Winston Churchill's 1946 "Iron Curtain" speech. Some would reach forward to the speech by Senator Joseph R. McCarthy in 1950 that alleged numerous (the number kept changing) communists in the State Department. But it can be cogently argued that, almost by chance, it was the rescue from oblivion by a close vote in January 1945 of what was to become the House Un-American Activities Committee (HUAC) that provided the genesis of the second Red Scare, even as fighting continued overseas. With the creation of a standing committee—the only permanent investigating committee in the House and one with subpoena power—the stage was set for those who would use and abuse these powers to create a witch hunt, seeking to identify the "extent, character and objectives of un-American propaganda activities in the United States."[33]

The fact that all HUAC's work was supposed to have a clear legislative purpose was to be lost in the headlines carrying the accusations of disloyalty against otherwise unknowns as well as against high-visibility Hollywood personalities. "Are you now or have you ever been a member of the Communist Party?" became the most famous question of Red Scare times. The failure to answer, the refusal to name names, could and did lead to contempt of Congress citations and jail for more than one hundred witnesses between 1945 and 1957. Between those years, HUAC conducted at least 230 hearings at which more than 3,000 persons testified. Its power to destroy lives and reputations has been well documented.[34]

While there had been a level of cooperation between the committee and the FBI prior to 1945, it was only after the creation of a standing committee in that year that a symbiosis between Hoover's agency and HUAC took place, resulting in a major power base for Red Scare activities. As one Hoover biographer has stated, "the anticommunist political style triumphed only when the FBI provided the type of assistance to HUAC and to other anticommunist interests that Martin Dies (chairman, 1938–44) had ached for."[35]

To another Hoover biographer, the nexus was most vividly demonstrated when Hoover, in effect, broke with the Truman administration (because he felt that the loyalty program was deficient and defective) and made a "spectacular appearance" before HUAC in 1947, contravening his own precedent of not appearing before any congressional committee (except Appropriations), in order to denounce communism and praise HUAC.[36] As one ex-FBI agent explained about his own resignation in the aftermath of the Red Scare: "Hoover was more interested in guys who were Communists for fifteen minutes in 1931 than he was in guys who were stealing New Jersey."[37] Thus the forces of a powerful House committee (the first of many) combined with the authority and potency of Hoover's FBI resources in an all-out war against "domestic disloyalty."

It is little wonder that various states, caught up in the fever of the search for "Reds," sought to imitate HUAC, as well as the strident tones of Hoover, who was for many decades the leading purveyor of Red Scare rhetoric. Furthermore, House committees instigated court cases (some reaching the Supreme Court) derived from their power to hold in contempt of Congress those refusing to answer questions about their political beliefs or affiliations. This weapon in the Red Scare arsenal was an innovation that had not been used in the first Red Scare era.

When did it end? By 1969 HUAC, a prime bulwark of the Red Scare, had retreated into a new name, the House Committee on Internal Security, and had stopped issuing subpoenas to hostile witnesses, a method that had been used extensively to gain popular attention as well as information by forcing testimony. The end came in 1975, when the committee itself was eliminated. The committee's files, including index cards on 750,000 alleged "subversive" Americans, were placed under seal in the National Archives.[38] Thus it can be argued that the Red Scare that had began in January 1945 with the establishment of HUAC did not finally end until thirty years later when the committee closed its doors.

Significant also was the death of the leading Red Scare warrior, J. Edgar Hoover, three years earlier in 1972. Realistically, however, the focus had already shifted in the 1960s from hunting down the old Reds of the Communist Party, left-wing unions, and dissenting groups and individuals, to the "New Left," which had coalesced in opposition to the war in Vietnam and in promotion of vigorous actions to gain civil rights for black citizens.

Larger questions and issues about the second Red Scare have continued to roil the national conscience. These address the whys and hows underlying the anti-communist witch hunt, focusing on and arguing the rights and wrongs involved. In the larger sense, the Red Scare touched millions personally through required loyalty oaths (teachers, union leaders, all armed services personnel, and all federal government and most state employees). For this reason alone, the second Red Scare stands in juxtaposition to the earlier one; then, only the very militant Industrial Workers of the World (IWW—known as the Wobblies), anarchists, some socialists, and, particularly, alien radicals were the focus of attention. The first Red Scare was essentially nothing more personal for almost all Americans than an elongated, dramatic newspaper story. The second Red Scare not only lasted for many years but touched countless lives and influenced ordinary people's political and personal conduct (how they voted; what they said; whom they were willing to be seen with; what they read or were willing to have others know they read). It also left many shattered lives. The stories of the controversy about the era persist to this day.[39]

Before rendering an oral history account of the involvement of Ring Lardner, Jr. and Frances Chaney Lardner with the "Hollywood Ten" (writers and directors who refused to answer questions at a HUAC hearing in 1947 on communist influence in the movie industry), the editors of *It Did Happen Here* set the stage by recalling some Red Scare events:

> Persons named at a Flint, Michigan, hearing were physically attacked by local vigilantes. A woman named at a Pittsburgh hearing, a mother of two children, was cut off from relief benefits. A Stanford University research scientist committed suicide after being served the committee's subpoena. Three days later, his wife was refused permission to present her statement in his place: "Is it a crime for a young man in his twenties to dream of a bright new world? Must the children of our country leave their idealism in the cradle so that their future careers will not be blighted by the Un-American Activities Committee?"[40]

Yet, too often, the focus of attention has been on prominent personalities of the era: actors and actresses, radio and television personalities who testified as "friendly witnesses," often naming names, or, because they were not cooperative, were blacklisted from working in these media. Or attention has focused on such prominent personalities as Alger Hiss, William Remington, and the Rosenbergs but has ignored what the Red Scare meant to multitudes of people caught up in its vortex. Realistically, the vast majority of those whose lives were touched by the Red Scare simply signed the oath, answered questions about their past, and had no active role in persecuting or being persecuted.

One of the ironies of the times was that those who were Party members or were willing to be Soviet agents would likely have no compunction about signing loyalty oaths or doing anything necessary to accomplish their purpose. Others faced problems of conscience when asked to swear to these "negative oaths," these demands to prove loyalty and good citizenship by saying what you have not belonged to, avowed, or associated with. Those who believed that citizenship alone provided the presumption of loyalty and that they had the right to face their accuser, and those who felt that HUAC was itself Un-American, were candidates for the public spotlight and sanction.

Thus, while the extensive American participation in World War II did not, during the war years, produce the hysteria, foolishness, and breaches of constitutionally protected rights that were evident during World War I, all, to some degree, were evident in the postwar years. An example of foolishness at least: Rockwell Kent, noted artist, illustrator, and left-wing political activist, who lived on a dairy farm, found that his neighbors stopped buying his dairy products under the influence of Red Scare times.[41]

The excesses and gross injustices of the Red Scare era are indefensible, and were so even before the collapse of the Soviet Union. It should be noted that a Red Scare response to the Cold War did not occur in any other Western country. Most historians agree that Russian expansionism justified the geopolitical reaction of the Truman administration. Winston Churchill's 1946 "Iron Curtain" speech represented a clear articulation of the view of most Americans that the world was truly divided; well into the 1980s, President Ronald Reagan's description of Russia as the Evil Empire continued the Cold War rhetoric. Heating up and cooling off for over forty years, it was the preeminent international theme, explaining, justifying, and labeling world events as well as reflexive internal postures. The Cold War carried with it the assurance that issues were clear cut—that there existed right and wrong, good and evil—all without compromise or doubt. Dictionaries accepted and defined the term, and nations armed themselves and developed global strategies in response to its existence.

A major Cold War component was fear of domestic subversion, or at least contamination of the population by the other side. With the United States taking on the role of superpower in a Cold War with Russia, there was a concomitant dread of Communist subversion, spying, and influence in this country. These fears gripped the nation with varying degrees of intensity throughout these decades and generated the era of the Red Scare. In the Soviet Union, parallel developments reflected fear of Western values and subversion. The Cold War for both sides was particularly hot from 1946 through the mid-1960s. But even in the cooled-down state of affairs in the 1980s, any reference to the Cold War still could be depended on to influence attitudes and actions.

Postwar disappointment that victory over the Axis had failed to provide a peaceful, secure existence and once again failed to make the world safe for democracy, turned the victory sour. On the international front, the Cold War continued hostilities, only against new enemies. On the domestic front, the Red Scare led to battles fought against those perceived to be internal enemies, particularly members of the American Communist Party. Peter Buckingham, writing of that time, stated,

"Anti-Communism has become so pervasive in American society that it has become an integral part of our culture."[42]

It is important, however, to distinguish the Cold War from its off-spring, the Red Scare. While the Cold War as an international phenomenon was inextricably interwoven with the anti-communist crusade carried on in the United States, the Red Scare had an active, virulent life that was shorter than that of the Cold War, which had nurtured it. The theme of this work is that by 1957, enough had changed in the domestic and international scenes that, in combination with changes in Supreme Court personnel, a dramatic departure from the role of the Court in supporting the government's position was to occur. The pragmatic effect was the substantial dismantling of the legal basis for the Red Scare. This theme, like many other aspects of Cold War-Red Scare issues, is itself controversial.[43]

Chapter 3
Red Scare at High Tide:
The *Dennis* Case

The death of Franklin D. Roosevelt, on April 12, 1945, cut short his apparent awakening to the deceptive, unreliable nature of Stalin and his regime. President Harry S Truman took little time to conclude that talking and acting tough with the Soviets was necessary if the Yalta agreements were to be fulfilled and Eastern European countries were to be saved from total Russian domination. The new president recognized the need to argue for a new foreign policy, a policy responsive to the threat of Stalinist expansionism.

An avid student of history, Truman knew that to rally support for continued American intervention in postwar Europe in the face of traditional American isolationism would be difficult. He believed that to accomplish this goal he had to arouse fears that would overcome isolationist sentiments, so he talked of a war against the communist plot to carry Bolshevist control throughout the world, destroying freedom and liberty wherever it succeeded. The idea was to scare and, through fright, to change American attitudes from isolationism to internationalism—no mean task.

The programs themselves—the Truman Doctrine (to supply military aid to any nation resisting internal or external threats of subjugation), the Marshall Plan (massive economic assistance to the war-ravaged countries in Europe), and ultimately the North Atlantic Treaty Organization (NATO), a military alliance to counter Russian threats—implemented this "containment of communism" policy. Under Truman the nation was thus firing urgent salvos of Cold War acts and rhetoric for worldwide as well as internal consumption.[1]

But there was a price to be paid by the Truman administration for selling a program of internationalism on the grounds of fear of communism, even as world events (such as the overthrow of the Czechoslovak government by communist coup and the Berlin Blockade) supported its position. That price was essentially political: Truman had uncorked the perception of communists, communism, and the American Communist Party as part of a worldwide conspiracy that threatened the nation. This strategy placed a needed and important weapon in the hands of Republicans, who had been out of power for so long; FDR was essentially invulnerable, but Truman and his administration were not.[2] World War II was over, the need for bipartisanship had ended, and political warfare could now resume.

Thus the Republicans accused the Democratic administration of being "soft on communism," of having Communist Party members and fellow travelers (those who are sympathetic to or follow the Party line, but are not members) in government or in agencies established by the federal executive branch. A simple answer began to emerge in response to most postwar issues facing the nation: Communists here and abroad were at fault. This explained why peace had not come with victory over the Axis, why China was "lost" to the communists, and why Russia got the atomic bomb. The reason produced the enemy: internal subversion and espionage.

The idea that any of this could happen because of failed U.S. policies, because of the reality of the Soviet presence in Eastern Europe, or because of Chinese Communist zeal was unacceptable. Therefore from 1946 to 1953 the Truman administration endeavored to appear (and act) tough against the Communist Party and other leftists. To do so, the administration had to counter the accusations, as well as the legislative moves, of right-wing Republicans. Particularly for the 1948 election campaign, Truman was advised to attack the Communist Party to garner votes by saying what the public apparently wanted to hear.

It may be argued that during the 1948 presidential election campaign the embers of the Red Scare were waiting to be ignited to blast furnace proportions, should the moderate wing of the Republican Party lose. Thomas E. Dewey of New York and his vice-presidential running mate, Earl Warren, governor of California, represented the internationalist and domestically moderate wing of the party. Because Truman defeated them, David Frumkin has concluded, "When they did lose, they [the Republican Party] felt cheated—and they were driven to desperate tactics."[3]

The Truman administration faced two linked problems: for political reasons, investigations and criminal prosecutions would never satisfy the right wing of the Republican Party (a fact that Eisenhower was to lament), and, once opened, the Pandora's box of investigations would not be limited to ferreting out provable disloyalty or espionage but would spread to all shades of leftists, liberals, New Dealers, and dissidents. The times would also induce Democratic members of Congress to attempt to outdo Republicans in their show of anti-communist zeal. Truman attempted, in some measure, to halt the forces he himself had unleashed—he spoke out against Senator McCarthy and bravely vetoed the Internal Security Act of 1950—but the Red Scare paid off far too many interests to be readily curbed or controlled.[4]

Shortly after the Republicans gained control of Congress in 1946, President Truman signed Executive Order 9806. This order established the Commission on Employee Loyalty, which was to help establish standards and procedures for investigating persons employed by the government. Its aim was removal of disloyal or subversive persons. This was the initial administration response to accusations that it was "soft on communism" and that it harbored subversives in government jobs. Thereafter, on March 21, 1947, came Executive Order 9835, which embodied the commission's findings, and the hunt for disloyalty was on. Attorney General Tom C. Clark, in his *Annual Report of the Attorney General of the United States* for 1947, put the best face on the program when he stated:

> The basic purpose underlying the establishment of the Departmental Loyalty Board is, of course, to protect the Government against the infiltration of subversive persons into the ranks of its employees. However, another and equally important purpose is served by the program, that of vindicating the innocence of those employees whose loyalty has been impugned.[5]

He did not add that this was the first peacetime federal employment loyalty program in U.S. history.

The attorney general's *Annual Report* for the following year stated that more than two million loyalty forms had been processed for employees and applicants, that full field investigations by the FBI were ordered in some 5000 cases, and that 435 employees stated had resigned during investigation to that date. The report found that these figures "are a source of deep gratification for they serve to vindicate the confidence which the Government has always reposed on its civil servants," as confirmed by the "infinitesimal number of cases in which evidence of divergence of allegiance has been found."[6] By 1952, the number of forms processed was nearly three million, with only 212 employees dismissed as potentially disloyal or as security risks. The work of these loyalty boards continued and in fact broadened during the Eisenhower years.[7]

In his report for 1948 (covering 1947), the attorney general created a new section dealing with "Subversive Activities"; in the prior year's report there had been no such heading. The 1948 report informed the reader that prosecutions were now taking place as a result of the loyalty oath program. It stated that "a large number of such cases are under active consideration by [the Department of] Justice and in several instances indictments have been obtained." These cases involved prosecu-

tions for contempt of court of persons accused of falsifying or conceal-
ing material facts or declining to answer questions or name names, or
for "unwarranted assertion of constitutional privilege."[8] Thus the court
system began to grapple with the legal issues presented by the loyalty
oath program.

Another significant source of Red Scare cases was alluded to in the
1948 report, the attorney general's creation in 1947 of a subversive organizations list. This list, which, according to Attorney General Clark, resulted from investigating hundreds of organizations, initially declared
123 of them as "subversive." Even though it was supposed to be used exclusively by the Federal Loyalty Review Board in its work,[9] the list soon
took on a life of its own. Published by newspapers and used by groups
involved in addressing issues of "loyalty" throughout the nation, the list
became the foundation for blacklisting, as well as for deporting aliens
tainted as "Reds" because they belonged to a listed organization. For
those accused of disloyalty simply by virtue of membership in one or
more of the listed organizations, it was clearly a case of guilt by association.

No public hearing or opportunity to challenge being listed as a subversive organization was part of the listing process. Once again, the
courts were to come into play as three of the listed organizations filed
suit to dispute their inclusion as subversive.[10]

By 1947, indictments for contempt of Congress came in increasing
numbers, resulting in federal court trials as the House Committee on
Un-American Activities (HUAC) continued its hearings and demands
for prosecution against those refusing to answer its questions or name
names. The political heat was intense; the Truman administration had
to demonstrate its anti-communist zeal without appearing to knuckle
under to right-wing Republican demands. The Subversive Organizations
List was trumpeted as proof that there was a network of groups of an
un-American nature being actively ferreted out by the administration.

Bills were introduced in Congress that attacked the domestic communist "problem" from many directions, all of which would infringe on, or
literally outlaw, the right of dissent. For example, the Mundt-Nixon Subversive Activities Control Act of 1948 would have required the Communist Party, its front organizations, and its individual members to register
with a federal agency. It proposed these legislative findings as a basis
for this radical legislation: that a clear and present danger existed in
the form of the communist movement and that this movement sought
to overthrow the government. If passed, the act would have made the
Communist Party illegal and required all members to register as persons having allegiance to a foreign power. Red Scare activities were also

directed at union leadership. Section 9(h) of the Labor-Management Relations (Taft-Hartley) Act required non-communist affidavits.

The result of all this was pressure that mounted in early 1948 on the administration for court action to stave off the Mundt-Nixon Bill and other anti-communist legislation that would embarrass the Democrats.[11] The Red Scare had, by 1949, metastasized to every appendage of the nation's body. Fear for oneself, one's family, one's job, and one's status in the eyes of society gripped tens of thousands in the wake of the Red Scare. This fear was elevated to the status of national paranoia for Americans caught in its grasp.

In the throes of the Great Depression, millions of middle-class Americans had feared losing their jobs. By analogy, the Red Scare era reintroduced this fear syndrome; this time it was a fear that they would be accused of some wrongdoing that could (as realistically as the loss of work in depression times) bring trauma, stress, and financial ruin. This is not to say that a majority of citizens were directly and personally confronted by accusations, but, for many, they were a serious threat, particularly since accusations could come from unnamed, unrevealed sources. Everyone had a "closet," and the fear and consequences of exposure were palpable.

Thomas Mann, the celebrated novelist, had made anti-Nazi speeches and statements in Germany, leaving that country in 1938 and becoming an American citizen. In 1947 he was brought before HUAC as a part of its investigation of communists in Hollywood. Mann was at the time a socialist, but he denied being a communist or fellow traveler. Nevertheless, he was branded a communist by the committee. In 1952, depressed by the Red Scare hysteria and often vilified by the press, he left for Switzerland and never returned.[12]

Edward G. Robinson, the nationally noted actor, when threatened with being blacklisted, had a representative go through his check stubs to prove he had not knowingly contributed to any so-called subversive organizations. Surely this was ironic, given Robinson's "tough guy" persona in the movies. To clear his name, Robinson appeared twice before HUAC, in 1950 and 1952. The extent to which he appeared and offered "proof" of his loyalty is but one demonstration of how profoundly the Red Scare had invaded American life.[13]

If such persons as Thomas Mann and Edward G. Robinson could be attacked and intimidated for their politics, beliefs, or associations, then tens of thousands of powerless people caught up in Red Scare threats or accusations were understandably fearful for their jobs, their families, and their status in society.

While most Red Scare incidents did not end up in courtrooms, those who attempted to obtain redress or defend themselves against charges of violating state or federal law were to find that American courtrooms offered little by way of sanctuary for their politics, their views of First Amendment freedoms, or their right to dissent. Those who were forced into court by government prosecution or to appeal a conviction had the additional obstacle of finding lawyers willing to represent them.

The Red Scare did not exempt the legal community. Attorneys defending dissidents could find themselves losing clients and being subjected to much adverse publicity. Because passions ran high in a number of these Red Scare cases, the threat of sanctions in the form of a contempt charge was very real. Contempt could lead not only to a fine but also to jail; all the attorneys representing the top Communist Party leaders in *United States v. Dennis* were found in contempt, as was Eugene Dennis, who represented himself. All the attorneys were given jail terms; some were brought up for disbarment proceedings. Broken lives, as well as smashed professional standing, was the price they paid for representing dissidents in those times.[14]

A further disadvantage for one accused during the Red Scare era was the lack of funds with which to try or appeal a case. Against the substantial resources of the federal or state government, even an affluent citizen could not compete. Almost invariably, the contest favored the government. None of the Smith Act defendants had a "dream team" on his side, nor did any have court-appointed lawyers or public defenders paid by the government, as defendants have today.

In 1952, Supreme Court Justice William O. Douglas, writing in the *New York Times*, took a realistic note of the difficulties unpopular defendants faced:

Fear even strikes at lawyers and the Bar. Those accused of illegal Communist activity—all presumed innocent, of course, until found guilty—have difficulty getting reputable lawyers to defend them. Lawyers have talked with me about it. Many are worried. Some could not volunteer their services, for if they did they would lose clients and their firms would suffer. Others could not volunteer because if they did they would be dubbed "subversive" by their community and put in the same category as those they would defend. This is a dark tragedy.[15]

Factually, Douglas was correct: getting counsel for those under attack as subversives was extremely difficult. Because of hearings before HUAC, deportation board hearings, state and federal loyalty boards, and criminal prosecutions of communists and communist-affiliated organizations, a significant demand was created for the few lawyers willing to defend accused individuals and groups.

At the very time when more lawyers were needed, HUAC launched a major attack against the National Lawyers Guild, an organization of liberal lawyers (some were Communist Party members) that provided many attorneys for the accused.[16] HUAC in 1950 labeled the organization an "appendage to the Communist Party" and accused it of serving as a "legal bulwark" of the Party.[17]

The atmosphere was one of chill, if not panic, among lawyers called on to act as counsel to those people and organizations.[18] The red brush painted broad strokes indeed when wielded by bar associations; additionally, some members of Congress, government agencies, and the media, as well as these private groups, made a crusade and a business out of anti-communism.

In his *History of American Law*, Lawrence M. Friedman observes the following about judges asked to rule on politically sensitive issues:

The judges were themselves middle-class; they could easily empathize with professionals and artisans. Their constitutional antennae were much more sensitive when they picked up vibrations of class struggle or proletarian revolt, things which they barely understood and desperately feared.[19]

Judges, in their approach to treating the issues, as well as the parties and their lawyers, were far from immune to Red Scare times. The Red Scare itself was palpably in court; given the pervasiveness of the scare evident in all forms of media, it could hardly be otherwise. Besides, an important Red Scare case could make a judge into an important or even a nationally known personality, a phenomenon exemplified by Harold R. Medina (judge in the *Dennis* case) and Irving R. Kaufman (judge in the *Rosenberg* case).[20] Conversely, being on the "wrong" side of a Red Scare case could also prevent promotion, as happened in the judicial career of Judge Learned Hand.[21] We have already noted Hoover's reaction to Supreme Court justices who were on the "wrong" side of anti-communist issues.

One central question was increasingly voiced in Congress and the media: why wasn't the Justice Department directly and forcefully prosecuting Communist Party members?[22] Heat poured in from all sides on this hottest of national political issues. Attorney General Clark, the focus of a great deal of this pressure, hoped that stepped-up deportations in late 1947 and early 1948 would dampen demands for other action. The answer, however, long and vigorously promoted by J. Edgar Hoover, was to use the Smith Act to prosecute the leadership of the Communist Party; in doing so, Hoover could fulfill the task he had begun in 1919 as director of Attorney General Palmer's Radical Division.[23] One biographer has stated, "In broad design, Hoover was replaying the 1919–20 assault on the American Communists, but he was avoiding, this time, the mistakes that had defeated him before."[24]

The machinations that eventually led a reluctant Attorney General

Clark to yield to FBI, HUAC, congressional, and public pressures to indict the top leadership of the Communist Party were byzantine. For
example, although the Bureau denied that the FBI had any role in initi-
ating these prosecutions, most sources agree that the FBI's role was "direct, persistent, and persuasive."[25] Hoover, at the same time, unknown
to Clark (his bureaucratic superior) or Truman, was assisting HUAC in
its war against communism and in its bitter opposition to the administration's record on dealing with the communist "threat." Thus, through
his public pronouncements, through his behind-the-scenes work with
HUAC, and by virtue of the pressure he brought to bear within the
administration, "Hoover was the catalyst for the decision to indict the
Communist party leadership."[26] He also handed Clark a legal brief in
support of the proposed indictments that, with exhibits, ran almost
2000 pages.

Hoover's aim was nothing less than the destruction of the Party and
"the detention of any persons whom the Bureau considered 'sympathetic' to communism, quite possibly an impressive number."[27]

Hoover also posited an educational purpose: to teach the American
public about the evils of Communists and their Party through this trial.
It was evident that such prosecutions would also justify the decades of
expenditures and staff time dedicated to this purpose. Another message
was that unorthodox ideology would bring down on dissidents the considerable wrath and power of the federal government. In fact, by 1948
the Communist Party was severely reduced in numbers and thoroughly
discredited in almost every sector of American society. As David Caute
has described the prosecution, "The government took a sledgehammer
to squash a gnat."[28]

Clark, caught between the Hoover/HUAC pressure, the political implications for the Democratic Party in 1948, and his own doubts, agreed
to commence prosecutions; he did not, however, give Hoover all he
wanted. Hoover wanted all fifty-five members of the Communist Party
National Committee to be arrested and prosecuted; instead only the
twelve members of the Communist National Board were tried for violating the Smith Act. Hoover wanted a repeat of the 1917 prosecution of all
national and local leaders of the radical labor organization the Industrial Workers of the World (called the IWW or the Wobblies), which
resulted in prison sentences for more than one hundred leaders and
successfully crushed that organization. He need not have worried; the
Communist Party was already terribly weak, and the use of former Party
members at the trial who were either FBI agents or Party members who
became informants detailing inner workings of Party plans, was devas-
tating to the Communists and their Party.[29]

Deportations, contempt of congressional prosecutions, and loyalty oath enforcements all became sideshows once the Smith Act prosecutions commenced. These Smith Act cases portrayed the heart of the domestic war against communism, Communists, the Communist Party, and those persons and organizations allegedly fronting their aims.

The Communist Party, through the trial of its leadership, was to battle for its life in *United States v. Dennis*, which lasted for almost nine months, from January 17, 1949 to October 14, 1949, and was the centerpiece of Smith Act legal action in the Red Scare movement. Meanwhile, communist hunting in other arenas, not bound by the limitations inherent in the American court system, continued full force.

HUAC went after Alger Hiss, the most prominent State Department employee to be accused of espionage. Elizabeth Bentley, the "Red Spy Queen," corroborated the testimony of another ex-Communist that Hiss was a Soviet spy. This was also the time when freshman Representative Richard M. Nixon climbed aboard the Red Scare bandwagon to become an effective anti-communist advocate and Hiss's major nemesis.[30] Also in the midst of the *Dennis* trial came the arrest of Judith Coplon, a Treasury Department employee accused of espionage and of having FBI documents in her possession at the time of her arrest. Thus the public had plenty of other Red Scare news to read and hear about on the radio as the trial of the top Party leadership slowly moved forward.

Dennis was different from the other Smith Act cases because it alone focused on what an entire political party represented—not just on individuals accused of espionage, perjury, or contempt. Whatever such individuals did or may have done for "the cause," that cause was symbolized by the Party, and now the Party, through its leadership, was on trial.

Twelve men were indicted on July 28, 1948 by a federal grand jury in New York; all were members of the national governing board of the Party. One woman, Elizabeth Gurley Flynn, was indicted later. Eleven of the twelve were tried; William Z. Foster was severed from the group because of precarious health. Into Foley Square, in the heart of New York City's financial district, came these twelve, having been charged with "willingly and knowingly conspiring"

(1) to organize as the Communist Party of the United States of America as a society, group and assembly of persons who teach and advocate the overthrow and destruction of the Government of the United States by force and violence, and (2) knowingly and willfully to advocate and teach the duty and necessity of overthrowing and destroying the Government of the United States by force and violence.

The indictment further alleged that Section 2 of the Smith Act proscribes these acts and that any conspiracy to take such action is a violation of Section 3 of the Act.[31]

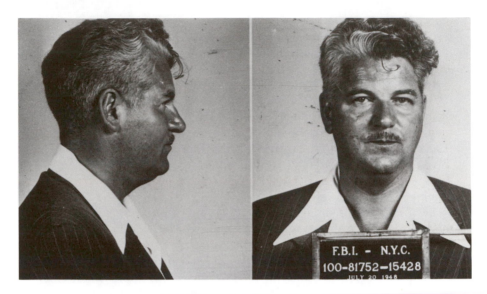

Figure 2. Eugene Dennis, general secretary of the Communist Party-USA, at the time of his arrest by the FBI in 1948. FBI photo; UPI/Corbis-Bettmann photograph.

The key words of the indictment tie into the Smith Act: "organize" (be a member), "teach," "advocate," and "conspire" to engage in all these acts for the purpose of overthrowing the government "by force and violence." At bottom, the leadership was accused of organizing the Party as a vehicle for advocating the illegal acts (Article 2), as well as for conspiring among themselves through their common membership for the purpose of teaching and advocating the overthrow of the government (Article 3).

What they were not accused of was actually attempting that overthrow, undertaking to develop a force of arms, or teaching the military techniques of revolt. No cache of arms was found, no technology for blowing up buildings was unearthed in Communist hands, and no militia-type exercises for engaging in the proposed overthrow were revealed, because none of these things existed. At most (but under the Smith Act it was sufficient for conviction), these Party leaders conspired to advocate the violent overthrow of the government at some future appropriate time and had joined together for that purpose.

It became clear even to the Party's leadership that there would be convictions and that there was an overwhelmingly favorable public response to trying and convicting Communist Party members. The Party's

Figure 3. Leaders of the Communist Party-USA, soon to be tried under the Smith Act, in front of the Federal Court Building. Left to right: Henry Winston, Eugene Dennis, Benjamin Davis, Gus Hall, John Williamson, Carl Winter, John Gates, Irving Potash, Robert Thompson, and Jack Stachel. Absent from this photograph are William Z. Foster, who was too ill to be tried, and Gilbert Green, who was not present for the picture but who was tried and convicted. UPI/Corbis-Bettmann photograph.

strategy, as it developed, was to lower its sights and seek instead to put pressure on President Truman and Attorney General Clark to stop the proceedings. In turn this brought continued legal maneuvers designed to delay the trial in order to yield the time felt necessary to press for a termination of the proceedings.

The strategy failed, and, in the end, the trial began on January 17, 1949, before an inexperienced judge, Harold R. Medina. As a presiding judge, this would be Medina's first criminal trial. An analysis of his personal traits, particularly on the bench, has led a leading historian of the era to conclude that the choice of Medina was an error.[32]

Ironically, Medina's name has been consistently linked with the *Dennis*

Figure 4. *Dennis* defense lawyers photographed after being held in contempt of court by Judge Harold R. Medina. Left to right: Abraham H. Isserman, George W. Crockett Jr., Richard Gladstein, Harry Sacher, and Louis F. McCabe. The prison sentences ranged from terms of thirty days to six months. UPI/Corbis-Bettmann photograph.

case, while his participation as lead defense counsel in a case tried in the same federal court just seven years before has been generally overlooked. That case was a treason charge against Anthony Cramer for aiding two Nazi saboteurs in 1942.[33]

Medina, assigned to defend Cramer, faced a "fevered wartime atmosphere." He apparently viewed his client as a "poor little fellow" and gave the equivalent of a year of his professional time to Cramer's cause; the value of his fee in 1940s dollars has been estimated at $100,000. Beyond money was the personal price Medina paid: he was "spat on in court, shunned by friends and neighbors, and bawled out by his mother for mixing with Nazis."[34]

Medina's performance in representing a man accused of treason in a highly charged wartime atmosphere won high praise. On appeal before the Supreme Court, after losing in the trial court, when Medina was questioned there about his assertion of a hostile trial atmosphere, he stated that "the problem appears differently from where you sit and

Figure 5. Federal Judge Harold R. Medina at the time of the *Dennis* trial in 1949. UPI/Corbis-Bettmann photograph.

down here."[35] Adding that treason charges in wartime create hostility toward any defendant, he recounted his own mistreatment as proof.

The Supreme Court's decision in *Cramer v. United States* came just before the end of the war in Europe. Given the imminent collapse of Germany and exposure of the European Holocaust, the *Cramer* decision received little news coverage. The Court majority found insufficient evidence of treason, leaving the government open to retrying the case; instead, Cramer pleaded guilty to a lesser crime.

The *Cramer* case, with its high evidentiary standards for proof of treason, influenced the use of "lesser" means such as the Smith Act as a safer

Figure 6. Hundreds of pickets marched silently at the Federal Courthouse, Foley Square, New York City, on October 21, 1949, during the sentencing of the eleven top Communists. UPI/Corbis-Bettmann photograph.

and more certain path than charges of treason for attacking internal enemies during the Red Scare era. The *Cramer* case also made Medina an exemplar of "a prominent advocate [who] braved hostility to defend an accused in a time of popular passion."[36]

Thus the irony: in 1949, where was the lawyer who had so bravely defended a very unpopular client in hostile times just a few years before? Indeed, perhaps the difference was where he now sat.

Medina the judge was undoubtedly biased against the *Dennis* defendants, was sensitive to anything he considered an insult, and believed the defendants and their lawyers were out to wreck his health and sanity.[37] This led to persistent confrontations between the Communists and their lawyers and what one historian has called "an antagonist on the bench."[38] On the other hand, the defendants' lawyers took orders from Party leaders, and their legal skills were basically used to promote

Party propaganda, at least once the initial goal of preventing the trial had failed.[39]

With a biased judge, an unsympathetic jury (one juror had declared before the trial that "we must fight Communism to the death" and during the trial spoke of his determination "to hang those Commies," the words and deeds (using false names, filing false oaths) of the defendants, the effective use of FBI spies and government informers who could make even innocent-sounding language into evil plots, and the sometimes circus-like atmosphere in the courtroom as the judge clashed with the defendants and their attorneys, a guilty verdict was a near certainty. After Judge Medina determined that as a matter of law (not for the jury to decide) there *was* a clear and present danger posed by the Communist Party, the jury had only two choices: it could reject everything the judge had declared or convict all defendants. The jury chose the latter.[40]

The guilty verdicts in *Dennis* were also assured by larger issues of the times: the Red Scare was in a state of high intensity and was tangibly in that courtroom. The nine-month-long trial spanned events that intensified the developing Red Scare: the Coplon espionage case continued; Alger Hiss awaited trial for perjury; Communists were being purged from unions and barred from holding union office; Harry Bridges, the West Coast labor leader, was accused of perjury when he denied being a Communist; the University of California required all faculty to take non-communist oaths; the Vatican announced that communists would be excommunicated; even the American Civil Liberties Union (ACLU) adopted an anti-communist resolution. In 1948–49, legitimate and defensible moves continued under the actual threat of Soviet power and expansion. American leadership formed NATO and organized the Berlin Blockade airlift, reflecting the hardening of Cold War lines. Unfortunately, these world events were used as justification for battle against a perceived internal "threat."

To these developments must be added two more of the greatest significance. On September 23, 1949, just a few weeks before the trial ended, President Truman announced that the Soviet Union had detonated an atomic bomb.[41] The presumed line of ultimate defense was gone: the communists had the Bomb. That same day, the defense in the *Dennis* case rested and the government attorneys waived the opportunity to rebut the defendants' case; given the times it was not necessary.

Also during the course of the *Dennis* trial, Chiang Kai-shek resigned and fled with the remnants of his supporters to the island of Formosa, and on October 1, 1949, the Communist leaders Mao Tse-tung and Chou En-lai declared the People's Republic of China. Russia had the Bomb, and China was now in communist hands. Who was to blame? The most agreeable explanations fueled the Red Scare: espionage and betrayal had stolen the A-bomb secrets and "lost" China to the Reds.

Thus the *Dennis* decision at the trial level reflected—in fact, mirrored—American society. World events were hardening into intractable lines between "free" (non-communist, though in some cases authoritarian, states) and communist-dominated countries. Friends and enemies were sharply delineated. In *Dennis* the internal enemy had been tried and found guilty. As to "losses" on the world scene, those might be beyond control, but similar defeats on home territory would be both unjustifiable and intolerable.

The *Dennis* trial encompassed many thousands of pages of record and resulted in not one, but more than a dozen, appellate-level decisions, including at least five United States Supreme Court opinions. These cases on appeal contained another important result, highly relevant to those times and since: the contempt proceedings initiated by Judge Medina against certain defendants and all of the defense lawyers.[42]

The defense strategy in the *Dennis* trial involved a two-fold approach: to show that the Party was a legitimate, constitutionally protected political organization and that the defendants' acts, writings, and statements were protected by the First Amendment and were nonviolent in nature. In effect, the argument was that there was no clear and present danger, only discussion and thinking. But along with this traditionally grounded defense there was the aim of using the trial as a challenge to the "system"—putting capitalism on trial. This reflected what the Communists called their "labor defense" strategy, developed years before this trial. It called for protests in and out of the courtroom predicated on the belief that no capitalist trial could be fair to any proletarian defendant.[43]

The result of this approach was to attack the method of selecting jurors for grand and trial juries and to highlight the faults and failures of a capitalist society. In the wake of this strategy followed quarrelsome bickering with, and attacks against, Judge Medina. The media, the Department of Justice, and other federal officials, including the president, were also disparaged. Melvin B. Lewis adds these observations:

No thoughtful lawyer would have believed that such tactics would persuade the jury to acquit. A reading of the turgid trial record instills the conjecture that the defense may have abandoned hope for an acquittal and was engaged in an attempt to provoke a mistrial.[44]

Such tactics did not produce a mistrial, but they did provoke Medina to retaliate against the defense attorneys and their clients. Even during the trial, in an atmosphere of overt mutual hostility, four of the defendants were jailed, one for refusing to answer a question on cross-examination, two others for vocally protesting the judge's action against the first, and the fourth for complaining to the judge "in an angry, sarcastic manner" about his ruling refusing to allow an article to be introduced into evidence.[45]

After the jury had found all defendants guilty, but before pronouncing sentences on the defendants, Judge Medina said, "Now I turn to some unfinished business." It was pay-back time for having, in his view, been abused. All the defense attorneys were held in contempt of court (meaning in contempt of Judge Medina) for their conduct during the trial. He read from a lengthy order he had prepared and proceeded to impose prison sentences on each of them. No attorney was allowed to speak on his own behalf, nor did Medina hold any sort of hearing to allow any argument in opposition to his order. Sentences ranged from thirty days to six months in prison.[46]

This contempt procedure, directing imprisonment for members of the trial bar, was unprecedented; one authority has termed it "freakish."[47] All these contempt citations and prison sentences were appealed, but there was little chance for success given the times and the inability of a reviewing court to decide whether the acts or words were delivered in contemptuous fashion. The legal ramifications of summarily sending lawyers to prison was the subject of a number of appeals. A Supreme Court majority essentially affirmed Medina's findings and method; Justices Black, Frankfurter, and Douglas dissented on the procedural issue of how Medina carried out his contempt findings. Black and Frankfurter wrote an analysis of the fifteen-volume trial record as the basis for their objection to Medina's method. Their view was that the court was deficient in handling the lapses in proper court decorum and often encouraged debate, repartee, and banter between the judge and the attorneys.[48]

The result of Supreme Court majority decisions was jail for these lawyers and significant expansion of the trial court's contempt powers. The only meaningful retreat from these contempt decisions since 1952 was when the Supreme Court in 1968 adopted the view expressed by Justice Black in his dissent in *Sacher v. United States* (one of the defense attorneys), by granting the right to trial by jury if the contempt sentence exceeded six months in prison.[49]

If the nature of the Smith Act prosecutions and other venues for Red Scare proceedings had deterred lawyers from representing leftist defendants, the jailing of the *Dennis* trial lawyers provided an even stronger disincentive to undertake such representation.

To these dangers of contempt and jail were added other potential threats: disbarment, suspension from the practice of law, or formal reprimand. Two *Dennis* attorneys (Abraham Isserman and Harry Sacher) were disbarred. Isserman regained the right to practice in 1961. An appeal to the Supreme Court of the United States was necessary before Sacher's right to practice law was restored. Other attorneys defending Smith Act defendants in years following *Dennis* frequently found themselves in trouble with licensing or regulatory agencies or courts. In trials that followed *Dennis,* two of the defendants who were also lawyers and were found guilty of violating the Smith Act were disbarred.[50]

It became more difficult after the *Dennis* trial for a defendant to obtain counsel when faced with a Smith Act charge or accused in a loyalty-security case. Because lawyers came to fear guilt by association, those who needed representation the most were often unable to obtain competent counsel. There were some brave lawyers who swam against this current, often at financial sacrifice, preferring principle to profit.[51] For defendants, being found guilty of violating the Smith Act or losing a security-loyalty battle almost invariably meant an additional punishment: no chance for employment and social opprobrium that might last for years.

This was the time (September 1950) when the American Bar Association's House of Delegates adopted a resolution urging that attorneys be required to file affidavits of nonmembership in the Party. The next year the ABA recommended that all Communists and advocates of Marxism-Leninism be expelled from the practice of law by state regulatory bodies. The attitude of the organized bar did not change until 1953, when the ABA recognized that, even in Red Scare times, it was the lawyer's duty to represent all defendants, no matter how unpopular.[52]

On the other hand, the National Lawyers Guild, which had supplied most of the lawyers for Smith Act defendants, was itself placed on the attorney general's Subversive Organizations List. A guild official stated, "the blow was paralyzing." The guild spent its energies defending itself, but with the exodus of many members the pool of attorneys willing to take on those accused was still further reduced.[53] The result was that defendants were disadvantaged and often desperate. Maurice Braverman, himself an attorney, after many tries gave up on finding counsel willing to defend him in a Smith Act case. Elizabeth Gurley Flynn, who was not tried in the *Dennis* case but who became a prominent defendant in the next round of Smith Act prosecutions, sought counsel for herself and fellow defendants. They approached approximately two hundred lawyers, all of whom refused to represent the group. Defendants even had difficulty finding attorneys to handle appeals, where the public exposure was much less.[54]

Nor could the Party raise the money necessary to pay lawyers. The final bill for the *Dennis* trial may have run as high as $500,000. The

cost of preparing appeals was also high, and losing on appeal could result in the government's costs being shifted to the appellants.[55] There
were insufficient funds available from within the Party, and attempts to
raise money for bail funds, attorneys, and court costs fell short of ever-
growing needs. For lack of bail funds, defendants languished in jail.

A major source of money to pay lawyers, court costs, and bail money
was the Civil Rights Congress and its ancillary Bail Fund group. Formed
after World War II by some leading leftists, civil rights advocates, and
communists, the group included Paul Robeson, Representative Vito
Marcantonio, Dashiell Hammett, and other nationally known names
among its supporters. When the Smith Act prosecutions produced the
need to raise defense and bail money, contributions were solicited with
the promise that names of contributors would not be exposed. Robeson's efforts to raise money for the organization in 1949 touched off riots
in Peekskill, New York.[56]

When four of the *Dennis* defendants, on orders from the Party, jumped
bail to go underground in 1951, the Bail Fund, which had provided the
money, was called before a grand jury investigating the disappearance
of the four. Hammett, a trustee of the Bail Fund, was famous for his
mystery books and screenplays. Called before the grand jury, he did not
know the name of any contributor and could have pleaded honest ignorance; instead he invoked the Fifth Amendment and was sentenced to
six months in prison. When he was released in December 1951, he found
he had been blacklisted from radio, television, and films. The IRS au-
dited his tax returns and presented a bill for more than $100,000. After
an appearance before McCarthy's subcommittee, his books (mainly his
detective novels) were removed by McCarthy's associates, Roy Cohn and
G. David Schine, from State Department libraries overseas. Actor José
Ferrer and actress Judy Holliday were others accused of Civil Rights
Congress and Bail Fund involvement and whose careers were similarly
affected.[57]

Following the *Dennis* case bond forfeiture, an all-out attack was
mounted against the Civil Rights Congress and particularly the Bail
Fund. The jumping of bail by the four cost the fund $60,000. Fifteen
other New York Communist defendants had their bail bonds canceled
because the Bail Fund had supplied the money. The government got
the names of some 4000 contributors, and in May 1952 the New York
attorney general obtained an injunction freezing the fund's remaining
assets and enjoining its activities. By June 1952, the attorney general announced that he had "broken" the Bail Fund and had a list of 6,442
names of individuals and organizations that had contributed. David
Caute called this and other related federal and state government ac-

tions a deliberate attempt to break organizations linked to the defense of Communists, leftists, and civil libertarians. As to the destruction of the Civil Rights Congress and its Bail Fund, he concluded, "The lesson for other citizens who might be tempted to champion the legal rights of political outcasts was clear." [58]

Chapter 4
The Aftermath of the *Dennis* Trial

When Harry "Rabbit" Angstrom, in John Updike's novel *Rabbit at Rest*, said, "The Cold War. It gave you a reason to get up in the morning," he was reflecting, in a satirical but nevertheless realistic sense, the pervasiveness of the Cold War and Red Scare times that percolated within the nation and its courts. The Red Scare was tangible nationwide, imposing a sense of war against Communists, leftists, and dissidents.

It would be historically accurate to state that in the normal course of war against an external enemy the law remains silent—silent in the sense of conforming to the Zeitgeist of the times, of placing no legal impediments in the way of waging that war. In Latin, this idea has been expressed as *inter arma silent leges*. This has been true even in countries such as the United States, where the judiciary is supposed to be independent of the will of the executive and legislative branches. When the judicial system is, however, made up of citizens drawn from and essentially reflecting the general population, it takes extraordinary trial or appellate judges to run counter to the times—especially when the times involve their nation at war. Both Red Scares proved that an ideological war against internal enemies generated a judicial silence, a conformity as strict as that produced during a war against an external enemy.

Sixty-three years before the *Dennis* trial, the Haymarket bombing occurred in Chicago. During an outdoor rally in 1886, labor anarchists were demonstrating for the eight-hour work day when someone threw a bomb, killing a number of people, including eight policemen. Just who was responsible for the bomb was never established. Nevertheless, eight leaders of the sponsoring organization were prosecuted for murder. All were found guilty, though none was actually linked to the bomb. Four were hanged and a fifth killed himself to cheat the gallows. Three remained in jail until 1893, when they were pardoned by Illinois Governor John P. Altgeld in a message that acknowledged the injustice of the trial.[1]

In a parallel to the *Dennis* defendants, the anarchists stood for the internal enemy. As Carl Smith wrote,

What had actually happened in the Haymarket, like the miscarriage of justice at the trial, was almost irrelevant, a technicality quickly disposed of as part of the larger purpose of making the accused responsible for the conflicts of the time.[2]

From the announcement of the indictments of the Communist national leadership on July 21, 1948, through the long trial that followed, the print media covered the major events. the *New York Times* ran the headline, "12 U.S. Communists Indicted in Anti-Government Plot. Foster [William Z. Foster, Party Chairman], Davis [Benjamin Davis, a New York City councilman and member of the Communist National Board], Others, Seized."[3] Newspapers and magazines covered the trial, and editorial comments overwhelmingly favored the government cause. Most of the focus was on the personalities of the participants, primarily Judge Medina. Increasingly, as the months at trial wore on, he was portrayed as demonstrating saintly patience in the face of diatribes, maneuvers, and explosive confrontations with the defense attorneys. Issues receded as the courtroom antics and sidewalk demonstrations were highlighted by nationally prominent newspapers and magazines.[4] Judge Medina made the cover of *Time* at the end of the trial; the magazine concentrated on his role in conducting the longest criminal trial in U.S. history.[5]

The *Dennis* trial, which had taken many months to present, with its thousands of documents and scores of witnesses, resulted in a jury verdict of guilty on all counts against every defendant after just seven hours of deliberation. The general consensus among the press and public was one of satisfaction with the outcome of the trial; the head of domestic evil had been duly severed, though the body still had appendages that were to be destroyed by further prosecutions.

There were, however, some warnings issued from the liberal and leftist press to the effect that all might not be well for the nation as a result of these convictions. Stating the case for caution and questioning the wisdom of the *Dennis* trial, the *New Republic* reflected on the meaning of the convictions. While not contesting the fact that the trial showed the nation that the Communist Party was a secret society and not a legitimate political party and that there was "some very wild talk" at secret meetings of Party cells, the editorial pointed out that what was said in private was also said publicly, as well as published in books and pamphlets. Labeling *Dennis* as "in fact a political trial, conducted in an atmosphere of political hysteria, with a background of the cold war with the Soviet Union," the editorial concluded:

In such an atmosphere, "Anglo-Saxon justice" in the old sense is impossible. Men's actions are judged, not by what they mean, but by what they might mean. Any accusation is in some degree a condemnation—as it is in Washington today, where the charge of disloyalty ruins a man's career no matter how completely he is afterward vindicated.

In these terms the Communist trial has been a disaster, or, rather, part of a long-continued and mounting disaster in which millions of Americans, under the whip of fear, are losing much of their sense of proportion, their sense of humor, and their adherence to democratic principles. It is no answer—though people often try to make it one—to say that in the Communist-controlled countries the same thing is even more true; if we respond to an attack on our democracy by adopting the attitude of the opponent, that opponent thereby wins a great part of his case. The Communists if they are as shrewd as we think they are will be delighted to be made martyrs and to be spared the necessity of any longer pretending to conduct themselves properly in terms of our national mores. It is the American people who have now suffered a defeat, a defeat from which only the Supreme Court can rescue us.[6]

In contrast, *Reader's Digest* contained a lengthy review of the trial, untroubled by any constitutional, civil liberties, or right-to-dissent issues. Instead, it fastened on Judge Medina's splendid role in bringing criminals to justice. The article stated that Medina received 60,000 pieces of mail after the verdict, only one of which was not laudatory. It concluded:

The mail now [as compared to early communications from prominent people] was from average American citizens who were grateful to the Judge for the outstanding service he had rendered his country.

No matter what happens in the future, whether the appeals from this trial are successful or not, no matter how many protestations the Communists make with some new "line," the fact of their criminal conspiracy against all decent Americans is established once and for all. By their own words, they have forever convicted themselves. Their unchangeable intention is to destroy, by force and violence, everything we hold dear. Let every American remember this.[7]

Among many government officials, local, state, and national, there was high praise for the verdict, the judge, and government prosecutors; the lead prosecuting attorney was soon appointed to a federal judgeship. Typical of the comments, and voicing the mood of the times, were remarks appearing in the *Congressional Record* in the wake of the guilty verdict:

Mr. Speaker, a deep debt of gratitude is owed to the American people for this magnificent democratic way of life which was resplendently mirrored in the conduct of the trial of the 11 Communists presided over by the patient and forbearing judge, the Honorable Harold Medina, who along with the jury, prosecutors, the witnesses, and the American people at large evidenced that the Constitution of the United States not only protects its citizens but also protects this great country of ours.[8]

And another:

Mr. Chairman, the verdict of "guilty" in the trial of 11 Communists in New York City represents a victory to the American people over the insidious forces which have been and will continue to attempt to establish world domination by Soviet principles, and the destruction of our free-enterprise form of economy.

Having attended a session of the trial, and having watched with admiration the untiring patience and unfailing fairness evidenced by Judge Harold Medina, I believe that he deserves a vote of confidence from the American public for thus exemplifying our American brand of justice. I take this opportunity to do so now.

I sincerely hope that the end of this long trial will be but the beginning of a crusade to wipe out forever the remaining forces of subversion and espionage in the United States of America.[9]

J. Edgar Hoover sent Medina a letter of praise dated October 17, 1949, which the judge received before the sentencing of the defendants. Hoover's letter complimented Medina "on the outstanding manner in which you conducted the trial" and added, "Your fair and impartial conduct of this trial certainly deserves a prominent place in the annals of American jurisprudence." On the FBI's file copy of this letter, there is a supplementary statement in a different typescript: "*Note*: According to current information the eleven Communist defendants are scheduled to be sentenced on October 21, 1949."[10] It can thus be argued that one aim of this letter, delivered before sentencing, was to encourage punishments as severe as the law would allow. After the sentencing, Medina wrote to Hoover thanking him for the FBI protection at home and in court.[11] FBI agents had surrounded Medina during the trial, both inside and outside the courtroom. The result was a close relationship between the judge, the prosecution, and the FBI.

Hoover and Medina continued to correspond, and when Medina was nominated for elevation to the Court of Appeals for the Second Circuit (New York area), Hoover waived the usual FBI check and instead sent congratulations.[12]

The public appeared gratified for what was portrayed as the triumph of good over evil with constant reminders that such a fair trial would never have taken place in Russia. The fact that many newspaper accounts were garbled and confused about the meaning of the decision did not alter the bottom line: the Red Scare war had produced a major victory on the home front, no matter what was happening overseas. Medina, the dispenser of right, became a folk hero to millions.[13]

Medina did not end his relationship with prosecutors of Communists and left-wing dissidents. The next year, 1950, the judge learned about the prosecution of the nation's largest communist-affiliated organization by the attorney general's office of the state of New York and sent materials drawn from his *Dennis* case files for the prosecutor's office to use. He did this through his former law office, the prominent Wall Street firm of

Cravath, Swaine and Moore. In turn, the prosecutors thanked him, returning the materials in April 1951 after making needed copies, and they addressed the letter "Dear Mr. Medina." Just what a sitting federal judge was doing seeking to aid the prosecution in a state case may well be questioned. The discreet funneling of materials through the law office indicated the care apparently necessary to avoid allegations of impropriety, if not outright wrongdoing.[14] That a federal judge would be willing to engage in such tactics and forge such a behind-the-scenes relationship indicated the passions of the times. Neither Medina's memoirs nor his official biography mentioned any of this correspondence or involvement.[15]

The figures for Party membership shrank dramatically in 1950 and still further in 1951. By 1953 the Party was one-half the size it had been in 1950. The explanations for this precipitous fall focus on the Smith Act prosecutions and the outbreak of the Korean War. The convictions of their top comrades frightened many of the Party faithful, especially since the *Dennis* trial had exposed many other trusted comrades as FBI informants or agents. The existence of these informants and agents led the Party to become even more paranoid, insisting that loyalty be proven and suspicions checked, with the result that many innocent members were expelled. Michal R. Belknap has concluded that "The CPUSA [Communist Party USA] carried on an internal witch hunt which at least equaled in intensity the worst excesses of McCarthyism."[16]

The Smith Act victory, combined with the internal battles within the Party following revelations of double-crossing and spying, left the party in shambles. Fearing the loss of top leadership, the Party ordered selected members to go underground, including four of the convicted leaders in the *Dennis* case, who jumped bail and disappeared. The use of the underground technique to preserve the Party fed Hoover's beliefs that the CPUSA was entirely clandestine and not a political entity. It was not until the climate had cooled that the underground was dissolved and those who had hidden from prosecution gave themselves up and went to serve increased jail terms. Finally, the Party itself, fearing the Smith Act and paralyzed by paranoia, ceased to function in terms of influencing even those segments of the population that may have been willing to hear its message.[17]

Considering that all regular members of the 1948 National Board of the Communist Party were jailed under the Smith Act except Foster (because of his age and illness), that prosecutions of so-called second-string, state Party leaders were commencing, and that the editors of its newspaper and monthly magazine were in jail, the impact of the Smith Act can hardly be overemphasized. Adding to this scenario the wounds the Party was inflicting on itself, one would think that the nation would have been rejoicing at the disintegration of the Communist Party.

Instead, the reaction throughout the nation—pressed by Hoover and many Republicans, including that rising star of anti-communism, Joseph R. McCarthy—was quite the opposite: more must be done to smash Communists, their Party, and their influence. The fact that only a minuscule portion of the American population still had any trust or belief in the Party, its doctrines, or its wisdom meant nothing to the anti-communist zealots. As Peter L. Steinberg has written:

Those who believed the prosecution of the top leaders of the American communist movement would end the gathering political hysteria were mistaken. Those who had worked so hard for this prosecution as a first step toward stringent political limitations were encouraged. A more restrictive political atmosphere had grown concurrent with the trial proceedings. The verdict could only foster this trend.[18]

Instead of calming down, the hysteria was just warming up. Hoover did not use the convictions in the *Dennis* case to reap his deserved vindication for his faith in the efficacy of Smith Act prosecutions, which substantially destroyed the Communist Party; instead, he declared that "Communists have been and are today at work within the very gates of America. Western civilization was at stake."[19] These thoughts were delivered a month before the outbreak of the Korean War and eight months after the *Dennis* trial decision.

The rhetoric carried on unabated. Before the House committee considering appropriations for the Justice Department, in arguing for increased funds, a department spokesperson stated that the FBI regarded 21,105 people as possible prosecutional subjects under the Smith Act. Of these, it was estimated that "roughly 12,000" would face indictment if the law's constitutionality was upheld;[20] a month later this estimate was raised to 15,000.[21]

In light of the Party's grossly diminished proportions, Hoover's explanation for these figures, and for the Bureau's Communist Index containing an estimated 200,000 people, was that the size of the Party made little difference because the U.S. Party was merely a branch of a worldwide underground movement. He declared that for every actual member there were ten others who followed the Party line and would do the Party's work. Thus, using Hoover's approach and inflated figures, there were 540,000 enemies dedicated to communism in this country.[22]

Exploitation of the *Dennis* decision took place in many arenas and by many persons and groups. "Fighting communism" was sufficient to get appropriations requests through Congress, to pass even tougher legislation against aliens, and to encourage Senator McCarthy to latch on to anti-communism as a method of seeking reelection to his Senate seat. Attempts by the Truman administration to control the fury were unavailing. The president continued to speak out against hysteria, but he was overwhelmed by the demands for more action and stronger measures. Truman was caught between his sense that the nation must not succumb to this consuming fear of communism and the need to appear strongly anti-communist.

The Hiss conviction for perjury in January 1950, followed by the Coplon conviction in March and the arrest of Klaus Fuchs in Great Britain on charges of giving atomic secrets to Russia, kept the anti-communist pot boiling. The Republican Party, still smarting from the loss of the presidency in 1948, exploited these developments and was eager to use the communist issue. The specific charge was that within the Democratic Party's New Deal/Fair Deal at home and abroad there existed a conspiracy in government devised and controlled by the "Reds." The communist issue directed against the Democratic Party had not been effective in 1948; by 1950 the scene had changed enough to make the wild claims of McCarthy about Communists in the State Department newsworthy, plausible, and gaining the endorsement of many in the Republican Party.[23]

Curiously, the Red Scare contagion did not spread outside the United States. Despite revelations of traitorous conduct, England did not have a Red Scare reaction. In fact, there was almost a universally negative attitude toward the American reaction, as characterized by an English critic as he reviewed two recent books on the Red Scare.

All of this was disliked in England, by Tories almost as much as the left. It was seen as hysterical over-reaction, and as a mistake worse than a crime; the late Lord Gladwyn (Sir Gladwyn Jebb at the time) used to advise his American colleagues that the Communist menace was best left to wither on the vine rather than nourished by persecution. There was a particular distaste, for the ritual of "naming names" (repugnant especially to anyone inculcated in the public-school hatred of sneaking), and of purging by formal self-abasement.[24]

In 1950 Congress passed over the president's veto a resurrected Mundt-Nixon bill. Included in this law was a definition of "Communist-infiltrated organization" and a prohibition on Party members being employed in defense facilities or holding office in a labor organization. The new law denied passports to Communists, required registration of all Communists, restricted use of the mails by Communist organizations, and created a Subversive Activities Control Board with which the Party and all members were to register. Perhaps most revealing of the extreme nature of the times, it established detention camps for the emergency confining of suspected security risks.[25] Under this law, camps were actually established in five states.

The camps would remain open and available for use through 1956, when the Federal Bureau of Prisons closed them. Hoover's response to the closing was to complain about the "growing public complacency toward the threat of subversion."[26] But that was in 1957; by that time his words were falling on a Red Scare scene that had significantly changed.

All walks of life were affected by the enlarging war against the "Reds." Walter Reuther, president of the Congress of Industrial Organizations (CIO), at the union's national convention in the fall of 1949, insisted there was but "one issue, and one issue alone, and that is . . . Communism." Thereafter, two Communist-oriented unions were expelled, followed by nine others in 1950. The Congress of Racial Equality, the National Association for the Advancement of Colored People, the American Civil Liberties Union, and the National Education Association all took stands against Communists and banned them from office and sometimes even from membership. Demands for loyalty oaths for teachers, lawyers, and state and local employees accelerated. Thus, M. J. Heale concluded,

Even before Senator Joseph McCarthy belatedly spotted Communists in the State Department in February 1950, the Cold War, in interacting with a political system in which precarious politicians were buffeted endlessly by a host of revitalized patriotic and conservative interests, had transformed American Communists and their sympathizers into public lepers.[27]

Not only the label of public lepers, but also the taint of homosexuality was used against Communists. In his work on the culture of the Cold War, Stephen J. Whitfield has said, "If only through innuendo, nothing in the political arena in the 1950s was more convenient than establishing some sort of connection between political and sexual 'perversion.'" Senator Kenneth Wherry (R-Neb.) made the point directly:

"You can't . . . separate homosexuals from subversives. . . . I don't say every subversive is a homosexual. But a man of low morality is a menace in the government, whatever he is, and they are tied up together."[28]

In kaleidoscope fashion, wherever one turned in the early 1950s, the Red Scare and Cold War were there. They were in print and on the radio, as well as in the new medium, television, keeping before the American public the events and personalities of the war between communism and anti-communism. The Red Scare was conspicuous in Congress, courts, schools, movies, and the workplace. HUAC made headlines; Congress almost continually debated the menace of communism and what new laws should be created, not only to smash communism, but, in a larger sense, to keep out aliens, alien thoughts, and dissident ideas. To help the public understand what was at stake, HUAC got the U.S. Government Printing Office to publish books and pamphlets designed to alert Americans. Typical of these was *100 Things You Should Know About Communism and Guide to Subversive Organizations and Publications.*[29] In a little more than a year, 850,000 copies were distributed free; the publication proved so popular that another 320,000 were printed and sold for ten cents each—the cost to the government to print them.[30]

The *Dennis* case convictions paved the way for further prosecutions for violation of the Smith Act. The assumption, made by the Justice Department and later proved correct, was that the appeals court and Supreme Court would affirm the convictions. Hoover and his FBI were certainly eager to move against more Party members. Soon after the United States Court of Appeals affirmed the guilty verdicts on August 1, 1950, the attorney general called U.S. attorneys throughout the country to plan the prosecutions of more Communist party leaders. Waiting only two weeks after the Supreme Court's affirming decision in 1951, the FBI moved against those top Party leaders not tried earlier. This was the all-out attack Hoover had been waiting for.

Of the 126 indicted after the Supreme Court decision in *Dennis*, only ten won acquittal at the trial court level. Others died before trial or were severed from the trial of codefendants because of bad health. In one case, there was a hung jury. For years not one conviction that went to an appellate court was reversed; the government won every time.

Thus, as Belknap has analyzed the trial results, "of the 105 Party leaders who stood trial and lived to see a judge and jury determine their fate, 93, or just under 89 percent, suffered conviction."[31]

From one perspective, the trials that took place from 1951 to 1956 should simply have been *Dennis* reruns of monotonous character. There was, however, one major factor that cannot be overlooked: the Korean War, involving the invasion by the Communist North of pro-Western South Korea, had begun in June 1950; during the next three years, as it yielded terrible casualties, it turned foul in the mouths of Americans. The Korean War became a war without victory, misunderstood and distinctly unpopular.

The Communist Party, whose leaders were to continue to come before juries, followed their Soviet masters in expressing opposition to U.S. involvement in the Korean War. Attorney General Clark, who had supervised the early planning of the post-*Dennis* cases, did not consider these new cases against lesser or minor Party functionaries to be strong. He need not have worried; where evidence was lacking or weak, the Korean War itself insured convictions.

A new approach was also tried against American Communists. Beginning in 1954 and lasting until the *Yates* decision on Red Monday in 1957, there were eight prosecutions of Communists under the Membership

Clause of the Smith Act; all who were tried were convicted. Until 1954 Communists were prosecuted for conspiracy under the Smith Act; the Membership Clause (joining an organization to conspire to advocate) was a new weapon in the war against the Party. As in the accusation of conspiracy, it was the Party that was essentially on trial in these membership cases, notwithstanding the fact that individuals faced the jury on the charge of having chosen to be Party members. Once more, the Korean War was in the courtroom, even though it had ended with an armistice in 1953. During one membership trial, a government witness testified at length about the Party's continuing opposition to the American role in Korea; his testimony was accepted as relevant evidence.[32]

A total of 418 years of imprisonment was levied in these Smith Act prosecutions, with $435,500 in fines for convicted defendants through 1956. Of that total, 108 years were actually served as of June 1958.[33] Three were still in jail as late as 1961; two were released in that year, and President Kennedy commuted the last defendant's sentence to time served on Christmas Eve, 1962.[34]

Statistics do not, however, accurately render even a portion of the toll of the *Dennis* decision. The lives of the defendants and their families were badly upset and often effectively destroyed. It may be argued that these front-line soldiers of the Party knew or should have known of the risks they took, but the impact also generated fear throughout the rank and file. Also affected were those who had for some time been Party members, attended Party functions, signed petitions, donated money, or associated with those who were members. The decision struck fear into those who belonged to left-wing organizations or even just subscribed to publications that were tainted as "Red." For all of these people and their families, the personal danger of the Red Scare victory in *Dennis* was real.[35]

The government's punishing power was brought to bear in the Red Scare war in the early 1950s. The IRS investigated eighty-one organizations that appeared on the attorney general's Subversive Organizations List and had tax-exempt status for contributions. Congress amended the Housing Administration Act to deny the right to anyone belonging to any group on the Subversive Organizations List to live in such housing. Only after successful challenges to this law did the government in 1956 stop enforcing it. Attempts were also made to cut off Social Security payments to Party members, to end veterans' disability payments to Communists and Communist sympathizers, and to terminate unemployment compensation benefits. Here Caute concludes that "these bureaucratic attempts to deprive radicals of the financial and welfare benefits to which all eligible citizens were entitled must rank among the meanest harassments of the purge."[36] Most of these attempts were thwarted in court challenges by 1956, but when they were instigated in the early 1950s the public reception was favorable, once again indicating the times.

The *Dennis* trial legitimized Red Scare passions in state and local governments even before higher courts had reviewed the verdicts. In one case, begun just two months after the *Dennis* trial was concluded, the state of New York, through its Department of Insurance, began a proceeding against the largest and most successful Communist-affiliated organization in the nation, the International Workers Order (IWO).[37]

The IWO in 1950 was some twenty years old. Headquartered in New York, it was licensed as a fraternal benefit insurance company. In that capacity, it offered low-cost life and medical insurance to working people. During the 1930s, when such low-cost insurance was generally unavailable, the IWO's ability to offer it through membership in the organization made it the fastest-growing fraternal benefit insurance company in America. By 1948 it had almost 200,000 members and operated in nineteen states and the District of Columbia. During its existence, perhaps one million people joined.

In the wake of the *Dennis* case, the New York Department of Insurance, having discovered that the IWO was on the Subversive Organizations List, decided to seek its liquidation as an insurance company and thus destroy it. The state was, however, in a difficult legal situation because the IWO had passed all audits of its books and operations. It was a financially sound, conservatively run company that paid claims promptly. The problem for the IWO was that, while 97 percent of its members were not Communist Party members, the remaining 3 percent were, and they constituted the majority of officers and directors of the IWO.

As a fraternal benefit insurance company, the IWO was unique in that, instead of serving just one constituency such as one ethnic, racial, or religious group, it was an integrated multinational and multiracial organization with some thirteen different ethnic foreign-language groups as well as a general group of English-speaking members. The IWO was the only national insurance carrier that offered blacks the same insurance at the same rates offered to whites; elsewhere, blacks had always been charged more. By offering insurance without employing salespeople or paying commissions, it was able to attract workers from high-risk employment groups, such as coal miners, charging them the same rates as others.

The offerings of all fraternal benefit insurance companies included social, educational, and sports activities. For tens of thousands (mainly first-generation immigrant groups) the IWO offered a full program including singing societies, marching bands, sports teams, health care, education, and dance and theater groups. But what made the state seek a way to destroy the IWO was that its political, economic, and social message followed the path of the American Communist Party.

Some of the political and economic positions taken by the Order (support for a broader Social Security system and for a form of national health insurance, along with endorsement of the cause of industrial-type unionization) do not appear from the vantage point of the 1990s to be very radical, but for the 1930s and 1940s they were exactly that.

The IWO has been credited for its active and, at times, crucial role in the early history of the CIO, particularly in the unionization of the steel-workers. The IWO lodges supported strike efforts, raised food, clothing, and money for strikers, and frequently provided the only available meeting halls for unions. As one historian has noted, no community organization gave so much to so many unions for such an extended period of time as the IWO gave to the CIO struggles between 1935 and 1941.[38]

Every official position of the IWO—from opposing racial discrimination (support for the unpopular black defendants in the *Scottsboro* rape case) to supporting social legislation, from militant industrial unionism to support for the Spanish Republican cause—mirrored the position of the Communist Party. This was never overlooked by those who attempted to discredit the organization by sole virtue of that fact, regardless of the merit of such positions.

What the state of New York did was develop a legal strategy that would have been untenable at any time other than the early 1950s. The insurance statute governing insurance companies allowed the state to move against any company that posed a "hazard" to present or potential policyholders. This had always been given one interpretation, that of posing a financial hazard. The state proposed expanding the concept to include posing a *political* hazard. That "hazard" existed because of the "subversive organization" designation and because the IWO had liquid assets of some six million dollars, which, the state argued, could be withdrawn by its officers and given to the Soviet Union. By this device the sound financial status of the IWO was turned into a liability. There was no evidence that any officer had taken or would take any IWO funds for this purpose, but there did not have to be. While the case was being tried, the Korean War posed the threat of a direct U.S.-Soviet confrontation. Thus the argument that these officers would take the money and run was accepted by the judge trying the case.

The trial, lasting four months from January through April 1951, was without a jury. Judge Henry Clay Greenberg would determine the guilt or innocence of the IWO. The government case involved thirteen witnesses, twelve of them paid professional informers (in the sense that they appeared in many cases and were well paid for their testimony services). They included the "star," Louis Budenz, former managing editor

of the Communist *Daily Worker*, who was a leading *Dennis* trial partici-
pant. Another prominent state witness was Matthew Cvetic, whose life
was fictionalized in the film *I Was a Communist for the FBI.*

The phenomenon of the government-paid professional informer was
unique to this Red Scare era. The paid informer per se is as old as human
history and can be found in trials for treason, subversion, and many
forms of criminality. What was different here was that these witnesses
held themselves out as experts on Communism and the Party, moving
from trial to trial, from committee to committee, using their "expertise"
and naming names on behalf of the federal and state governments. Their
paid-for testimony constituted the backbone of the state's case against
the IWO; no then-current member of the Order testified against it.

While the use of paid ex-Communist informers was common in Red
Scare trials and tribunals, it was a troublesome practice then and continues to raise questions about our legal system. These witnesses, having
seen the wrongs of their ways, claimed that they alone could properly
expose the evils they had forsaken. This posture put them on federal and
state government payrolls for their willingness to level such accusations.

The questionable logic involved was expressed by Bernard De Voto
in an article published just as the IWO trial had these informers taking
the stand:

Understand, I am right now *because* I was wrong then. *Only* the ex-Communist
can understand Communism. Trust me to lead you aright *because* I tried to lead
you astray. My intelligence has been vindicated in that it made all-out commitment to error.[39]

These witnesses testified that the IWO was closely aligned to the policies of the Communist Party, not by ideological choice, but because
it was controlled by leaders who were also disciplined members of the
Party. The IWO, they asserted, was a "transmission belt" for moving
masses of working people from mere membership for insurance purposes to class consciousness and then to Party membership.

Despite vigorous cross-examination of the state's witnesses, and notwithstanding the testimony of IWO officers and rank-and-file members
about the Order's insurance programs and its social, cultural, and chari-
table activities, the essential ties of the IWO to the Communist Party
predominated. What Judge Greenberg wanted to hear was repudiation
by the IWO of its radical ties and leaders, but this would not be forthcoming.

With the exception of Rockwell Kent, president of the IWO and noted
artist and author, all the IWO officers used their Fifth Amendment privilege when the prosecution asked whether they had been or were still
members of the Communist Party. In doing so, they sought to convince

the judge that their personal political preferences were constitutionally guaranteed as well as irrelevant to the operation of the Order. On the other hand, what Judge Greenberg read about in the daily press were the continuing exposes of the "Communist menace" in Hollywood and in unions, schools, and government. Proceeding at the same time in the federal court very near to Judge Greenberg's own courtroom was the Rosenberg atomic bomb spy case. During that trial, the only organization Julius Rosenberg admitted to being a member of was the IWO.

After generating a trial record of more than four thousand pages, the *IWO* case closed. Both sides prepared extensive briefs, reviewing the legal issues and evidence. Dipping its brush deeply into a Red pot, the state painted "communist" on virtually every page of its work. By contrast, the IWO barely mentioned the word and instead attempted to focus Judge Greenberg's attention on the legal issues it had raised before the trial began.

What the IWO wanted the judge to see was that the law favored its position because the concept of "hazard" was clearly directed toward and had always been interpreted as involving a financial issue. The Order argued for a conservative, "original intent" interpretation of the law, in effect asking the judge not to engage in "judicial activism" by adopting any broader meaning. This argument was also used in response to the state's allegation that because of its politics, the IWO had acted beyond the legal scope of its corporate insurance powers; in the law this is called an allegation of *ultra vires* activities. The state argued that the Department of Insurance should have the authority to destroy this communist "evil," and therefore legal interpretations should expand to incorporate the ability to deal with this politically radical insurance company.

On June 21, 1951 Judge Greenberg issued his long-awaited decision, in which he adopted every major legal contention argued by the Department of Insurance: "hazard" could mean "political hazard"; the political activities of the IWO were *ultra vires*, thus violating its state charter; and the superintendent of insurance had the power to liquidate an insurance company because of its politics. On factual issues, he found the IWO to be linked to the Communist Party, and in answer to the admittedly excellent financial position of the Order, he even accepted the "take the money and run" theory as valid.[40]

There followed appeals through the New York State court system. The Appellate Division quickly affirmed the trial court's decision, even expanding on what Judge Greenberg had written by defining a "moral risk" in addition to a "political hazard." The appellate court also accepted the "take the money and run" argument.[41]

Two years after the IWO trial ended, on April 23, 1953, after thousands of pages of record and hundreds of pages of briefs, the lower courts' decisions were unanimously affirmed by the highest New York court, the Court of Appeals, in a scant two-page decision. In its opinion, the court seemed to say that the "hazard" concept correctly applied only to financial matters, but that the *ultra vires* political acts described above justified liquidating the IWO.[42]

Only one legal option was left to the IWO—seek review by the United States Supreme Court by applying for a writ of certiorari.[43] In this procedure, the IWO was asking the Supreme Court to review its case because significant constitutional issues were involved. The problem was that the odds were against obtaining the required four affirmative votes from the justices required to take the case; only 15 percent of petitions for review were taken by the Court during the October 1953 term.[44] In an attempt to send a message as to the importance of the case, the IWO gathered some 15,000 individual members' petitions addressed to the Court asking it to hear the case and also held a demonstration on the steps of the Supreme Court building as its term opened.

Of the justices who voted (Justice Tom C. Clark took no part in the matter since he had promulgated the Subversive Organizations List containing the IWO), only Justices Hugo L. Black and William O. Douglas voted for hearing the case. Newly appointed Chief Justice Warren joined the other members of the Court in denying the petition.

Lacking two votes, the IWO had reached the end of its legal remedies. The state of New York took over the Order's assets and, after lengthy hearings, awarded the Continental Assurance Company of Chicago the right to take over the insurance policies; to this day, a separate department of the company is maintained for IWO policyholders.

No one was put to death; no one went to jail or was fined because of the IWO case, although leaders and members who were aliens were deported simply because of their association with the organization. However, after a twenty-three-year existence, the state of New York, with the assistance of the federal government, was able to put a thriving but politically radical insurance company out of business.

Before leaving this singular case, two factors should be noted. This was the only Red Scare case where the defendant had ample funds to defend itself, but that fact made no difference. Notwithstanding the ability to pay for the best counsel possible, the IWO could not get the attorneys it wanted; the lawyers it initially approached turned them down. The IWO had to settle for those who were willing to withstand guilt by association.

When the lead prosecuting attorney in the IWO case was asked in 1988 whether New York would have won if the matter were tried then instead of 1950–51, his answer was that there would have been no case in 1988; the fact that the prosecution had happened at all was itself a reflection of Red Scare times.[45]

"In those times" is an expression used by those who lived through the era to explain, justify, and contrast other "times"—usually the present. There were the Great Depression times of the 1930s, the war and post-war 1940s, and, as it is generally expressed, the Cold War-Red Scare times of the 1950s. These labels, used to evoke the outstanding traits of a decade, are, of course, generalizations subject to criticism, not the least of which is recognition that the use of a decade as the beginning or end to which descriptive labels are attached is a convenient but faulty construct. Yet it cannot be denied that "times" do change and do validly exhibit certain general conditions and attitudes; in other words, there is validity in recognizing that changes have evolved. Furthermore, contrasting aspects of earlier times using the decade-labeling device serves to illuminate both past and present.

Consider these examples of changing times. The use of four-letter words and of open sexuality, evident in all media in the 1990s, was unacceptable and generally unavailable in the 1950s. On the other hand, the obscenities of overt racism and anti-Semitism were acceptable in the 1950s but no longer acceptable in the 1990s. In the 1950s it was objectionable for movies to portray the president of the United States as being involved in a murder plot, as insane, beaten up or demolished by alien creatures, but it became commonplace in the 1990s.

The Smith Act cases, the loyalty-security requirements, even large numbers of contempt of Congress proceedings were all creatures of the 1950s. It was a time of consensus in American life, expressed in terms of conformity to the broad proposition that leftist or communist dissent was a serious evil, a cancer in the body of the nation that threatened its health and even its survival.

Certainly there were those who did not join in this consensus and who warned of the dangers to American freedom in succumbing to the Red Scare. Among these who carried the message against McCarthyism were Edward R. Murrow, Elmer Davis, and Henry Steele Commager. Newspapers such as the *Chicago Sun* (later the *Sun-Times*) and the *New York Times*, and magazines including the *Nation*, the *New Republic*, the *Reporter*, and the *New Yorker* were consistently critical of McCarthy and the entire Red Scare scene. Nevertheless, the times reflected a consensus that accepted and approved of manifestations of the Red Scare in government, courts, unions, churches, and the media. That consensus survived and, as we have seen, enlarged after the *Dennis* case in 1949, as it was later to survive the replacement of a Democratic president by a Republican one in 1953.

The anti-communist consensus as endorsed by the courts of the late 1940s and into the mid-1950s included the concept that it was a federal crime to advocate revolutionary ideas and programs, even without any show of force or actual act of revolt. Talking, writing, or meeting was sufficient to justify imprisoning people where the "times" appeared to yield a clear and present danger. The *Dennis* trial said so in 1949, as the appellate level federal court was soon to confirm; the Supreme Court followed in 1951 by placing its sanction on the sufficiency of the evidence justifying guilt.

Chapter 5
On Appeal

Criminal trials historically have been a major form of entertainment in American life. Well before modern media allowed people vicarious access to trials, actually attending a trial and then viewing the punishment of the guilty were diversions from everyday work life. Until the end of the nineteenth century, almost all lawyers were trial lawyers. It was also well toward the end of that century before executions ceased to be held in public.[1]

Once a trial ends, a guilty verdict in a criminal case under American law entitles the convicted to at least one appeal. Appeals lack the drama of testimony, cross-examination, and the anticipated jury verdict. The appeal process is basically a matter of counterpointed legal arguments addressed by attorneys before a panel of appellate judges. Under these circumstances, the spotlight of public interest is considerably dimmed, if not entirely turned off.

Unlike a trial, the drama in an appeal lies in the clash of ideas and arguments contained in the briefs prepared by the opposing sides. Here the appealing party states the issues to be reviewed with the demand to overturn what has taken place in lower courts. After briefing and response by the opposing side (which seeks to affirm what the trial court did), oral arguments are generally allowed. Weeks, months, or even longer thereafter, the appeals court renders its decision. The process is generally slow and costly, and public attention attenuates. Smith Act and related Red Scare cases were no exception; they did not begin to appear at the federal appellate and Supreme Court levels until 1950, reflecting trial decisions of the late 1940s.

The first important case to come to the United States Supreme Court was argued in October 1949 and decided on May 8, 1950, under the title *American Communications (CIO) v. Douds*.[2] At issue was a provision of the National Labor Relations Act, section 9(h), that had been added in 1947 by the Taft-Hartley Act. President Truman had vetoed the Taft-Hartley Act as antiunion, but his veto was overruled. The union challenged the constitutionality of section 9(h) because it required affidavits from union officers asserting they were not Communists in order for the union to have certain benefits of the National Labor Relations Act and access to the National Labor Relations Board (NLRB). Most important, without non-Communist affidavits from its leadership, the union could not bring charges of unfair labor practices against an employer.

Congress had stated that the purpose of section 9(h) was to hinder communists from disrupting the flow of commerce through "political strikes," that is, strikes undertaken with a Party objective rather than legitimate labor aims. The basic issue before the Court was whether Congress, consistent with the First Amendment, could use section 9(h) to exert pressures on labor unions to deny positions of leadership to certain persons who were identified by particular beliefs (overthrow of the government) or political affiliations (membership in the Communist Party).

By a vote of five to one, the Court held that Congress could demand a negative oath—an oath of what one is *not* (a Party member) or of what one does *not* believe in (violent overthrow of the government). Chief Justice Frederick (Fred) M. Vinson wrote the majority opinion, joined by Stanley F. Reed, Harold H. Burton, Felix Frankfurter (except as to one portion), and Robert H. Jackson (who concurred in part and dissented in part), leaving only Hugo L. Black dissenting from the majority opinion. Sherman Minton, William O. Douglas, and Thomas (Tom) C. Clark did not participate in the decision.

What the majority said was this: the fact that the legislation identified people with political beliefs did not, in and of itself, render the statute invalid. Certain classes could be barred from certain occupations consistent with the Constitution because of a reasonable relationship between the classification and a perceived evil. Prevention of political strikes (which would yield unwarranted business disruptions) was a legitimate government interest sufficient to support this kind of regulation.

While it lessened this threat to interstate commerce, section 9(h) also discouraged the protected exercise of political rights; therefore the majority had to confront the constitutional question of First Amendment protections for speech, thought, and political affiliation. To the argument that no "clear and present danger" existed to justify the limitations imposed, the majority responded:

Government's interest here is not in preventing the dissemination of Communist doctrine or the holding of particular beliefs because it is feared that unlawful action will result therefrom if free speech is practiced. Its interest is in protecting the free flow of commerce from what Congress considers to be substantial evils of conduct that are not the products of speech at all. Section 9(h), in other words, does not interfere with speech because Congress fears the consequences of speech; it regulates harmful conduct which Congress has determined is carried on by persons who may be identified by their political affiliations and beliefs.[3]

Evidence that "political strikes" organized by the Communist Party had occurred was taken from the record of congressional hearings, with special focus on a 1941 strike at the Milwaukee plant of the Allis-Chalmers Manufacturing Company. What was not discussed or placed in perspective in the 1950 decision was that the strike had taken place during the period between the onset of the European war, September 1, 1939, and June 22, 1941, when the Soviet Union was invaded. This was a time when, after the Hitler-Stalin Pact, the Communist Party obeyed the Moscow line of nonbelligerency and nonintervention. Immediately after Hitler's invasion of Russia, the Party became ultra-patriotic, joining in no-strike pledges and urging all-out intervention in the war. Thus the Party was far from wanting—much less organizing—political strikes in the years following the Allis-Chalmers strike. Not until the Cold War and Red Scare did the potential of "political strikes" as "harmful conduct" become possible; yet the Court cited no strikes that took place after the 1941 example. It should also be noted that the *Douds* decision came down just prior to the outbreak of war in Korea, so the Court's view could not have been influenced by that event.[4]

What was the message of *Douds* in 1950? One immediate signal was that a majority of the Vinson Court would uphold Congress in cases where the First Amendment clashed with a law addressing the perceived threat of Communists. Yet to come would be the situation where there would be federal prosecution of those whose beliefs ran afoul of the House Un-American Activities Committee (HUAC) or who were Communist Party leaders.

Four justices had not voted. Of them, only one, Douglas, was known for favoring civil liberties. Clark, Reed, Burton, and probably Jackson could be counted on to vote as did the majority in *Douds*. The next major case (*Blau v. United States*), however, demonstrated that certain issues involving constitutionally protected rights would generate a pro-protective stance where a particularly egregious wrong was involved.

The *Douds* case was also relevant for introducing names of attorneys and groups that would appear time and again on behalf of defendants. With a union as plaintiff, the name of Arthur J. Goldberg (then counsel to the Congress of Industrial Organizations [CIO] and later Supreme Court justice) appeared on the brief along with *amici curiae* (friend of the court) briefs from the CIO itself, the American Civil Liberties Union, and the National Lawyers Guild. Frank Donner and Osmond K. Fraenkel appeared as attorneys for the union; both were involved with the later International Workers Order (IWO) and many other Red Scare cases.[5]

Later in 1950 another Red Scare case, *Blau v. United States*, moved to the Supreme Court.[6] Patricia Blau had been brought before a federal grand jury, apparently for the investigation of a criminal offense unrelated to certain questions put to her. When she was asked about her employment by the Communist Party of Colorado, she refused to respond to those questions on the constitutional ground (Fifth Amendment) that her answers might tend to incriminate her. Taken before the district court judge, she repeated her claim of constitutional privilege against self-incrimination and refused to testify. The judge found her in contempt of court and sentenced her to one year in prison. The court of appeals affirmed and the Supreme Court granted certiorari based on the constitutional issue.[7]

A unanimous Court (with Justice Clark not participating) reversed her conviction in a short opinion authored by Justice Black. Because the Smith Act made it a crime to advocate the overthrow of the government or to organize or be a member of a group that so advocated, being compelled to answer questions "would have furnished a link in the chain of evidence needed in a prosecution of petitioner for violation of (or conspiracy to violate) the Smith Act."[8] Thus Blau had the right to remain silent.

Reaction to the *Blau* decision presented divergent views. The *Washington Star* was fearful the decision might provide Communists with "a shield to hide their conspiracy against the Constitution and everything it stands for."[9] The *New York Herald Tribune* stated that "we may like to punish Communists for contemptuous silence, but the Constitution still comes first."[10]

Both articles raised the issue of the impact of this decision on the operation and effectiveness of the McCarran Act, which called for registration of Communists and other "subversives" with possible internment under certain emergencies; both articles expressed the hope that *Blau* and other forthcoming decisions would not hamper or destroy that law. On the other hand, an editorial in the *Nation*, "The Constitution Wars," not only rejoiced in the decision ("It is extremely good to know that even in these irrational days the Supreme Court can adhere, unanimously, to the basic law of the land"), but also hoped it would cast a shadow on the McCarran Act as a violation of the right not to incriminate oneself and on the "device" of the loyalty oath.[11]

Justice Black received letters from people who commented on the decision. One was from a lawyer who protested that communists did not behave in accordance with the ethical and moral precepts of others. He wrote, "by the opinion in the Blau case, the members of the Supreme Court have shown us how to destroy our nation and have given us leadership in that destruction." The letter concluded, "I suppose that we may now expect the Supreme Court to release the eleven traitors convicted at New York on the ground that Judge Medina one afternoon spoke harshly to them."[12]

A contrary position was taken by the famed New Dealer Harold L. Ickes, who wrote:

The decision handed down on December 12 [*sic*] by you, speaking for a unanimous court, was like a breath of swiftly-moving fresh air down a mountain side into the smog-laden atmosphere of Los Angeles. It came at a time, during our surrender to hysteria and fear, that ought to give us a good start back toward sanity and some degree of equanimity.[13]

In all these reactions was a consistent underlying theme: the *Blau* case was not, in and of itself, that important. Rather, what it did was portend how the Court would decide more controversial issues, issues that would go to the heart of the legal foundation for the Red Scare.

On October 11, 1950 the Supreme Court heard oral arguments in *Joint Anti-Fascist Refugee Committee v. McGrath*, in which organizations challenged their inclusion on the attorney general's Subversive Organizations List.[14] Three organizations that Attorney General Tom Clark included in his list for use by the Loyalty Review Board of the United States Civil Service Commission sought an injunction to have their names removed. The litigation had commenced in late 1947; it was not until three years later that arguments over the issues came before the Supreme Court. All appeals by these three organizations, which included the IWO, were defeated at trial and in the appellate courts.[15]

The Subversive Organizations List, created in compliance with President Truman's Executive Order 9835, had taken on a life of its own, moving into use in the private as well as the public sector. Accusations of disloyalty, blacklisting, loss of employment, and deportation were among the consequences of belonging to a listed organization. For example, the IWO's legal troubles commenced when a New York Insurance Department auditor who was routinely reviewing the company's financial records saw the IWO's name on a newspaper copy of the list.[16] The list also caused trouble for as mainstream an organization as the National Advisory Council of the National Institute of Neurological Diseases and Blindness, which complained about the use of the list as well as other secretive methods to justify denying grants-in-aid for research.[17]

What these organizations complained about was the lack of due process; no hearings had been held and no notice given before the decision to designate an organization as subversive was made. All three cases were combined for hearing and decision making. The Court majority in *Joint Anti-Fascist Refugee Committee* agreed that the conduct of the attorney general was patently arbitrary and tantamount to defamation. Though no legal consequences resulted per se from inclusion in the list, the "effect [was] to cripple the functioning and damage the reputation of these organizations."[18] As a practical matter, the list was used as evidence of disloyalty and guilt by association before loyalty boards, as well as in a variety of formal and informal venues throughout the nation.

The majority decision in *Joint Anti-Fascist Refugee Committee* was not based on any substantive constitutional question because the case could be decided on just the facts revealed by the pleadings—that the listing procedure lacked due process and therefore wronged these organizations. Justice Black, concurring in the result, would, however, have carried the matter further. As the Court's most vocal guardian of First Amendment rights, he would have held the executive order authorizing the list to be an act of censorship (as well as a form of bill of attainder) that violated the First Amendment. Justice Frankfurter's concurrence reflected his persistent concern with due process, which he found was clearly violated. He also felt that inclusion on the list itself violated the Fifth Amendment. Justices Douglas and Jackson added further reasons for joining in the majority's decision.

Each member of the majority wrote his own opinion. For that reason, Michal Belknap has pointed out that the Court's surprising decision favoring the organizations (surprising given the times and makeup of the Court) not surprisingly "lacked a coherent rationale."[19]

Additionally, on the same day the decision in the *Joint Anti-Fascist Refugee Committee* case was announced, a Court majority let stand a lower court's decision that allowed the dismissal of a government employee who had challenged the Loyalty Review Board's action. The employee faced charges from unnamed accusers whose identity was undisclosed to both the board and the employee. Notwithstanding the patent unfairness inherent in such a procedure, the Court majority found in favor of the government. The mixed signals sent by the Court as to the loyalty program, due process, and constitutional rights indicated a badly divided Court at a time when clarity was most needed on these matters.[20]

In the *Joint Anti-Fascist Refugee Committee* decision, Justice Reed wrote a dissent joined by Chief Justice Vinson and Justice Minton. The dissent argued that the country had the right and the duty to protect itself from any force seeking its overthrow and that the tolerance mandated by the First Amendment could not reach the point where the government could become indifferent to manifestations of subversion. Arguing that the organizations were not ordered to do anything and were not punished for anything, the analogy was drawn to a grand jury hearing:

all that the listing amounted to was enough evidence to go forth to a trial, where defenses could then be raised. The argument was made that while the nation must respect the First Amendment, it need not tolerate espionage, disloyalty, or sedition.

From a procedural viewpoint, the majority decision went no further than to return the three challenges to the district court because each had stated a valid claim of having been listed wrongly without due process. The majority position did not exclude the possibility that these organizations could, after a hearing, be listed or that such listing in and of itself violated any constitutionally protected rights.

The victory for these three organizations (the Joint Anti-Fascist Refugee Committee (JAFRC), the American Council of Soviet-American Friendship, and the IWO) successfully challenging their listing was entirely pyrrhic; it changed nothing. The day after the decision was announced, U.S. government attorneys declared that membership in the three organizations "would continue to carry weight in federal employees' loyalty investigations." They added that the Supreme Court decision "would not eliminate the groups from consideration, even temporarily." [21]

The decision did not halt the ongoing prosecution of the IWO, which was still on trial in New York when the decision was announced. Furthermore, there was every indication that executive branch government offices continued to use the list and that prosecutions proceeded on the basis of belonging to these organizations. [22]

It was also clear that organizations and groups outside government exploited the list. Redbaiting and blacklisting were well established as businesses prior to the Korean War, consisting of selling lists of names of persons allegedly involved with one or more so-called subversive organizations and (for a fee) conducting background checks for "subversive activities." American Business Consultants put out a blacklisting publication called *Counterattack*; a spin-off publication, *Red Channels*, concentrated on radio and television personalities. These organizations and others like them were highly effective in having persons blacklisted, frequently for years. They used the attorney general's list as authority, as well as membership in or support of the three organizations that were supposed to be delisted. [23]

The Joint Anti-Fascist Refugee Committee was a particular and continuing target for HUAC and government prosecutors. The group was organized in 1939 by veterans of the Abraham Lincoln International Brigade, which had fought against General Francisco Franco's Nationalist forces in support of the Republic in the Spanish Civil War. Their announced aim was to aid war refugees.

HUAC claimed JAFRC was a clearinghouse for funds for various Communist-front organizations. Elements supporting the Franco regime, particularly the Catholic hierarchy, pressed for action against JAFRC. J. Parnell Thomas, chairman of HUAC, had close ties with the Franco regime and used the power of HUAC to attack the Brigade. In February 1946 HUAC demanded that JAFRC bring its financial records and correspondence to the investigating committee. The chairman, Dr. Edward K. Barsky, responded, informing HUAC that JAFRC's board had directed him not to produce these records. HUAC then had Barsky cited for contempt. Next, HUAC issued sixteen separate subpoenas for all members of the board, directing them to appear on April 4, 1946. All appeared, but not the records. All were cited for contempt and sentenced to prison terms.[24]

The contempt convictions were affirmed by the District Court of the United States for the District of Columbia.[25] On March 18, 1949 the U.S. Court of Appeals for the District of Columbia affirmed the right of Congress to carry on such investigations, even if the threat did not meet the criterion of "clear and present danger." Dr. Barsky and others (including the noted author Howard Fast) went to prison and paid fines for their willful failure to produce the records. The Supreme Court refused to hear the case; a writ of certiorari was denied on June 14, 1949.[26]

The importance of this case was that it taught HUAC how to deal with witnesses who refused to give the committee what it wanted and how successfully to punish such people with jail.

During the next year, 1949, the Supreme Court did hear a case brought to it by another executive board member of JAFRC, Ernestina A. Fleischman, in the continued effort to litigate the guilt of board members for failing to deliver the organization's records. The essential issue was whether Fleischman had individual responsibility to produce the records or at least to demonstrate that she had made every effort to urge that they be turned over. The majority confirmed her guilt as a willful failure, again strengthening HUAC's hand. Justices Douglas and Clark did not participate; Justices Black and Frankfurter wrote dissents.[27]

For Dr. Barsky, a prominent New York physician, the matter was not over with his prison term and fine. The Department of Education of the State of New York (which controlled licensing) sought to punish him by suspending him from the practice of medicine. After a number of administrative groups heard testimony, he was suspended for six months because of his conviction for failing to produce the subpoenaed records. Courtroom proceedings in state courts followed, all of which affirmed the suspension and upheld the state law under which he was punished. Then appeals were made to the federal courts, and finally, in 1954, the Supreme Court heard oral arguments and decided the case.

By a six-to-three decision, the majority upheld as constitutional the

New York law under which he was punished. The state had a legitimate interest in maintaining high standards of professional conduct; Barsky's conviction, the Court agreed, was proper grounds for what followed.[28]

Justices Black, Douglas, and Frankfurter dissented, arguing that no moral turpitude had been shown and that Dr. Barsky's right to practice medicine was violated without due process of law. Justice Black pointed out that the organization, JAFRC, had been listed as subversive and that the state grievance committee had heard the matter made a formal finding that it had been so listed. The list, Black pointed out, was used despite the Supreme Court's decision in the listing case. Thus, it could be argued, even the Court's own majority was ignoring the Court's decision. Black said, "Dr. Barsky had a constitutional right to be free of any imputations on account of this illegal list. That reason alone should in my judgment require reversal of this case."[29] For Dr. Barsky, the journey that commenced with the HUAC subpoena in 1946 thus ended with his suspension for six months from the practice of medicine in 1954.

By mid-1951, whatever positive impact the *Blau* case (the right not to incriminate oneself) and the *Joint Anti-Fascist* case (due process violated by listing as subversive without hearing) may have had apparently had been overwhelmed by cases that narrowed First Amendment rights or resulted in decisions being ignored in practice. The listing case exemplifies the latter. Even the right to refuse self-incrimination was substantially diluted just a few months after the *Blau* decision.

Jane Rogers was convicted of contempt before a grand jury for failing to name the person to whom she had delivered the membership lists and dues records of the Communist Party of Denver, Colorado. She did not deny that she was formerly treasurer of the Party; she only maintained that she did not want to give the name of, in effect, her successor. The district court judge held her in contempt, did not allow her counsel to speak, and sentenced her to four months' imprisonment. The Court of Appeals for the Tenth Circuit affirmed, and the Supreme Court allowed certiorari. In a decision decided on February 26, 1951, the majority opinion, written by Chief Justice Vinson, affirmed her conviction.[30]

Notwithstanding the *Blau* decision, the Vinson opinion in *Rogers* significantly narrowed the right to refuse to incriminate oneself. In effect, the Court's finding was that Rogers was required both to properly claim the right and to claim it at the proper moment or lose the Fifth Amendment protection. The Court held that Rogers had done neither.

Justices Black, Frankfurter, and Douglas dissented. Black's dissent opened, "Some people are hostile to the Fifth Amendment's provision unequivocally commanding that no United States official shall compel a person to be a witness against himself."[31] Black went on to call for no retreat from a broad construction of that principle. He and his dissenting colleagues argued that Rogers had not waived her rights and that, given the Smith Act, the question she was asked demanded an answer that could be self-incriminating. Black pointed out that, realistically, intimate association with the Communist Party was itself an incriminating fact.

Justice Douglas, writing thirty years later in his autobiography *The Court Years, 1939–1975*, made this comment about the *Rogers* case:

> Thirty years ago the plea of self-incrimination fell into popular disrepute. The phrase "Fifth Amendment Communist" was freely used to condemn recalcitrant witnesses. What people forgot was that the plea of self-incrimination preserved by the Fifth Amendment was made for the protection of the innocent as well as the guilty. Innocent people are often caught up in ambiguous circumstances that might lead to prosecution or even conviction.[32]

As the crucial *Dennis* case moved to oral argument and consideration by the Supreme Court in late 1950, it was clear that First Amendment rights were on the defensive in the court system. Congressional statutes were upheld (the union non-Communist affidavit), as were contempt actions by congressional and state anti-Communist investigating committees. The executive branch could deport aliens for political affiliations; its loyalty program, using the Subversive Organizations List, survived and in fact thrived despite the Supreme Court ruling striking down the listing process as violating due process of law. Perjury indictments for those who wrongly professed they were not Communist Party members could result in five years' imprisonment. The alternative—relying on the Fifth Amendment—might result in a contempt finding with a maximum of one year in jail. They were not pleasant choices for those caught up in the Red Scare.

Cases and issues decided prior to the *Dennis* case paled by comparison to what the decision in that case portended. Here was the heart of the Red Scare: was it a crime in America to believe and advocate as the Communist Party leadership did? Would a statute making belief and advocacy—without more than writing, speaking, meeting and teaching—a crime that would pass constitutional muster?

While the question of how the Supreme Court would come down was of utmost consequence, those attuned to the operation of the legal system focused first on the U.S. Court of Appeals for the Second Circuit, where the intermediate appeal would be decided. On the panel of three judges that would hear the case was the highly respected jurist Learned Hand; many in the nation's legal community thought he should have been on the Supreme Court.[33] His views on the issues involved in the *Dennis* appeal would, and in fact did, carry considerable weight with the Supreme Court.

Hand was sensitive to the deleterious affect the Red Scare was having on the country. His biographer, Gerald Gunther, has stated that Hand perceived "from the start the domestic damage that American obsession with international communism was inflicting."[34] As early as mid-1947, Hand wrote to a friend that "the frantic witch hunters are given freer reign to set up a sort of Inquisition, detecting heresy wherever non-conformity appears."[35]

In the time of the earlier Red Scare, his decision in the *Masses* case[36] and his influence on Holmes in formulating the *Abrams* dissent demonstrated his sensitivity to the preservation of First Amendment rights.[37] Hand frequently spoke out about his concern over the growing public intolerance toward aliens and radicals "and the strange doings of the FBI."[38] He was hostile toward McCarthy and those following in his footsteps, owing to the sensational, unsupported charges and innuendo that constituted McCarthyism. Hand reacted particularly to the ceaseless attacks on Dean Acheson, Truman's secretary of state, by McCarthy and the China Lobby. His biographer states, however, that Hand did not speak out publicly against McCarthyism because of his role as a judge and because of what Gunther has described as Hand's innately fearful nature. When he did speak out publicly in 1951, it was after he had retired from active judicial service.[39]

Before Hand went public on McCarthyism, however, he had played a very significant role in two Red Scare cases and one espionage case. Hand participated in and wrote opinions in these cases despite his concern that enough was known about his views to have perhaps prevented his involvement with these appeals. He wrote the opinion in the appeal of Judith Coplon's espionage conviction, finding, among other reasons for reversal, that the illegal arrest and use of wiretaps by the FBI violated the Fourth Amendment.[40] While favoring the defendant, his opinion was anything but sympathetic to spies. He clearly acknowledged the threat of communism, but his position reflected the overriding importance of the constitutional guarantees that had been violated.

The *Dennis* case, in which Hand wrote the opinion for the court of appeals, was his most important judicial statement on Red Scare issues. Written for a unanimous three-judge panel and affirming the conviction of the eleven top Communist Party leaders, Hand's opinion came as a shock to those who believed he stood solidly for the interests of civil liberties and constitutional protections. One must bear in mind that this was not the opinion of any judge, but of a judge whose intellect and legal acumen were held in the highest regard.[41] The Supreme Court majority was to affirm not only the result but also the reasoning of Hand's opinion.[42]

Hand's biographer rejected the attitude that blamed Hand for strengthening Red Scare forces in American society, stating that "the ruling does not truly cast doubt on Hand's strong hostility to McCarthyism or the genuineness of his long commitment to civil liberties."[43]

The explanation offered by Gerald Gunther was that Hand believed his *Masses* case had provided a far more speech-protective formula and that it was preferable to the Holmes "clear and present danger" standard. By the time of *Dennis*, his *Masses* approach had failed; thus, he was bound to accept the Holmes standard, updated by his own rephrasing. "In each case they [the courts] must ask whether the gravity of the 'evil,' discounted by its probability, justifies such invasion of free speech as is necessary to avoid the danger."[44]

Gunther also argued that Hand took seriously his obligation as a lower court judge to follow Supreme Court precedents. This obligation, he argues, unavoidably led to the "clear and present danger" test being modified by Hand's language in order to incorporate the world situation.

What Hand argued was that the *Douds* case (holding that Congress can deal with the threat of political strikes through use of non-Communist affidavits to insure that commerce could not be hampered) taught a balancing test in which a court could find that the public interest outweighed an indirect abridgment of the right of free speech. He opined that though *Douds* did not control this case, the threat there was more imminent than in *Dennis* and the gravity in *Dennis* was far greater. That, in turn, yielded the redefined test wherein the court had to look at the gravity of the evil, discounted by its probability, to justify the invasion of free speech.

Hand justified his holding that there was a "clear and present danger," thus allowing these prosecutions, by looking at the summer of 1948 — the time when the defendants were indicted. Hand briefly reviewed Cold War history to that point, concluding that "any border fray, any diplomatic incident . . . might prove a spark in the tinder-box, and lead to war."[45]

Therefore the United States, acting to suppress a danger, could properly prosecute those who appeared to seek overthrow of the government by force. The Smith Act as applied to such a conspiracy did not unconstitutionally abridge freedom of speech. Other challenges raised by the defendants were reviewed and found wanting.

Oral arguments before the court of appeals in *Dennis* took an exceptionally long three days, ending June 23, 1950. The next day North Korea invaded South Korea, and by the time the decision was issued on August 1, 1950, the United States was deeply involved in the war. Judge Hand did not need to describe in detail the world situation down to 1950; in effect, "judicial notice" of the threat of communism and of the

Communist Party had been taken at the trial and was sufficient in providing the "clear and dangerous" circumstances by the summer of 1948, the time when the defendants had been indicted.

Finally, in defending Hand's opinion in the case, his biographer states, "Clearly, Hand's performance in *Dennis* was neither a sudden surrender to McCarthyism, nor an act of cowardice. Thus, Hand insisted repeatedly that he thought the Smith Act prosecutions of the Communist leaders a mistake," but explained that he "was bound by and faithful to Supreme Court precedents."[46]

The Supreme Court, to which the *Dennis* case next moved in late 1950, was headed by Chief Justice Frederick (Fred) M. Vinson, nominated by President Truman. Vinson served from 1946 to his death in office on September 8, 1953. Of the nine justices who were to decide the *Dennis* case, five were Roosevelt appointees and four were appointed by Truman. The fact that the entire Court in 1950 was composed of liberal Democratic presidents' choices, however, was no assurance as to how any justice would vote, even on politically charged issues. The same was to be the case with respect to the Eisenhower nominees; this unpredictability is part of Supreme Court lore.

Fred Vinson was fifty-six years old when President Truman nominated him to be chief justice. Truman admired this Kentuckian who had successfully handled important jobs in the administration; when nominated in 1946, Vinson was secretary of the treasury. Roosevelt had found Vinson to be a valuable ally in Congress and had placed him on the United States Court of Appeals for the District of Columbia in 1937, a position he held until he resigned in 1943 to take on a wartime administrative assignment.

President Truman faced a difficult situation when Chief Justice Harlan F. Stone died in April 1946. The infighting on the Supreme Court was intense; there were threats of resignation over which justice should be elevated to chief justice. Sidestepping further controversy and hoping his good friend Vinson could calm the waters, Truman nominated a person from outside the Court.

Vinson's credentials were good; he had experience in all three branches of government. Truman found him compatible in terms of political philosophy and was impressed with his sociability, friendliness, and sense of humor; overall, he seemed an excellent choice to conciliate conflicting views and to work out compromises—traits Truman admired. These qualities, rather than legal acumen and jurisprudential scholarship, were what motivated the president to appoint him.

Vinson was a pragmatist whose philosophy and principles included upholding the power of the office of the president and of government in general. Because he believed in strong government and a broad interpretation of congressional and executive power, Vinson was already committed to allowing the government to exercise its powers against the communist threat, particularly in what he considered the perilous times facing the nation.

Vinson's arrival on the Court came at a time when a majority of the justices were civil libertarians: Black, Douglas, Murphy, and Rutledge joined with Chief Justice Stone to form this bloc. With Vinson replacing Stone in 1946, and the added loss of Murphy and Rutledge later that year, the balance shifted. To Vinson, Burton, and new justices Minton and Clark, the four Truman appointees, was added the vote of Reed, an FDR appointee, to create a conservative majority in civil liberties cases that rarely ruled in favor of individual freedom. For example, Sherman Minton had, as a senator from Indiana, voted for the Smith Act in 1940; given his strong belief in the limited role the Court should play in dealing with congressional or presidential prerogatives, he consistently voted against interfering with government actions, notwithstanding any civil liberties considerations. Further, he was firmly convinced that the Red Scare was a serious national threat.[47]

The result was a new majority, which favored allowing Congress and the executive branch wide authority and discretion in combating the perceived threat of internal subversion, so prevalent in the late 1940s and 1950s. Thus the majority held that for a proper response to the Red Scare authority, not freedom, ought to prevail when a choice had to be made.[48] As one commentator has noted, the Vinson majority posed one answer to the continuing, perhaps inevitable conflict: sacrifice individual rights and freedoms to the common good or mandate through judicial decisions the opposite.[49] Another view, expressed by David Caute, was that under Vinson, "from 1949 to 1954 the Constitution was concussed in the Courts," and that Vinson remained so much a Truman confidant, interested in party political intrigue, that he "rubber-stamped the administration's position on almost every occasion."[50]

Thus far, history has not been generally favorable in its evaluation of Fred Vinson. Bernard Schwartz, in *A Book of Legal Lists: The Best and Worst in American Law*, names Vinson to his "Ten Worst Supreme Court Justices" list. This assessment of Vinson included his failure to accomplish his mission to unify the Court; the Vinson Court was the most fragmented in the Court's history, with only 19 percent of the cases decided unanimously in his last term. Vinson was also regarded as having a second-class mind; fellow justices regarded him as their intellectual inferior and assessed that his death opened the way to obtaining unanimity in *Brown v. Board of Education* under the leadership of the new chief justice, Earl Warren. Frankfurter is said to have remarked on hearing of Vinson's death, "This is the first indication that I have ever had that there is a God."[51]

A poll of legal scholars taken in 1970 rated Vinson as one of the eight failures as justices and the only chief justice so delineated. Other scholars have attacked this rating as unfair, given his short tenure on the Court, during which he presided over a divided and divisive group.[52] Undoubtedly, a sizable portion of the ill will one comes across regarding Vinson is attributable to his *Dennis* decision. James A. Thompson has offered this appraisal:

The evidence here is indisputable: individuals and their constitutional rights were, for the chief justice, subordinate to federal and state powers. . . . For others, particularly leftists ensnared in the Cold War and McCarthyism hysteria, Vinson's Supreme Court tenure offered no protection against repressive congressional laws and committees, executive investigations or criminal prosecutions.[53]

Though it heard oral arguments in early December 1950, the Supreme Court took until June 4, 1951 to issue its *Dennis* decision. Chief Justice Vinson was joined by Justices Reed, Burton, and Minton in writing the majority opinion; Frankfurter and Jackson wrote separate concurring opinions. The result was to affirm the trial and appellate courts' conviction. As was expected, Justices Douglas and Black dissented.

The crux of the case was whether the sections of the Smith Act under which the defendants were tried violated the First Amendment. The majority stated that government had the power to prevent an armed rebellion; given this power, the issue was whether the Smith Act would pass constitutional muster as a means of protecting the existing government. The Court held that it did.

Recognizing that the Supreme Court had never even decided an important case involving free speech before the 1919 *Schenck* case, the Court in *Dennis* sought for rules and guidance that had been displayed by past decisions resulting in the determination that free speech was neither unlimited nor unqualified. The majority argued that the societal value of free speech must, on occasion, be subordinated to other values and considerations.

This led to the use of the "clear and present danger" test to determine when circumstances were of such threatening nature that Congress had the right to act to prevent their occurrence. In response to the argument that no acts had taken place, the Vinson opinion stated:

Obviously, the words cannot mean that before the Government may act, it must wait until the putsch is about to be executed, the plans have been laid and the signal is awaited. If Government is aware that a group aiming at its overthrow is attempting to indoctrinate its members and to commit them to a course whereby they will strike when the leaders feel the circumstances permit, action by the Government is required.[54]

The threat posed may not realistically have had a chance of success; nevertheless, it was a sufficient evil that Congress could act to prevent it. The majority held that when the government becomes aware of a group attempting to indoctrinate members and commit them to a course where they will strike when propitious, government has an obligation to act.

Recognizing that Holmes and Brandeis had modified the "clear and present danger" standard and narrowed its application, the majority attempted to distinguish between what was involved in cases where they had dissented and the situation the Court faced in *Dennis*:

They [Holmes and Brandeis] were not confronted with any situation comparable to the instant one—the development of an apparatus designed and dedicated to the overthrow of the Government, in the context of world crisis after crisis.[55]

The Court then adopted the Learned Hand formulation of the rule: "In each case [courts] must ask whether the gravity of the 'evil,' discounted by its improbability, justifies such invasion of free speech as is necessary to avoid the danger."[56]

The majority concurred with Hand that the requisite danger was present, justifying the invasion of freedom of speech. There followed a finding that the trial judge, Harold Medina, had correctly handled the presentation of the issue to the jury and that the Smith Act sections involved did not violate any constitutional limitation because of being indefinite or vague.

Felix Frankfurter, apparently uncomfortable with the majority's statement but willing to join in affirming the conviction, wrote his views in a concurring decision that ran twice as long (including an appendix) as the majority's.

Roaming through history generally and many cases specifically, Frankfurter examined arguments brought forth from all directions. Ultimately, his belief in the right of the government to protect itself in the interests of national security predominated. While citing arguments for preserving a broad tolerance for free speech, he found the Communists' exercise of their rights to free speech to be ill deserving of protection.

Justice Jackson's argument would have followed a different path while concurring in the guilt of the Communists. His argument was that a clear and present danger need not be found where a conspiracy is proven. Conspiracy was, in itself, a crime; the defendants were found guilty of a conspiracy. That, for him, seemed to be sufficient.

Having returned from his role in the Nuremberg Trials, Jackson quoted from the German Criminal Code under the Weimar Republic, which outlawed the Communist and Nazi parties. Yet Germany had fallen to the Nazis. With this in mind, he closed his concurrence with these thoughts:

I add that I have little faith in the long-range effectiveness of this conviction to stop the rise of the Communist movement. Communism will not go to jail with these Communists. No decision by this Court can forestall revolution whenever the existing government fails to command the respect and loyalty of the people and sufficient distress and discontent is allowed to grow up among the masses. Many failures by fallen governments attest that no government can long prevent revolution by outlawry.[57]

Short dissents by Justices Black and Douglas followed. Justice Black made his views clear that:

At the outset I want to emphasize what the crime involved in this case is, and what it is not. These petitioners were not charged with an attempt to overthrow the Government. They were not charged with overt acts of any kind designed to overthrow the Government. They were not even charged with saying anything or writing anything designed to overthrow the Government. The charge was that they agreed to assemble and to talk and publish certain ideas at a later date: The indictment is that they conspired to organize the Communist Party and to use speech or newspapers and other publications in the future to teach and advocate the forcible overthrow of the Government. No matter how it is worded, this is a virulent form of prior censorship of speech and press, which I believe the First Amendment forbids. I would hold §3 of the Smith Act authorizing this prior restraint unconstitutional on its face and as applied.[58]

From that point, he argued that no clear and present danger existed and that the First Amendment "is the keystone of our Government, that the freedoms it guarantees provide the best insurance against the destruction of all freedom."[59]

Justice Black closed his dissent with a prescient prediction:

Public opinion being what it now is, few will protest the conviction of these Communist petitioners. There is hope, however, that in calmer times, when present pressures, passions and fears subside, this or some later Court will restore the First Amendment liberties to the high preferred place where they belong in a free society.[60]

At the present time, when the nation has so recently been confronted by acts of domestic terrorism, the opening words of Justice Douglas's dissent are particularly meaningful:

If this were a case where those who claimed protection under the First Amendment were teaching the techniques of sabotage, the assassination of the President, the filching of documents from public files, the planting of bombs, the art of street warfare, and the like, I would have no doubts. The freedom to speak is not absolute; the teaching of methods of terror and other seditious conduct should be beyond the pale along with obscenity and immorality.[61]

Douglas then stated that the *Dennis* case was argued as if these were the facts when in fact they were not. He argued that communism was a bogeyman and really inconsequential as a political force. Douglas quoted Justice Brandeis extensively on the value of free speech: that more speech, not enforced silence, was the proper response to falsehoods and fallacies. In Justice Douglas's view, free speech had already destroyed the effectiveness of the Communist Party. Looking back to the Great Depression, he noted that communists had had little success at a time of economic trouble. With the conditions of the country so greatly changed, he argued, "The country is not in despair; the people know Soviet Communism; the doctrine of Soviet revolution is exposed in all its ugliness and the American people want none of it."[62]

Douglas, in his conference notes, gives insight into the decision making process behind *Dennis*. The conference he wrote about was one in which the justices convened to vote on a case after oral discussion. The most junior justice voted first, working up to the chief justice. Then the chief assigned who was to write the majority opinion.

Of the *Dennis* conference, held five days after oral arguments ended, Douglas remarked that "the amazing thing about the conference in this important case was the brief nature of the discussion. Those wanting to affirm [the convictions] had minds closed to argument or persuasion. The conference discussion was largely pro forma. It was more amazing because of the drastic revision of the 'clear and present danger' test which affirmance requires." Chief Justice Vinson, Douglas said, would affirm the convictions with "practically no discussion."[63]

The less than satisfactory discussion, however, was followed by months of circulating drafts of opinions by the justices. What developed was that the Vinson majority was apparently ready to do all that was necessary to affirm the convictions, including taking "judicial notice" of the communist peril as a substitute for conformity to the "clear and present danger" test. When a court takes "judicial notice" of a fact it means that the party asking for this device has satisfied the burden of proving a fact without the formal presentation of evidence. Use of "judicial notice," modifying the "clear and present danger" test to the Hand expression, supported the majority's conclusions. Criticisms by Black and Douglas were fruitless; Douglas had pointed out that the majority was willing to modify any standard to get the desired result.

Douglas, in his autobiography, reflecting on *Dennis*, placed special importance on the times, which produced a Zeitgeist that encompassed even the courts of justice:

In the 1950s, when the Cold War flourished, the resulting climate of opinion made the dispensation of justice very unlikely when one was merely charged with being a Communist, let alone a person who was, in fact, a hard-core member. Juries were almost bound to reflect the dark suspicions which most Americans harbored about dispensers of a foreign ideology. Judges were not much more independent; it often seemed that they were being whipsawed by public passions and transformed into agents of intolerance. State judges, elected to office, were often mere mouth-pieces of the most intolerant members of the community . . . even federal judges, named for life, were affected, as is illustrated by the long series of sad episodes which resulted in federal prosecutions.[64]

The reaction to the *Dennis* decision in the mass media was predictably positive. In the few months preceding *Dennis*, the press had reported on Remington's guilt in his second perjury trial (a typical example was the *Chicago Tribune* front-page headline of February 8, 1951 "Remington Guilty! Jailed!"). On March 29, 1951 Julius and Ethel Rosenberg were found guilty of wartime espionage on behalf of the Soviet Union and the following week sentenced to death. And Alger Hiss lost his attempt to bring his case to the Supreme Court on March 12, 1951, thus sending him to jail for perjury for saying he never gave government secrets to Whittaker Chambers, an acknowledged former communist spy courier.

The guilt of the top Party members was welcomed in headlines and editorials. The war in Korea was not going well; American blood was being shed in the battle against communism overseas, making these court victories on the domestic scene that much more welcome. In an editorial reviewing the decision (and ignoring the dissents), the *Los Angeles Times* stated:

A time may come again when a Communist will be a harmless member of a political splinter party, when he can holler from his soapbox that it would be a good thing to burn the Capitol, hang the Cabinet and start on the way to a true "people's government." But that time is not now or in the foreseeable future. We are fighting Communism with blood and money on both sides of the world; now the Supreme Court permits us to fight it at home. The weapon is an awkward one, but it is better than none at all.[65]

Many responses anticipated and welcomed a roundup of more Communist Party leaders; some warned of "Red violence" in the wake of the decision. Eugene Dennis, Party secretary, said the Court's action could be "reversed by the people."[66] Both assertions were patently absurd: the idea that there would be a violent uprising of the remnants of the

Communist Party was as realistic as Dennis's belief that the "people" disagreed with the majority's verdict and would somehow "reverse" it.

James E. McInerney, assistant attorney general, announced prosecution of local Communist leaders in various parts of the country; he estimated that "nearer 2,500 than 25,000" federal indictments under the Smith Act would be sought, which was a gross exaggeration of even the lowest figure.[67] This was echoed by *Newsweek* on June 18, 1951, when it predicted, "Communists: Worse Days Coming," as it speculated on a list of new targets for further Smith Act prosecutions.[68] Both *Dennis* dissenters, especially Justice Douglas, were vilified by some of the more extreme voices; a Republican representative called for Douglas to resign for giving "aid and comfort" to America's enemies.[69]

Douglas's dissent also raised the ire of syndicated newspaper commentators such as Fulton Lewis, Jr., who stated, "Douglas peddles a lot of the same stuff mouthed by liberals, who come crying out of the woods every time a Communist gets into trouble." The article was clipped by a reader and sent to Douglas with a note that included the question, "How in the Name of God did a nut, screwball and crackpot like you get on the Bench of the Supreme Court?"[70]

There were dissenters among newspapers, though few in number. Some major exceptions were the *St. Louis Post-Dispatch*, the *New York Post*, and the *Louisville Courier-Journal*, all of which criticized the *Dennis* majority.[71] As the weeks went by, some publications had second thoughts about the verdict. In an editorial on June 20, 1951, the *Christian Century* commended the result, but after reading the editorials in the *St. Louis Post-Dispatch*, and the *Louisville Courier-Journal*, as well as an advertisement placed in the *New York Times* by some leading civil libertarians, it felt uncomfortable with the deeper implications of the Court's majority opinions and said so.[72]

The *New Republic* editorial under the title, "What the Court Has Destroyed," opened with the line, "On June 4, 1951, the Supreme Court of the U.S. paid tyranny the tribute of imitation." Calling the majority decision "the most dramatic delinquency of the Court," it concluded that "the great damage lies in the deterioration of the American spirit of freedom."[73]

In an October 1951 article appearing in *Fortune* summing up the work of the Supreme Court for the year, the magazine's legal expert contrasted the Supreme Court's liberal approach to regulating the economic system with the "Court's stern treatment of intellectual orthodoxy," exemplified in the enforcement of the Smith Act. The author attributed the latter as "inevitable [given] the climate of opinion being what it is in this country today." He added that it is "inconceivable" that Justices Murphy and Rutledge would have voted "to uphold the Smith Sedition [*sic*] Act, America's first peacetime sedition law since the ill-starred Alien and Sedition Acts of 1798." The author concluded by pointing out that the "libertarian" concept of limiting First Amendment rights developed by Holmes and Brandeis "has been unable to stand the stresses and strains of a cold war," instead requiring the looser standard of Judge Hand to support a theory that would uphold the convictions.[74]

Overlooked by almost all commentators was another decision of the Supreme Court issued the same day as *Dennis*. By a vote of six to three, seventeen people who worked for the city of Los Angeles and who had been fired for refusing to execute non-Communist affidavits and take an oath relating to their political views lost their appeal to the high court.[75] As the *New Republic* editorial pointed out, the *Dennis* case, "whatever its ultimate impact may be on all citizens, through weakening the First Amendment, its immediate impact falls on only a small band of conspirators [Communist Party members]." In contrast, the *Garner* decision was important to some three million public servants. In validating the Los Angeles loyalty-test scheme and enabling already hired civil servants to be fired without fear of prohibitions based on arguments of ex post facto or bill of attainder, "the Court has placed constitutional force behind the efforts of states and municipalities to use test oaths to drive political non-conformists from public office."

Claiming the decision would sustain such programs in at least thirty-three states and several cities, the editorial argued that "all of these expurgatory oath programs have now been judicially anointed and sanctified." With a bare majority upholding the legality of the oath, the editorial lamented the change in the Court brought on by the deaths of Justices Murphy and Rutledge, whom they presumed would have joined the dissenters, thus creating a majority that would have overturned the oath as unconstitutional.[76]

Thus, in one day, two foundation stones of the Red Scare were laid: the *Dennis* case confirmed the use of the Smith Act to prosecute communists, and the *Garner* decision enabled local governments to use negative test oaths and affidavits to screen potential employees, as well as to discharge those who were already working but who refused to subscribe. The use of non-Communist affidavits in unions had been confirmed in *Douds* a year earlier.

The ability of HUAC and other bodies to prosecute through contempt of Congress or other criminal proceedings was basically well established by 1951 in cases involving Dr. Barsky, Jane Rogers, and Ernestina Fleischman, as well as in a contempt of Congress (HUAC) case involving Eugene Dennis.[77] A few months later, a Supreme Court majority with Douglas and Black dissenting affirmed a broad interpretation of the government's ability to deport aliens under the Smith Act for political noncon-formity.[78] By early 1952 the Court's majority had also sent a significant signal to the legal community when it confirmed the contempt of court convictions by Judge Medina against all the lawyers in the *Dennis* case.[79]

There were few judicial refuges from the onslaught of Red Scare decisions that endorsed prosecutions and convictions. The *Blau* decision had been considerably narrowed in its protection against self-incrimination. The *Joint Anti-Fascist Refugee Committee* subversive organization case was pragmatically only a pyrrhic victory. In effect, the Supreme Court majority had placed its powerful endorsement on the prosecution of dissent. The Court had essentially remained silent as a force that could have dampened, discouraged, or even halted the strongest weapon in the arsenal of those waging this domestic war—the weapon of legal prosecution. Instead, it anointed and sanctified prosecutions.

Chapter 6
"The Courts Were of No Help Whatsoever"

Victor Rabinowitz, a leftist lawyer whose work goes back to the Red Scare era, was speaking only from the defense view when he asserted, "The courts were of no help whatsoever."[1] They were of no help for him and the cause of dissent; however, they were of significant help in endorsing and validating the Red Scare.

The planning that had taken place earlier in the U.S. attorney general's office in anticipation of a favorable result in the *Dennis* case meant the government could spring into immediate action in prosecuting more leaders of the Communist Party. Cabell Phillips, Washington correspondent for the *New York Times*, wrote on June 10, 1951:

> The decision of the Supreme Court Monday upholding the conviction of the eleven Communist Party leaders is one of the most momentous in the recent history of that tribunal. . . . [T]he inescapable fact remains that, for the first time, a political party in the United States has, to all intents and purposes, been put beyond the pale of the law. That, under any circumstances, is a sobering thought for the citizens of the world's freest democracy. . . .
>
> The court has given the Department of Justice a long-awaited green light to go after suspected groups and individuals whom it could not touch as long as the party's dogma enjoyed the protection of legal status. . . . [I]t is no secret that in the internal-security section there is a huge backlog of potential prosecutions under the Smith Act which they [department officials] have been sitting on pending the outcome of this case. . . . It is inconceivable that the Department of Justice, with this devastating new weapon in its hands and under the insistent pressure that comes from powerful segments of Congress and the public, will fail to use it freely.[2]

The press picked up the story as eighteen more Party members were arrested in New York City on June 21, 1951; these arrests were followed by arrests across the country and even in Hawaii. Political scientist Robert Mollan was later able to define sixteen groups of Party members who were indicted and prosecuted under the "advocacy" section of the Smith Act and one group prosecuted under the "membership" clause, for a total of 129 people.[3]

Michal R. Belknap called these arrests, indictments, and trials "Repeat Performances" and vividly described how one hundred FBI agents went after the second group of New York Communists "[a]s the first light of dawn colored the Manhattan sky" on June 21, 1951. The result, given the *Dennis* case, was to produce "repeat performances" of the Foley Square trial in cities from New Haven to Honolulu, "staged not only to destroy the Party but also to educate the public about the menace of communism and to advance the interests of politicians and internal security bureaucrats."[4]

The following week, the *New Republic* asked, "Do the new indictments presage a wave of further arrests?" Answering their own question, the writers said they believed the arrests would only pertain to top Party members (who gave orders) and not to rank-and-file members (who took orders). The writers concluded that the Party had been weakened, but also that the "Bill of Rights has not escaped unscathed."[5]

The *Dennis* decision encouraged other groups and individuals to pursue Red Scare goals; after all, when the Supreme Court of the United States, the most powerful and prestigious court in the world, placed its seal of approval on convicting Communists of criminal behavior, the legitimacy of all anti-Red activities received a significant boost. Wittingly or unwittingly, the Court's decisions were encouraging smear campaigns by Senator McCarthy, blacklists, loyalty oaths, attacks on aliens, and prosecutions for contempt on the state and federal levels.

Illustrating the impact of *Dennis* is this article in the *New York Times* published three days after that decision was announced, relating to New York public schools:

JANSEN TO WIDEN RED INVESTIGATION
Several More Teachers Will Be Questioned on Ties to Communist Party
Spurred by the United States Supreme Court's decision upholding the conviction of the eleven Communist leaders the Board of Education will investigate several more teachers to determine whether they are, or ever have been, members of the Communist Party.
Dr. William Jansen, Superintendent of Schools, confirmed yesterday the forthcoming investigations and said he was gratified by the court's recent ruling. Dr. Jansen, who last year started action that led to the dismissal of eight teachers who refused to answer questions about alleged Communist affiliation, declared:
"The nation's highest court has held that the Communist Party is a criminal conspiracy against the United States of America. That is what we contended in the trial of the eight teachers. We also contended that it was their duty to state whether or not, as teachers, they were or had been members of a conspiratorial group."[6]

As time passed, it was not uncommon for newspapers and magazines to publish "box scores" summarizing Communist prosecutions. For example, on August 10, 1952 the *New York Times*, published an editorial "Score on C.P.," which stated how many had been convicted by that date (thirty-one), how many were awaiting trial (twenty-one), how many were in prison (eight), how many were fugitives (seven), and how many were free on bail pending appeal of guilty verdicts (twenty). The *Nation* gave its own box score update and comments in its December 12, 1953 edition.[7]

Notwithstanding the weaknesses of the cases, particularly against lower-echelon leaders, it generally took juries little time to return guilty verdicts; appellate courts promptly and overwhelmingly sustained those verdicts. Belknap has characterized these trials as a "kind of grinding monotony . . . , for although there was some variation between individual Smith Act cases, on the whole they were extremely repetitious, both of *Dennis* and of each other."[8]

While the trials that followed in the wake of *Dennis* were essentially repeat performances, often using the same government evidence in the form of the writings and speeches of Communists and using the same traveling band of paid informers to identify the defendants as active Communists, there were differences. The "literary debates" involving the meaning of Communist doctrine, a "battle of quotations," as it has been called, were less acrimonious than *Dennis*, although still very lengthy. The trials were less circuslike than was *Dennis*, with more capable judges and with defense attorneys who were more restrained in their courtroom work and less the tools of the Party and its "labor defense" strategy.

What also came more clearly into focus was that Cold War events were a major driving force in these trials and appeals. World events were explicitly linked to "judicial notice" that communists constituted a clear and present danger. Thus, in 1954, Judge John Marshall Harlan, while on a federal court of appeals (before elevation to the Supreme Court in 1955), wrote in affirming the convictions of the second set of New York defendants (the *United States v. Flynn* case): "if the danger was clear and present in 1948, it can hardly be thought to have been less in 1951, when the Korean conflict was raging and our relations with the Communist world had moved from cold to hot war."[9] Harlan pointed out that the trial judge in *Flynn*, as the Supreme Court had in *Dennis*, properly relied on world events to justify the finding that a clear and present danger existed. In *Flynn*, Harlan noted, all that the trial judge had done was to bring those Cold War developments down to the date of the trial. Harlan's opinion included an extensive footnote that recited the trial judge's wide-ranging statement of Cold War developments that provided the basis for taking "judicial notice" of a clear and present danger.[10]

With such reliance on world events, two significant implications can be deduced from the *Dennis* and post-*Dennis* convictions. If world events changed significantly, the foundation for sustaining further convictions would begin to crumble. Also, given the fact that the *Dennis* decision had made the relevant precedent binding on all lower courts, there would be little chance that the Supreme Court would take any of these post-*Dennis* cases for review unless significantly new issues were raised or the Court was willing to change *Dennis*.

It could be inferred that, if the times changed, views held by at least some members of the Court might change, or new justices would be seated who would come there with a different view, or both. Thus the potential for a changed view of the dialectic between First Amendment rights and the perceived threat from Communists, their Party, and other dissenting voices was inherent in this reliance on Cold War developments. In turn, this fed the Red Scare. Because they were intertwined, if internal developments dampened Red Scare zeal, that too would be a factor of "changed times," a factor that would likely influence how the Court viewed further Red Scare cases. These, together with changes in Court personnel, kept open the potential that the Supreme Court would shift its position.

Law does mirror society; form ever follows function. Let American society reflect major changes in attitude and the law must also react, perhaps slowly, perhaps too slowly to help those who have already lost their cause, but react it will. In rare instances, the Supreme Court may indeed be ahead of public views.

So long as the function was to respond to the threat of communism and to wage a domestic war against it (and, in a broader sense, all dissent), the forms taken would confirm the use of the Smith Act, loyalty oaths, or other means endorsed as lawful weapons in the battle. Once the mirror reflected significant change, the form the law took would alter or shift.

The cases involving the many defendants following the *Dennis* decision were long in trial, often lasting months, and each generated a record for appeal purposes that was daunting for appellate judges to read and digest. Occasionally, one or more of these cases generated a dissent. William H. Hastie, a circuit judge for the United States Court of Appeals for the Third Circuit, on a panel of judges, heard the appeal of the fifth group of convicted Communists. The appeal was from guilty verdicts rendered in the District Court for the Western District of Pennsylvania. This group of Communists was arrested in August 1951; the appeals court did not hear arguments on the case until June 9, 1954. One year later, on June 13, 1955, the majority confirmed the conviction of the five defendants.

Judge Hastie, joined by one other judge, dissented. Hastie noted that the prosecuting attorney conceded in open court that the government could not prove the guilt of four of the five defendants, so weak was its case. Judge Hastie concluded that in the face of such an admission, given the Red Scare times, the jury would have only sent Communists to jail.

Hastie then proceeded to discuss the Smith Act requirement of some "overt act" by each individual. Judge Hastie's review of the record was that at most, the evidence demonstrated that the "overt act" was the defendants' participation in Party meetings—nothing more. There was, he found, no evidence that any "defendant or any alleged co-conspirator said or did anything advocating insurrection or even making arrangements for such advocacy." Because the government's case was, by its own counsel's admission, unproven against four of the five Communists, and because no overt acts were proven beyond the bare fact of having attended meetings, Hastie would have reversed these convictions. Against him, however, were five other judges on this appellate panel, as well as the Red Scare mentality that called for convictions regardless of proof.[11]

One apparent result of these post-*Dennis* prosecutions was the virtual cessation of the Communist Party as a viable force in politics and unions and as a platform for dissent. Because some of the convicted had jumped bail and others for whom arrest warrants had been issued had fled, efforts to determine fair bail amounts and to seek lowered bail required numerous court hearings and appeals, many of which the defendants won, but at a cost: the lack of funds available to the Party and to defendants meant jail because even the lowered bail could not be raised.[12]

Who would be next? That was a question that state as well as national Communist Party members had to ask themselves, and it was certainly on the minds of their families. The publicity given to these post-*Dennis* prosecutions raised the specter of arrest and criminal prosecution for anyone considering joining the Party or remaining a member.

There was also a clearly political and bureaucratic aspect to the continued Smith Act prosecutions. As Democrats fought to hold onto the presidency in 1952, the Justice Department pressed new attacks on the Party, with President Truman describing his administration's drive against the Communists as a major feature of the national campaign to eliminate subversion.[13]

The new Republican president elected that year, Dwight D. Eisenhower, had used the very unpopular Korean War, as well as the domestic "soft on communism" issue, to win the presidency. His administration continued the prosecutions already underway, defending on appeal the verdicts obtained under Truman's administration, and pressed for new prosecutions in 1953 and later. The Republican Party, fractured by splits between moderates and right-wing elements, found common ground in pressing the domestic subversion issue, leading the president to take a hard anti-communist line as a method of insuring congressional victories in 1954. Vice President Richard Nixon during the 1954 campaign charged sinister ties between Democrats and the Communist Party. New legislation stripping citizenship from persons convicted of Smith Act violations won quick congressional approval in 1954; this was the Expatriation Act. The Smith Act, however, remained the mode of choice for most prosecutions.[14]

It was also a time when prosecutors, judges, and bureaucrats bridging both administrations were rewarded for zeal in pursuing the Red Menace. J. Edgar Hoover pumped up demands for appropriations based on the communist threat, though his one-time assistant, William Sullivan, admitted that "the Party didn't amount to a damn."[15] Historian Eric F. Goldman has described this period as one in which "Everywhere in the United States, the fury against Communism was taking on—even more than it had before the Korean War—elements of a vendetta against the Half-Century of Revolution in domestic affairs [the New Deal-Fair Deal], against all departures from tradition in foreign policy, against the new, the adventurous, the questing in any field."[16]

What is to be understood is that these trials, set against the intensified Red Scare times, produced a plethora of appeals, not only on the central issue of convictions under the Smith Act, but on ancillary issues as well. It was not unusual for defendants on trial who took the stand in their own defense to be cited for contempt for refusing to answer questions that required implicating others. These contempt proceedings often generated their own appeals. Sometimes, too, bail bond issues were tied to these contempt proceedings. Indictments and contempt findings generated bail issues; guilty verdicts generated appeals in a constantly repeating cycle.

What this also indicated was that these Smith Act convictions, along with contempt of court, bail bond, and deportation issues, moved slowly through the American court process, involving appeals courts in the various federal appellate districts from one end of the nation to the other. It was not unusual, particularly in bail bond matters, for appellate courts to send back cases for further hearings, which then might once again be appealed.

Because the essential precedent had been set in *Dennis* by the Supreme Court, attempts to obtain the four votes to allow review of lower court decisions most often failed. For example, the fourth group of Communists arrested in Baltimore and Cleveland in August 1951 were all found guilty on July 31, 1952. Certiorari was denied by the Supreme Court on January 19, 1953.[17]

The IWO filed appeals (there were two) to the Supreme Court after its losses in the New York State court system. Only Justices Black and Douglas voted to grant a hearing of the case; the voting took place at the conference held on October 19, 1953, two weeks after the new term commenced, with a new chief justice, Earl Warren.[18]

The second group of Communists, headed by Elizabeth Gurley Flynn, consisted of eighteen defendants, most of whom were arrested in New York as part of that dawn raid. All of them were found guilty at the trial and appellate levels. Their petition for review by the Supreme Court was turned down in January 1955.[19] As Justice Harry A. Blackmun stated in a speech on March 6, 1991, "The power of the [Supreme] Court is awesome, and it is the end of the line."

The fact that these Smith Act conviction appeals were turned down did not, however, mean that the Supreme Court was inactive in related Red Scare cases in the years between *Dennis* and Red Monday in 1957. Nine months after the *Dennis* decision, a majority of the Court affirmed the right of the attorney general of the United States, as the executive head of the Immigration and Naturalization Service, to deny bail and thus to immediately jail four people who were "active alien Communists" while that official was deciding where they could be deported. Section 23 of the Internal Security Act of 1950 appeared to grant that power to the attorney general; the defendants argued that this power violated the Eighth Amendment's prohibition against excessive bail, excessive fines, and cruel and unusual punishments.[20]

The majority stated that "changes in world politics and in our internal economy bring legislative adjustments affecting the rights of various classes of aliens to admission and deportation." The changed attitude toward aliens who were Communists left the justices with "no doubt" that Congress could act to expel known such persons. In essence, the Court was concluding that if citizen Communists could be sent to jail, aliens who were Communists could be deported and kept in jail without bail until the process was completed.[21]

Four justices—Black, Frankfurter, Burton, and Douglas—dissented, variously arguing that the Eighth Amendment did apply and that the majority position would allow an INS agent to jail people merely because he thought jail is where Communists should be. Furthermore, they argued that the case demonstrated the use of illegal detention without proof of seditious conduct.[22]

The year 1952 brought oral arguments to the Supreme Court in the case of *Adler et al. v. Board of Education of the City of New York*. Public school teachers brought an action to invalidate section 12-a of the New York Civil Service Law as implemented by the Feinberg Act. The Feinberg law made membership in any organization the Board of Regents determined, after a hearing, to be sufficient evidence of ineligibility for employment or continued employment in any New York school. The issue thus posed was whether the Feinberg Act violated constitutional guarantees of freedom of speech and association.

Justice Minton answered in the negative for a majority of the Court. The Court reasoned that people have no right to work in the school system on their own terms; rather, the right to work is limited by those reasonable terms laid down by proper authorities. If teachers chose not to work on those terms, they were free to retain their beliefs and associations and go elsewhere.

The thinking at the time was that teachers worked in sensitive areas and had the ability to shape young minds, which were not discriminating enough to raise objections. Thus associations, past and present, were held to be proper considerations for determining one's fitness and loyalty as necessary for school employment.

Three justices dissented. Frankfurter felt that the constitutional question had not been properly reached; that to the point of this appeal, there had been no move to enforce the law. One week before the decision was announced, on February 25, 1952, Justice Frankfurter wrote a note to the other justices urging his view on them with these words:

Dear Brethren:
Narrow division on a serious question is always a matter of regret and therefore, if fairly avoidable, to be avoided. Therefore I venture to ask careful consideration of what I really believe to be the proper method of disposing of the case, however strong may be the convictions as to the merits on either side of what was discussed at the Bar.
F. F.[23]

Justice Douglas wrote a dissent, joined by Justice Black. It was immediately apparent that Douglas felt very deeply about the related subjects of academic freedom, guilt by association, and the movement to a police state as an aegis against communism. Douglas then did what few justices have done: in a slightly different version, he had his dissent published in *Education Digest* for April 1952.[24]

The files of some of the justices contain reprints of articles and letters concerning the decision. Justice Minton, who wrote for the majority, meticulously preserved these letters and envelopes, personally responding to each letter. Every one of the communications was congratulatory; newspaper editorials favoring his decision were sent to him, including one that appeared in the *New York World Telegram* of March 4, 1952, where Minton was complimented for his "positive and firm" language. Where letters implied criticism of the dissenting justices, Minton included variations of this thought: "I am glad you agree that the majority reached the right result, and I beg of you to believe me that my colleagues who did not agree reached their opinion only upon the most conscientious consideration of the constitutional law problem involved."[25] On the other hand, the Teachers Union of New York sent a letter of "deep appreciation" to Justices Douglas and Black for their dissents, stating, "you have given hope to all those who must meet the constant and persistent assaults on freedom of thought and freedom of inquiry."[26]

One week later, on March 10, 1952, the Court issued its decision in another case generated by the Red Scare, now involving an appeal by the lawyers for the Communists in the *Dennis* case, all of whom Judge Medina held in contempt of court for what they said and did during the trial. He had summarily sentenced all to prison, not allowing any of them to speak in response to his finding and punishment, meted out immediately after the eleven Communists were found guilty. The lawyers appealed their convictions and sentences, which were affirmed by the court of appeals.

Initially the Supreme Court had refused to review the case, but it reconsidered the importance of certain narrow issues and took the case. In essence, the question was whether Medina could do what he did—wait until after the trial instead of when the contemptuous conduct had taken place—to find the lawyers in contempt. Then without giving the attorneys notice or a hearing or the opportunity to defend themselves, he sentenced them to jail, without recusing himself and having the matter adjudged by some other judge.

The majority, with Justice Jackson writing the opinion, held that Judge Medina had acted within his proper discretion under court rules, thus confirming the convictions and jail sentences. To the argument that the sentences would have "an intimidating effect on the legal profession," Jackson responded by acknowledging "that persons identified with unpopular causes may find it difficult to enlist the counsel of their choice," but he felt that "few effective lawyers would regard the tactics condemned here as either necessary or helpful to a successful defense." While promising that the Court would stand by counsel in their "fearless, vigorous and effective performance," it [this Court] "will not equate contempt with courage or insults with independence."[27]

The dissenters were Justices Black, Frankfurter, and Douglas. Only Black and Frankfurter wrote extensively of their views; Douglas joined in concurring with the sentiments of the other two. Black found grounds for full reversal of the convictions, and he believed that Judge Medina should not have passed on the contempt charges he himself had imposed. The defendants were denied a fair opportunity to defend themselves, and the lawyers were constitutionally entitled to a jury trial since this was a matter of criminal contempt.

Justice Black did not hesitate to make the point that Medina's judg-
ments "against the lawyers were colored, however unconsciously, by his
natural abhorrence for the unpatriotic and treasonable designs attributed to their Communist leader clients."[28] Effectively, he was saying that
this was Medina's way of personally getting back at Communists.

Justice Frankfurter's dissent with an appendix of illustrations drawn
from the trial record ran more than sixty pages. In essence, Frankfurter,
ever sensitive to procedural regularity and fairness, found neither here.
"Due regard for such procedural questions, too often misconceived as
narrow and technical, alone justifies the truth of one of the great boasts
of our democracy, the essential fairness of our judicial system."[29]

He then argued that the procedure was all wrong, and that during
the trial

> The judge acted as the prosecuting witness; he thought of himself as such. His
> self-concern pervades the record; it could not humanly have been excluded
> from his judgment of contempt. Judges are human, and it is not suggested that
> any other judge could have been impervious to the abuse had he been subjected
> to it. But precisely because a judge is human, and in common frailty or manli-
> ness would interpret such conduct of lawyers as an attack on himself personally,
> he should not subsequently sit in judgment on his assailants, barring only in-
> stances where such extraordinary procedure is compellingly necessary in order
> that the trial may proceed and not be aborted.[30]

With Frankfurter on the side of dissent, the majority was five, dissenters three, with Justice Clark not participating.

Two years later, in 1954, an appeal came to the Supreme Court from
one of the attorneys, Harry Sacher, who, after to serving six months in
prison, was then disbarred by the Bar Association of the City of New
York. Sacher was successful in having the sanction of permanent disbarment reversed by a Supreme Court majority that felt the punishment
unnecessarily severe. Justices Reed and Burton dissented.[31]

Evidence that the Court was changing in its view of issues generated
by the Red Scare can be seen, not only in this case in early 1954, but
perhaps more significantly in a case decided later that same year. In
that case, a lawyer, Dorsey K. Offutt, was held in criminal contempt and
ordered to jail as a result of his conduct while defending an accused
abortionist. Offutt's trial judge followed in the footsteps of Judge Medina in imposing jail time after finding Offutt in contempt of court. In
the appeal to the Supreme Court, the government relied on the first
Sacher case, which had sustained the procedure and punishment.

This time Frankfurter wrote for the majority, in effect ignoring the
Sacher decision of two-and-one-half years earlier and basing the decision
on the same procedural grounds he had argued on in his dissent in 1952.
The majority included the new (1953) chief justice, Earl Warren. Jack-

son, who had written the majority opinion in 1952, died on October 9, 1954. His replacement, Justice John Marshall Harlan, was not confirmed until the following year. Though this was not a case generated in the defense of Communists, defending an abortionist was close. The indications were that by late 1954, the Court and the times were changing.[32]

There were instances where the Red Scare resulted in such egregious acts or events that even the most conservative members of the Court were repelled. That happened in 1952, when certain college faculty and staff members of an Oklahoma college failed to take a loyalty oath as prescribed by state statute. A taxpayer filed suit to stop the college from paying them. The state courts upheld the validity of the act, and in October 1952, the Supreme Court heard oral arguments in the case of *Wieman v. Updegraff.*[33]

The oath required the affiant to affirm that within the past five years he or she had not been a member of the Communist Party or of any party, association, group, or organization named by the U.S. attorney general as subversive. Just the fact of membership disqualified employment, regardless of any knowledge of the organization's disloyalty; disloyalty was presumed by membership alone.

This was too much even for Justice Clark, who, as attorney general, had prepared and promulgated the Subversive Organizations List. Writing for a unanimous Court, Clark quoted from none other than J. Edgar Hoover in support of the idea that one could join an organization or be "trapped" into joining "because one of the great weaknesses of all Americans, whether adult or youth, is to join something."

The decision also noted that being excluded from public employment on loyalty grounds was a "stain," "a badge of infamy" in "time of cold war and hot emotions."[34] To inhibit freedom in this manner, the Court held, offended due process. Given earlier cases on loyalty oaths such as *Douds* (union leadership requirement) and *Adler* (Feinberg Law upheld), the majority took pains to distinguish those and other pro-oath cases from *Wieman.* In those earlier cases, the Court had found that the defendants had knowledge and were in agreement with the organization's goals—in effect a truly "guilty" association.

A line had been drawn—one that Clark, Burton, Minton, Reed, and Vinson could accept—beyond which constitutional freedoms and rights would be deemed violated. Justices Black and Frankfurter wrote concurrences, joined by Justice Douglas, which took the issues involved to a higher plane. Said Black, "The present period of fear seems more ominously dangerous to speech and press than was that of the Alien and Sedition Laws. Suppressive laws and practices are the fashion. The Oklahoma oath statute is but one manifestation of a national network of laws aimed at coercing and controlling the minds of men. Test oaths are notorious tools of tyranny."[35] Frankfurter, in his concurrence, concentrated on the importance of intellectual freedom in the educational system.

Under a Supreme Court rule, if a lawyer licensed to practice before the Court was disbarred by a state court, the Supreme Court required that the lawyer show cause (prove) why he should not be disbarred from practicing before the Supreme Court. One of the *Dennis* lawyers faced this rule. Not only had Abraham Isserman served jail time and been suspended for two years from practicing before the United States District Court, but he had also been disbarred by New Jersey, his home state. Now he faced this further sanction.

Chief Justice Vinson and Justices Reed, Burton, and Minton ruled that Isserman failed to prove he should not be further sanctioned. Justices Jackson, Black, Douglas, and Frankfurter believed he should not be disbarred by the Supreme Court. The evenly split Court decision on April 6, 1953, meant, under Court rules, that Isserman lost.[36]

Behind the scene was some intense maneuvering that yields insight into how the justices related to each other and how alliances were being forged and shifted. Douglas apparently wanted to write a strong statement in favor of Isserman. Frankfurter appears to have favored letting Jackson's opinion stand for the four of them; Frankfurter wrote to Douglas on March 23, 1953:

Let me put it to you why I am strongly of the view that it would hurt the very thing that you are after to emit your *Isserman* opinion. I don't know much about warfare but I do know that it is important to choose one's battle ground and the time for attack. I am as sure as I am of anything that if the four of us speak through Bob's [Justice Jackson's] opinion as we have modified it, it will have a powerful impact. It will enlist sympathy for Isserman; it will make people feel a sentence is being meted out to him out of all proportion to his wrong; it will throw the force of suggestion to recall what some of us [the dissenters] said about Medina's performance in the original contempt case. The fact that we make Bob our spokesman will of course greatly emphasize that aspect.

A new direct attack on Medina [which apparently Douglas's dissent contained] will deflect attention from the new wrong to Isserman and will tap the current almost obsessive regard for Medina not only by the McCarthy feeling in the country but by all but a relatively few fellows like you and me who have taken his measure. I am as sure as I can be, that is, that instead of subtly undermining the Medina cult you will reinforce it. Since you ask me I tell you what I very strongly feel.[37]

Douglas, though his battles with and disdain for Frankfurter were legendary, joined in the Jackson opinion. Thereafter, the Supreme Court amended its rules to read, "no order of disbarment will be entered except with the concurrence of a majority of the justices participating," thus avoiding what happened in *Isserman*.

Isserman then filed a petition with the Court for a rehearing of the earlier disbarment ruling. The petition was granted because Vinson had died, reducing those who had wanted him disbarred to three and leaving Frankfurter, Jackson, Black, and Douglas as a majority, since the new chief justice, Earl Warren, and Justice Clark did not participate.[38] Apparently, Frankfurter was correct in his attempt to hold the four together; the "time for attack" became evident with Vinson's death. The rules were changed, and Frankfurter's group won. Frankfurter and Douglas had been on the same side in opposing the contempt and jail sentences for the *Dennis* lawyers imposed by Medina; the appeal was to Douglas to bide his time for the larger goals described by Frankfurter. It is questionable, however, whether the "Medina cult" was dissuaded by this *Isserman* reversal or that much sympathy for Isserman resulted.

Called "the crime of the century," a leading Red Scare era case was, incredibly, never reviewed by the Supreme Court. Nine times, in different forms and raising different issues, the guilt and death sentence for espionage of Julius and Ethel Rosenberg came before the Court, each time receiving a rebuff. In each instance not enough justices voted to hear the case. When the final vote on the final attempt was before the Court, its refusal to stay the Rosenbergs' execution resulted in the death of the first persons convicted of espionage in American history since the Civil War.[39]

The espionage trial opened on March 6, 1951, in New York's Foley Square. The trial lasted only a little over three weeks; a guilty verdict was rendered on March 29, 1951. During the entire Rosenberg trial, in the same court complex, the IWO trial, which was to last four months, was still going on.

In the midst of the Rosenberg trial, the prosecutor, Irving H. Saypol, obtained an admission from Julius Rosenberg that he belonged to the IWO, which Saypol characterized incorrectly as exclusively an organization of Communist Party members. He knew this was untrue, but since Saypol could not get Rosenberg to admit he was a Party member (Fifth Amendment pleaded), he got the next best thing: an admission of membership in an organization then on trial which, with just a few false words, made every member a Communist. Not only did the Rosenberg jury hear this, but the judge trying the IWO case undoubtedly read and heard about the connection, dooming the IWO and helping to assure the guilt of the Rosenbergs.[40]

Saypol, who as U.S. attorney was described by *Time* magazine as "the nation's number one legal hunter of top Communists," was deeply involved in the second Hiss trial and in the *Dennis* case as a supervising attorney. He used Roy Cohn as his assistant, the latter moving on afterward to work with Senator McCarthy. Saypol was rewarded with a judgeship and continued his anti-communist crusade from the bench.[41]

On April 5, 1951 Judge Irving Kaufman sentenced the Rosenbergs to death with a speech from the bench that was laced with heated Red Scare rhetoric. Calling their crime "worse than murder," Judge Kaufman slid into accusing the Rosenbergs of treason—a crime for which they were not even tried. This was the spring of 1951, when the death count in the Korean War mounted to more than 50,000 and fear of an expanding war involving the atomic bomb was felt inside as well as outside the court.

The appeals process began shortly thereafter, continuing until the day of the executions itself. Why the Supreme Court never heard the case remains a subject of considerable dispute: why did not at least four justices vote for certiorari in this very special case involving peacetime espionage with a death sentence?[42]

Worthy of a Hollywood film or a television documentary, the cliffhanging decision making process was all too evident. The *Rosenberg* case exacerbated underlying tensions between the brethren as accusations flew between them. For example, Frankfurter claimed his had been the most consistent vote, time and time again, for certiorari or to stay the Rosenbergs' execution. He excoriated Douglas for the latter's alleged inconsistency over a number of votes and even challenged Douglas's machinations in failing to provide that crucial fourth vote for certiorari.[43] Douglas, on the other hand, in his autobiography totally ignored the Frankfurter accusations and portrayed himself as a deeply concerned judge who behaved consistently with respect to the case.[44]

Douglas focused on the fact that he stayed the executions after hearing new arguments by Rosenberg attorneys to the effect that the defendants were tried under the wrong statute (the Espionage Act instead of the Atomic Energy Act), the latter providing for the death penalty only in case the jury recommended it; in *Rosenberg* the jury had made no penalty recommendation. Douglas felt that these issues called for Court review; he issued a stay of execution on June 17, 1953, then left town by car. By chance, as he drove, he heard a news bulletin on the radio stating that the chief justice (who did not try to reach Douglas) had called a special term (meeting) of the Court for noon the next day to review Douglas's stay. Douglas hurried back, and, angered over the move, asserted that Vinson had no authority to do what he had done. After several hours of argument over the issue of lifting the stay of execution (the argument over calling a special term having been dropped), only Douglas, Frankfurter, Black, and Burton voted to retain the stay. The unequivocal fifth vote was lacking.[45] As the arguments and the voting were taking place, a mass demonstration was taking place across from the White House, consisting mostly of well-dressed middle-class people holding signs demanding that the Rosenbergs burn and shouting intensely anti-Semitic remarks.[46]

Black's biographer, Roger K. Newman, fills in other dramatic details. Attorney General Herbert Brownell had met with the chief justice and reported that Vinson was angry with the Douglas move to stay the executions; Brownell suggested that Vinson convene a special session to get around the stay. Hoover got into this judicial crisis by apparently having agents posted in the courtroom to report to him what was being said and by whom. Brownell later felt that Vinson most likely had requested FBI involvement. What took place and was apparently overheard by Hoover's agents were passionate arguments from Black, Douglas, and Frankfurter. Nevertheless, lacking the fifth vote, the hour for the executions was fast approaching. Black left the court building in a laundry van to avoid FBI surveillance. But a Rosenberg lawyer came to his home, hoping Black would grant another stay. Newman, who claims Black was the only justice to vote to hear the case every time it came before the Court, ends the scene with this description:

Black was playing tennis with JoJo when Lizzie Mae said someone was at the door, JoJo answered it. When she came back to tell him, he was standing on the tennis court, in his shorts, racket in hand, facing her, crying. "I can't do it," he said before she could say anything. "Josephine, tell them I can't do it."
The Rosenbergs were executed that night.[47]

Like dissent in the *Dennis* case had, Douglas's act in staying the executions seems to have generated some of the strongest attacks of any leveled at the justices who had supported the Court's review of the *Rosenberg* case. Douglas has suggested that his act, which would have sent the case back for full hearing on the issue of whether Judge Kaufman had properly imposed the death penalty, threatened to deprive the country of the thrill of seeing the federal government execute a woman for the first time since the Civil War. Douglas, as well as the other dissenters, was aware that the hysteria of the times "touched off the Justices also. I have no other way of explaining why they ran pell-mell with the mob in the *Rosenberg* case and felt it was important that this couple die that very week—before the point of law on the legality of their sentence could be calmly considered and decided by the lower courts."[48]

Frankfurter reflected on the *Rosenberg* case, stating, "My brethren may well be bored to have me repeat that the Court's failure to take the case . . . has presented for us the most anguishing situation since I have been on the Court." His unalterable contention was that "without an affirmance of the fairness of the trial by the highest court of the land there may always be questions as to whether these executions were legally and rightfully carried out." [49]

There were substantial procedural and substantive issues outside the question of whether the Rosenbergs were spies. These included the allegation that in effect they had been tried and convicted of treason without the safeguards granted in Article III, Section 3 of the Constitution; that federal prosecutors had not performed their duty in meeting their responsibilities under the federal criminal code; that the defendants had been tried under the wrong statute; and that their death sentences constituted cruel and unusual punishment in violation of the Eighth Amendment.

The rush to have the Rosenbergs executed has been highly criticized. Two years from verdict to execution was speedy in the 1950s; today it is unheard of. Two other capital cases were actually the subject of Supreme Court opinions the very week in 1953 when the Court refused any further *Rosenberg* delays. In fact, both cases were in the judicial system substantially longer than *Rosenberg.*[50]

While the arguments and proofs continue to mount on the matter of the Rosenbergs' guilt, there is little or no argument—even among those who believe proof of guilt was overwhelming—that the Rosenbergs were wrongly denied the right of review by the Supreme Court, particularly since there had been a dissenting voice in the appellate court, which traditionally signals grounds for review. There are also the arguments that the defendants were not able to obtain or afford really competent counsel at the trial level and that the request for the death penalty for Ethel Rosenberg was only a ploy (that failed) in the attempt to get Julius to confess.

What decision the Vinson Court would have rendered if review had taken place is, of course, speculative. The argument may be made that the Court, which was, after all, willing to allow a hurried execution, contained a solid majority that would have confirmed guilt and the death penalty in any event. The times dictated the result.[51]

Even for those opposing certiorari and the staying of execution, this case and the lack of Supreme Court review were troubling. Douglas told this story as related to him by his brother: Douglas's brother happened to be at the same hotel where the American Bar Association was meeting in August 1953. Vinson called him and invited him for a drink in Vinson's suite. Over drinks, the chief justice said he was sorry about the *Rosenberg* case and the Court's treatment of Justice Douglas. Vinson declared that Douglas had been right and he, Vinson, wrong. Whether this conversation presaged a change of heart for Vinson on Red Scare matters is impossible to say: within a month Vinson—who smoked heavily, was overweight, and never exercised—was dead of a heart attack.

Chapter 7
Transitions

The sudden death of Chief Justice Fred M. Vinson on September 8, 1953, at age 63, heralded a number of transitions for the Supreme Court. At the same time, the nation and the world were witnessing changes that were bound to impact the justices and their work.

Even those who have objected to categorizing Vinson as a failure admit his weaknesses—most important, his inability to provide the Court with sorely needed, effective leadership.[1] There is no argument, however, that the man President Eisenhower named to replace Vinson furnished dynamic and effective leadership for the still-riven Court. While there are debates about the extent of Earl Warren's influence and his talent as a jurist,[2] the Warren Court and Earl Warren's sixteen years of leadership as chief justice continue to comprise a significant, ever-growing arena for popular and scholarly writing.

One readily encounters many biographies, retrospective papers, and symposia devoted to Warren's years as chief justice. A major retrospective drew leading lights to comment on the Warren Court in 1994, the twenty-fifth anniversary of his departure from the Court. Biographies continue to be written; reevaluations of the Warren Court years continue to be composed.[3]

The consensus is that Justice Warren and his Court had tremendous influence on the law and the life of the nation. The foremost scholar on Warren and his Court has written, "In terms of creative impact, the tenure of Earl Warren can only be compared with that of John Marshall."[4]

In the history of the Supreme Court, its decisions have rarely touched the lives of a majority or even a substantial minority of people or institutions. However one assesses the major Warren Court decisions, one can only conclude that they truly affected the very lives of Americans, especially those previously underrepresented groups and minority causes. Landmark decisions include *Brown v. Board of Education* (1954), ending the reign of segregation in education that the Court had condoned in *Plessy v. Ferguson* (1896); *Mapp v. Ohio* (1961), extending Fourth Amendment protections as incorporated into the due process clause of the Fourteenth Amendment; *Baker v. Carr* (1962), setting forth the one person-one vote principle to correct unfair apportionment; *Engel v. Vitale* (1962), holding that prayer and Bible studies are not allowed in public schools; *Gideon v. Wainright* (1963), giving indigent criminal defendants, at least in serious criminal cases, state-supplied counsel; *The New York Times v. Sullivan* (1964), extending constitutional protection to those who criticize or defame public officials or public persons; *Griswold v. Connecticut* (1965), overturning state convictions of those counseling on contraception, opening up the expansion of the right of privacy; and *Miranda v. Arizona* (1966), holding that the accused must be given warning concerning their rights, including the right to remain silent and the right to have an attorney.

Lists of prominent cases vary; generally, they expand rather than contract this one. What is noteworthy about them is the absence of cases that significantly modified the Vinson Court's Red Scare positions. Yet, after the shambles of the Court's handling of the *Rosenberg* appeals in 1953, there was, under the influence of changing times, a discernible shift in the Court's rulings that culminated in the Red Monday cases. That there was some backsliding from this rethinking of Red Scare issues is also evident; a few decisions of the late 1950s and early 1960s seem egregiously at odds with what the Red Monday cases evinced in their approach, which was protective of dissent and civil liberties. These cases do not, however, denigrate or detract from the pragmatic importance of those decisions of June 17, 1957.

The Warren Court also reflected transitions in the larger life of the nation. On January 20, 1953 Dwight D. Eisenhower was inaugurated as the thirty-fourth president, ending twenty years of Democratic leadership. Elected on a "had enough" platform, Eisenhower appealed as a great war hero without a political background who promised to do something about (win or end) the Korean War. Then Stalin, who was thought to be the decision making power behind the North Korean and Chinese Communist efforts, died on March 5, 1953. Not only was the supreme enemy of the non-communist world dead, but the inevitable problems following a dictator's demise created what appeared to be an opening for an end to the Korean War.

The weeks following the Russian dictator's death were full of reports of power struggles within the Soviet Union and stirrings of unrest in Russian-dominated lands. Four months later, on July 27, 1953, the Korean War ended with an armistice-type stalemate that established a demilitarized zone dividing North and South Korea. The next week, the Soviet Union announced its capacity to make a hydrogen bomb, putting itself just one year behind the United States, which under President Truman had moved ahead on its own H-bomb development and had successfully tested a bomb in 1952. Clearly the Cold War and arms race were in a dynamic state, but the new administration demonstrated continuity with Truman's foreign policy.

What about the Red Scare? On one level, nothing seemed to change: HUAC continued its work, Senator Joseph R. McCarthy persisted in his accusations and headline grabbing, the loyalty program ground on, deportations for leftist activities and Communist Party membership proceeded, and more Smith Act and contempt of Congress prosecutions went to trial and were appealed. Headlines still announced Red Scare developments, such as Dr. J. Robert Oppenheimer, the "father of the A-Bomb," being denied access to all classified scientific documents and, later that year, losing his security clearance. And the willingness to attach the absurd to the war against the Reds continued: the 1953 book *Sexual Behavior in the Human Female,* by Alfred C. Kinsey and his associates, was attacked as not only helping the communist cause but helping Americans "to act like Communists."[5]

The very fact that a Republican was now in the White House meant that changes were inevitable. It was one thing for McCarthy and HUAC to attack the existence of subversion and subversives under a Democratic president; it was quite another to implicate the new administration as anything but tough on communists and their "ism" or to imply that subversives were still in the executive branch of the federal government.

One opportunity to insure that a hard line on communists and dissenters would continue was in the filling of vacancies on the Supreme Court. From 1953 to the end of President Eisenhower's second term, he was able to nominate and have confirmed five Supreme Court justices. Of the five, three were active in deciding Red Monday cases: Chief Justice Warren and Justices Harlan and Brennan.[6]

Of these three Eisenhower appointees, all voted against the federal or—in one case—state governments' positions in the Red Monday decisions.[7] The ironies abounded: two of the majority Red Monday opinions were written by Warren, the other two by Harlan. The usual dissenters, Justices Black and Douglas, were now able to join the majority. It was the replacement of two Truman nominees—Vinson by Warren and Burton by Harlan—that made the difference, along with the replacement of two Franklin D. Roosevelt nominees, Minton by Brennan and Reed by Whittaker. That Eisenhower thought he was putting conservatives on the Court is evident; that he was terribly disappointed, particularly in Warren and Brennan, is clear.[8]

As was to be expected, the new chief justice proceeded cautiously in exerting leadership and influence on the Court. At sixty-two years of

age, the former governor of California had made his name as a politi-
cian. Now he was chief justice of the United States without having had
any prior experience on the bench. In this he joined several prior chiefs,
among them John Marshall. It was evident that his finely honed political
skills were more in demand than his legal abilities.[9]

Much has been conjectured about what motivated Warren to become
an activist judge willing to lead the brethren to rule in favor of the powerless, to see "American life as a struggle by disadvantaged individuals
against entrenched forces—an impersonal government, powerful interest groups, economic conglomerates, guardians of racial prerogatives." [10]
It appears that his strong sense of fairness and his willingness to use
the power of the Court to remedy wrongs was a basic component of his
character.

Confident as he was in his own powers, Warren was aware of the daunting task he had sought and undertaken. He said, "I've always thought
that perhaps the most lonesome day I ever had in my life was the day
I arrived at the Supreme Court." [11] The Court he arrived at was one divided by feuds and significant policy differences, one where each justice
would be taking his measure, seeking his support, and hoping he would
use his power and prestige to favor their positions.

Warren learned quickly and worked hard to understand what was
needed and expected of him. His personality won favor with the brethren and with all Court personnel; initial caution and even some hostility
about him apparently diminished as he sought guidance from long-
tenured colleagues. Initially, he took a back seat at Court conferences
until he felt confident he could lead; within two months he was in
charge. In his role as governor of California, Warren had exercised the
power of leadership; now he found himself comfortable in this further
executive challenge.[12]

Yet most commentators on Warren emphasize what a wrenching experience the move from governor to chief justice of the United States
must have been. He was to undertake a new occupation in a new area of
the country; he was to engage in tasks he had never done before (he had
not even practiced as a lawyer for ten years prior to 1953); he could not
change the Court personnel (including the justices), as he could have
done as an executive; he could not use his public persona as he had
been doing; he had little financial control of the Court and few perqui-
sites of office. Warren could only lead and persuade, not command. He
had to accept the harness of Supreme Court traditions covering minute
as well as major aspects of how the Court and his office would function.[13]

In retrospect, he succeeded as chief justice in remarkably quick fashion, gaining the appreciative comments of the brethren, even though
they (and he) realized he was not a legal heavyweight in terms of scholar-

ship or as a proponent of any school of constitutional thought. Also, his political and public positions on the grave issues that were to come before the Court were not clearly disclosed by examining Warren's words and acts prior to his becoming chief justice. As one authority has succinctly stated:

Of the major themes that were to characterize Warren's years on the Court —opposition to racial segregation, support for the reapportionment of state legislatures, opposition to wide-ranging legislative investigations in the name of national security, the abolition of prayers in the classroom, strong support for organized labor and for the economic regulatory powers of the federal government, and increased legal protection for criminals and persons suspected of committing crimes—only a handful surfaced in Warren's governorship, and he was not prominently identified with any.[14]

The dramatic change in the course of history for the Supreme Court, for the United States, and for the Warren chief justiceship came very early in his reign. Warren inherited the issue of school segregation as assuredly as his was the center chair in the Court's public chamber. For at least fifteen years the issue had been the subject of cases brought to the Court, all challenging aspects of the "separate but equal" doctrine of *Plessy v. Ferguson*.[15] The decision to end educational segregation handed down in the Kansas case, *Brown v. Board of Education*,[16] on May 17, 1954, involved a frontal attack on the issue; it not only ended the legality of segregation in seventeen states but symbolically announced the goal of ending racial discrimination and second-class citizenship for blacks in all areas of American life.

In comparison to most Supreme Court decisions, this was a case presenting an issue that deeply affected everyday life for most citizens. The unanimous decision became the benchmark for all that was to follow from the Warren Court. Whether it was the rights of those accused of a crime, the reapportionment of legislative districts to yield fairness in voting, or substantial dismantling of the use of the courts to further the aims of the Red Scare, the decisions following *Brown* could be understood as emanating from one essentially seamless line of thought and leadership.

The immediate background for the *Brown* decision emerged in late 1952, involving arguments over the case within the Court itself. Vinson had opened the regular conference four days after oral arguments by defending *Plessy* and questioning whether the numerous precedents that supported segregation could be overturned. He had also stressed that segregation had never been questioned by Congress. One Warren biographer has concluded that by his views at that moment, Vinson "missed his opportunity for judicial greatness." [17]

At that point Reed and Clark were essentially with Vinson. Black, Douglas, Burton, and Minton were ready to overturn *Plessy*. Jackson failed to see how segregation could legally be outlawed, and Frankfurter sought narrow grounds that would be acceptable in terms of his view of the law and would be politically acceptable to the majority of the country, as well as one that would reflect an overwhelmingly committed Court. As of this conference on December 13, 1952, the vote would have been five for and four against ending segregation in schools. This, Frankfurter believed, would be a disastrous result.[18] It would present the country with a Court seriously divided on a crucial issue.

Here the *Brown* story focuses on Frankfurter: he sought delay with the hope that further argument before and within the Court would create the needed larger majority. When changed positions did not seem likely, he sought further delay to the October 1953 term. To accomplish such a delay, he used a tactic of drafting five questions that he wanted the brethren to adopt as grounds calling for further argument by the opposing sides before the Court; his success yielded the delay that he felt was imperative.[19]

Frankfurter's gamble for time paid off. The death of Vinson and his replacement with Warren made the difference. By December 1953 Warren was comfortable enough with his post not only to take a minor role in the open court reargument but also to exert strong leadership in the conference that followed on December 12. Interestingly, Warren had not indicated his views on the constitutionality of segregation prior to that conference. There was, however, no question as to his views after he spoke; he delivered a ringing declaration that segregation was unconstitutional.

Warren not only questioned the *Plessy* decision for its justification of racial inferiority but added, "Personally, I can't see how today we can justify segregation based solely on race."[20] In essence, Warren raised the issue of the human values involved and faulted any legal arguments that attacked or ignored these overriding values.

What makes Warren's role remarkable is that he recognized the importance of a unanimous decision in favor of ending the legal basis for segregation; not even a substantial majority would suffice. This Warren was able to accomplish through astute leadership in the justices' conferences that followed, by his crafting of an opinion that would satisfy all, and by his acts of personal persuasion. By creating an opinion that could satisfy Frankfurter, Clark, and Jackson, he could get all but Justice Reed. Reed had apparently decided to stand alone in continued support of *Plessy*'s view that segregation by itself did not violate equal protection. Only through personal contact and persuasion was Reed finally won over. The role of Justice Minton in convincing Reed was apparently significant; they had very cordial relations.

The fact that Minton abandoned his commitment to judicial restraint and accepted the need for an activist Court in ending segregation must have influenced Reed. Minton's departure from the role he had consistently played in loyalty, alien, and civil liberties cases to this point was a crucial change for this former senator from Indiana. On the other hand, the courage it took for Reed, a born and bred small-town southerner, to join in creating a unanimous decision is noteworthy.[21]

The drama of writing, then convincing, then reading the unanimous decision in Court on May 17, 1954 has been well told and constitutes one of the most exciting episodes in all of American legal history.[22] An important element of the *Brown* decision was the public response. Justice Black correctly stated that *Brown* would give rise to a "storm over the Court."[23] That storm took the form of hate mail directed to the justices and diatribes by extremist white supremacists inside and outside Congress as well as in some southern legislatures. For the old Confederate South, the date of decision became known as "Black Monday." For the rest of the nation, *Brown*'s significance was the subject of intense and lasting exposition.

The decision really did affect the lives of Americans of all races and in almost all areas of the country. The intensity of reaction was palpable and increased over the months and years that followed as enforcement rulings and cases involving implementation continued through the federal legal system.

The issue of race in all its manifestations became a dominant theme that took center stage in American life from *Brown* forward. That decision and others that followed, along with congressional action in the field of civil rights, changed the lives of both black and white citizens. As such, whether the Court was ahead of the times or in mesh with them in dealing with race issues is less significant than that they were, in the view of most Americans, the result of the preeminent role assumed by the Supreme Court.

The *Brown* case meant that all other issues, including Red Scare cases, were relegated to a position secondary to what the Supreme Court and other federal courts were doing in the area of racial discrimination and integration. A Court that could end segregation in schools and enforce its mandate "with all deliberate speed" could commit lesser acts such as changing its position on Red Scare issues. Without *Brown*, all the judicial activism in other areas during the late 1950s and 1960s would have been less acceptable and much more controversial. In terms of the Supreme Court and the nation, *Brown* created a new relationship between the two under the leadership of this new chief justice.

Vinson's exit and Warren's entrance highlighted the importance of leadership. Who leads and who decides at what point in history makes a difference. That a new Supreme Court was before the American people was a direct cause of *Brown* and its progeny. That this Court would expand its activism into other socially and politically sensitive areas over the next decade was foretold by *Brown*. Even those who found the areas of judicial activism of the Warren Court repugnant were, like those who approved of the Court's decisions, bound to confront a Court that was willing to be on the cutting edge.

The nation, meanwhile, was made persistently aware of the reaction to *Brown*, its ancillary cases, and the enforcement of desegregation. These cases roiled through the federal court system, which, on a local level, had to deal with enforcement. Bitterness increased in the South with the passage of time. The Court was attacked, and special hatred was directed against its chief justice. The origin of the "Impeach Warren" campaign was in the *Brown* and other desegregation decisions.

With so much heat over years directed at the brethren and their leader because of race decisions, the additional criticisms that were to result from the Red Monday cases pale considerably. In the aftermath of *Brown* and its growing progeny of cases, the path to Red Monday was rendered significantly easier. Segregation in the Washington, D.C. schools,[24] recreational facilities,[25] the bus system in Montgomery, Alabama,[26] and many ancillary segregation laws and practices were struck down time and again over the next decade. By 1963 a Court opinion could declare that "it is no longer open to question that a State may not constitutionally require segregation of public facilities."[27]

Personally, Warren had traveled a good distance. From ending segregation of toilet facilities in the Supreme Court building when he became chief justice to ending the legality of racial segregation nationwide was a record of leadership that few could match and none could exceed. That he paid a price in estrangement from President Eisenhower became clear. The president did not support the Court and its decision in *Brown*, and Warren resented it. He believed that the president could have substantially smoothed the path by demanding that good citizens support the decision.[28] Yet it was not over the desegregation cases that, in a face-to-face meeting years later, Eisenhower expressed his disappointment in Warren's Court. Instead, it was Warren's position in the "Communist cases" that he criticized. When pressed, Eisenhower said he was disappointed in all those decisions. When Warren attempted to explain that he was obliged to judge Communists by the same rules applicable to others, Eisenhower rejected that position, and when Warren asked, what "would you do with Communists in America?" Eisenhower answered, "I would kill the S.O.B.s!"[29]

There was a further distinct and palpable connection between the *Brown* decision and the Cold War-Red Scare. This pertained to the issue of moral leadership claimed by the United States as the guide of the "free" world against communist-dominated areas. The Soviet challenge, directed most pointedly to third-world countries where majorities were other than white, emphasized the rampant racism and the second-class citizenship of blacks in the United States. Stories of lynching, of segregation in all avenues of life, and of economic exploitation were constantly publicized. All this was more than a little embarrassing for the country's leadership. Without difficulty or falsification, news of the egregious mistreatment suffered by blacks, pictures of slum conditions almost in the shadow of Capitol Hill, and racist pronouncements in the halls of Congress were telling barbs directed at the claim of the United States to be the leader of those who sought to live in liberty.

The nexus between the civil rights movement and the Cold War was understood by those proposing an end to segregation in the *Brown* case. The brief for the United States as amicus curiae (friend of the Court) in the case stated:

It is in the context of the present world struggle between freedom and tyranny that the problem of racial discrimination must be viewed . . . [for] discrimination against minority groups in the United States has an adverse effect upon our relations with other countries. Racial discrimination furnishes grist for the Communist propaganda mills, and it raises doubts even among friendly nations as to the intensity of our devotion to the democratic faith.[30]

The National Association for the Advancement of Colored People (NAACP) brief warned that "Survival of our country in the present international situation is inevitably tied to the resolution of this domestic issue."[31]

The *Brown* decision was the result of a number of converging factors. The times favored those advocating an end to segregation. The place, the Supreme Court, was amenable to accepting the need for change when the executive and legislative branches were not.[32]

The short opinion in *Brown* itself did not mention or acknowledge this global impact, although certainly it was in the minds of the justices. As early as 1945 Justice Black had noted with concern how Soviet propaganda effectively exploited the contradiction between America's espousal of freedom and the South's system of racial segregation.[33]

The media response to *Brown* almost invariably included what *Brown* would mean in the ideological war that was part of the Cold War. *Time* magazine in its first issue following the Court's decision in *Brown* wrote:

The international effect may be scarcely less important. In many countries, where U.S. prestige and leadership have been damaged by the fact of U.S. segregation, it will come as a timely reassertion of the basic American principle that "all men are created equal."[34]

Chicago Sun-Times columnist Roscoe Drummond, two days after the *Brown* decision came down, wrote that "The U.S. Supreme Court has given a new definition to un-Americanism. It has ruled that segregated public schools are unconstitutional and, therefore, un-American." Furthermore, "it comes at a moment when our leadership of the free people demands the best—not the next-best—of what America is and can be."[35]

The editors of the *New York Times* spoke similarly the day following the decision in *Brown* concerning the international message:

A constitutional principle inherent in the Declaration of Independence and never entirely forgotten, even in the days of human slavery, has, however, been restated. This nation is often criticized for its treatment of racial minorities, and particularly of the Negro. . . . When some hostile propagandist rises in Moscow or Peking to accuse us of being a class society we can if we wish recite the courageous words of yesterday's opinion. The highest court in the land, the guardian of our national conscience, has reaffirmed its faith—the undying American faith—in the equality of all men and all children before the law.[36]

Across the country editors of papers large and small echoed this refrain.[37]

Within one hour of the Court's ruling, the Voice of America began broadcasting the message of *Brown* in English and thirty-three other languages throughout the world.[38] The response in the international community was front-page news, except in communist-dominated countries or where communists controlled a specific newspaper. Its implications in the war for the allegiance of peoples and nations were evident.[39]

Among academics and intellectuals, praise for the decision often included recognition that *Brown* would aid the country's cause in the Cold War. For example, a social psychologist at Columbia University stated,

we will take away from the Communists one of their most effective arguments against the American way of life. . . . [The decision] would increase our prestige immeasurably in foreign countries, such as India, where the people have dark skins. These countries are now being made particular targets of Communist propaganda.[40]

There was, however, another aspect to the dilemma of a nation claiming to represent a free society and engaging in political, economic, and moral combat with those behind the Iron Curtain and for the allegiance of the third world. That was the American domestic Red Scare and all its manifestations, primarily the prosecution of people for their political beliefs. With the single word "McCarthyism," the cartoonist Herbert Block (Herblock) had created a rubric that expressed all the negatives attached to the anti-communist paranoia with its demands for unquestioning loyalty and its search for "Reds under the beds."

Thus the Red Scare was an issue that similarly went beyond the borders of the United States to an international ideological battlefield. While opposition to the Red Scare was evident from its inception, criticisms drawing parallels to racial segregation were in greater evidence both before and especially after the *Brown* decision.

In April 1953 the *Nation* published an article by a prominent English author, Alex Comfort, which discussed the European concerns with McCarthyism. The editors placed the following statement at the head of the article: "This article and the one following by Andrew Roth make it abundantly clear that the problem of McCarthyism has burst out of this country's boundaries and become an important international issue."[41] Comfort himself stated:

Europe is worried not because the witch hunt and the Eastern purges are "kif-kif," one as bad as the other—which they are manifestly not—but because it knows what they are symptoms of. . . .

America will never have a Hitler, but it may none the less become a land where liberals and scientists are silenced, and where the effective direction of policy is divided among General Motors, the madhouse [McCarthyites], and some destructive military men. . . .

In a world split between Marxism and an America isolated behind its own Padded Curtain, the cause of reason would be in a precarious state. Nobody wants to see a fascist, outcast America. This has not yet happened. Americans can prevent it. But they will need the vigor of the most rebellious moments of their history.[42]

Echoed over the years 1953–57 were concerns about authoritarianism, suppression of dissent and prosecution of dissenters, and how these forces affected the image of America and its leadership of the noncommunist world. A London newspaper's concerns were summarized by the *New Republic* in August 1954:

McCarthyism is a national problem in so far as it is interpreted by our friends abroad as an *American* trend toward authoritarianism. As the head of McCarthy's party, the President should long ago have read the Senator out of his ranks. Eisenhower's hands-off policy has helped undermine American prestige.[43]

In that same issue, an essay on the status of the British press's views of the United States concluded, "perhaps no other single factor has so damaged American prestige abroad as the rise of McCarthyism and all that it signifies to Europeans: bigotry, intolerance, persecution, unnatural power, government by irresponsible pressures—a trend that has for them distressing parallels to the rise of Fascism in Germany and Italy in the 1930s."[44]

At times, the linkage between *Brown* and McCarthyism was directly expressed. In a *New Republic* article in which "Six Leaders of World Opinion Assess Our Leadership," Herbert Tingsten, editor of a liberal Stockholm daily, wrote that the decline in American prestige was "above all . . . caused by the appearance of McCarthy and everything connected with that; reports of intervention against teachers and schools in different states and many other things. It is a matter of course that the decision of the Supreme Court banning segregation in public schools has worked in another direction."[45]

Anti-American sentiment abroad was linked to McCarthyism by the antics of two of Senator McCarthy's staff members, Roy M. Cohn and G. David Schine. They were sent in April 1953 to investigate the contents of U.S. embassy libraries in Europe. They became infamous for ordering the removal of works they felt were "Red-tainted," including American classics. They made shambles of State Department libraries and fools of the United States.[46]

The times were, however, changing. The views of those who saw McCarthyism as damaging to America's international relations as well as dangerous to the internal health of the country were summarized by Richard Pells in his study of the relationship between Europeans and American culture following World War II. Pells stated that by mid-1953, "Except for the McCarthyites, few people in or out of Washington believed that censorship, book burnings, and tirades against modern art were the best ways to wage the cultural Cold War. It should have been possible to defend freedom without resembling the totalitarian state."[47] The irony was that "McCarthyism should blossom in the United States at precisely the moment when the country was trying to present itself to the world as the home of civil liberties and high culture."[48]

The McCarthyism bloom was soon to wither and McCarthy was to confront an early death. His fall from grace was a major transition for the nation in these Red Scare years. To generations that did not live during his years of power, it is difficult to convey or explain the strength of this single senator to make and break careers and lives, even those of other senators. At least three senators, Scott M. Lucas, Millard E. Tydings, and William B. Benton, were defeated in reelection bids because McCarthy actively opposed them.[49] Perhaps McCarthy's most ominous use of power was silencing Eisenhower from defending his mentor, General George C. Marshall, against vicious, unfounded attacks by McCarthy in the 1952 campaign.[50]

Commencing with the Hiss perjury conviction in January 1950, the hunt for Reds had gained credence, since so many liberal, New Deal, and Fair Deal personalities, including President Truman, had placed their trust in Alger Hiss and believed he would be exonerated from any

wrongdoing.[51] That Hiss was found guilty left Hoover, Nixon, and thereafter McCarthy in the position to increase in volume and intensity their
charges of disloyalty and press forward with Red Scare tactics.[52]

McCarthy and Hoover had been on friendly terms since 1946, and
Hoover was pleased to have him aboard in the quest against the Reds.
Hoover's FBI became McCarthy's essential source for information prior
to 1952, as well as after the national elections, when McCarthy gained
his own investigating committee, the Senate Investigations Subcommittee of the Committee on Governmental Operations. Hoover supplied
McCarthy's subcommittee with three chief investigators. They were each
former FBI agents who had continued access to FBI reports, although
they no longer worked for the Bureau. This access was the crucial link between McCarthy and Hoover and was the linchpin of McCarthy's power.
Hoover had similarly fed information and files to the two other investigating committees, one of which was his oldest Red-hunting client,
HUAC. Hoover, of course, publicly denied any involvement with the
Red-baiting process. He was willing to let Nixon and McCarthy gain the
political advantage so long as they served the anti-communist crusade.[53]

McCarthy's power also stemmed from his ability to play on Cold War
fears, exacerbating a general paranoia about internal subversion. He
acted the role of superpatriot, exposing evildoing in high places by
eastern Ivy League elitists. His tactics included making accusations and
then, before allowing countervailing responses, moving on to other accusations. He bullied, threatened, sneered, and smeared without regard
to truth or fair play. Often the result was to confuse dissent with disloyalty, to encourage distrust and fear in the land, and to cause chaos
and ruin.

None of this could he do without the media's assistance. Frequently
those who despised the man and his methods paid him attention because his accusations made news. As president, Eisenhower worked only
behind the scenes to oppose him, arguing that he should not dignify
McCarthy by direct attack. For the millions who read of McCarthy's
doings during these years, many would say, "I don't like the man or
his methods, but he is doing an important service for the country; his
ends are good." For millions of others, both his means and his ends
were good.

Although McCarthy fed on the media and they fed on him, they were
instrumental in bringing him down in 1954. The election of a Republican president in 1952 probably foredoomed McCarthy's power because
his continued tirades after that year placed the Republican administration in the same target area for accusations that the Truman administration had been in. This was unacceptable, even to Hoover. Hoover had
signaled his break with Truman by appearing before HUAC in 1947, but

he moved close to Eisenhower and his administration, ultimately deciding that the nation's future and his own were with Eisenhower, not
McCarthy.

Hoover believed that only communists attacked legitimate authority,
"so anticommunism, to be authentic, had to defend that authority, not
attack it," as McCarthy continued to do.[54] Hoover apparently had had
enough of McCarthy and deliberately cut ties to him in July 1953.[55] To
Hoover, McCarthy had become a loose cannon, reckless and liable to
taint the FBI and its image of lofty impartiality by disclosing the supportive link between Hoover, the FBI, and McCarthy. Hoover's decision to
back Eisenhower and the administration's attempts to control McCarthy
were the crucial decisions that doomed the senator. All that was needed
was a vehicle for his downfall. That was to come in the late fall of 1953
when McCarthy, without the support of Hoover, first launched an investigation of doings at Fort Monmouth and then, in 1954, attacked the
U.S. Army.[56]

McCarthy's tactics and excessive hubris had made many enemies by
1954, including even conservative Republican members of the Senate.
In March 1954, Edward R. Murrow presented his take on McCarthy
in an episode of his television program, *See It Now*. Using film clips of
McCarthy in action, Murrow presented the public with, to say the least,
a view of the senator as reprehensible. It was a view that most Americans
had never had of McCarthy, an approach that was disquieting. Yet Murrow ended the program with a resolution of hope. "We will not walk in
fear," he said, "one of another."[57]

In 1954, television was the medium that allowed the American public
to witness the spectacle of McCarthy taking on the U.S. Army. McCarthy
had conducted an investigation of subversion in the Army Signal Corps
Research Center at Monmouth, New Jersey. Claiming that the army
was blocking his inquiry, McCarthy set off an explosion of charges and
countercharges about the army's treatment of G. David Schine, Roy
Cohn's friend and McCarthy staff consultant. The matter escalated to the
point of hearings before McCarthy's own subcommittee (McCarthy gave
up the chair for the hearing), pitting the U.S. Army against McCarthy —
a McCarthy who no longer had access to the vital records of the FBI,
which had been his major source of information in confronting his witnesses and his enemies.

The issue was coercion: had the army coerced Schine or had McCarthy and his staff attempted to blackmail the army into preferential treatment for Schine? Beginning on April 24, 1954, the nation for thirty-six
days watched what has been called a "brute soap opera." It became a
matter of personalities rather than of civil liberties. McCarthy delivered
himself "as a bad guy, a bully, and a loner." Joseph Walsh, the army's at-

torney, conducted what became a famous confrontation with McCarthy, demolishing the senator before some 20 million viewers.[58]

On June 11 the end came quickly in the form of a resolution introduced by Senator Ralph E. Flanders, Republican from Vermont, condemning McCarthy's conduct and resulting in the formation of a committee to hear the matter. Despite counsel from famed attorney Edward Bennett Williams, McCarthy was condemned on two narrow counts by a Senate vote of sixty-seven to twenty-two. It was enough, however, to break McCarthy as a powerhouse. He could be, and was, ignored by the media, the administration, and members of Congress. McCarthy's outburst against Eisenhower (he publicly apologized for backing him in 1952) caused further desertions from his camp and put him on the extremist fringe. His fall from grace was followed by physical deterioration as he sank into alcoholism and died on May 2, 1957, at the age of forty-nine.[59]

The relevance of the McCarthy story is this: the fall of the man tainted the "ism" (McCarthyism) that he had come to represent. McCarthy's fall from power and his death were significant factors also contributed to the calming of the times. Many other developments made their contribution, including Stalin's death in 1953 and Soviet Premier Nikita Khrushchev's amazing his nation and the world in 1956 with a long speech denouncing Stalin and his crimes. These revelations shattered what was left of the American Communist Party.

The Korean War was over. Europe had substantially recovered from the economic collapse that followed in the war's aftermath. NATO and other alliances had shored up defenses against further communist expansion. A Republican administration was running the country; with its credentials untainted by perceived Democratic administration errors, it could pursue a course of detente with the new Soviet leadership. In the words of Richard M. Fried, "the tide of all-pervasive anti-communism had crested and was moving out."[60]

Yet, as Fried himself acknowledges, while by 1954 the underpinnings of the second Red Scare had eroded, anti-communism was far from collapsing. Anti-communist laws were still being introduced, debated, and passed by huge majorities in Congress (for example, the Communist Control Act of 1954); HUAC was continuing its investigations of unions, churches, and the entertainment industry; and the Senate Internal Security Subcommittee (SISS) was joining HUAC in focusing on institutions of higher education in the search for Reds and communist influence.

J. Edgar Hoover, of course, never let up. Throughout the 1950s he continued to persuade the American public and its president that the threat from communism was greater than ever, despite the near-total collapse of the Communist Party. The easing of tensions in the Cold

War, demonstrated by the evacuation of Russian troops from Austria in May 1955 and Eisenhower's meeting with leaders of the World War II allies, including Russia, in July 1955, failed to move Hoover. When the detention camps established under the Security Act of 1950 were dismantled after 1956, Hoover's reaction was to complain about "growing public complacency toward the threat of subversion."[61]

Furthermore, after *Brown*, some southerners, both in and out of Congress and state legislatures, found a common enemy in what was perceived to be the nexus of civil rights and communism. By 1955 Supreme Court cases limiting state activity in the areas of subversion, sedition, and loyalty matters or favoring civil liberties and the right of dissent were viewed by some as extensions of desegregation decisions. Thus an alliance of segregationists and ultraconservative anti-communists was formed that blamed the Supreme Court for its woes. McCarthy, unwelcome elsewhere, found comfort and unity of purpose with the segregationists. To southern Senators Herman Talmadge (D-Ga.), Strom Thurmond (D-S.C.), Richard Russell (D-Ga.), and James O. Eastland (D-Miss.), civil rights and communism were one and the same. Now they were joined by northerners such as McCarthy, Sen. Karl Mundt (R-S.D.), Rep. Francis Walter (D-Pa.), Rep. Noah Mason (R-Ill.), and Sen. Styles Bridges (R-N.H.), who were willing to find fault with the Court because of decisions on Red Scare issues.[62] Those who excoriated the Court because of the *Brown* decision joined hands with those who were concerned that the Court was turning away from *Dennis* and other cases that had judicially validated the Red Scare. But giving credence to the link between communism and race issues was the persistent ideal of racial equality promoted by the Communist Party.

The Supreme Court continued to issue decisions that found racial segregation unconstitutional, and, in 1955–56, the Court also exhibited a different attitude toward Red Scare issues. Yet this anti-Court coalition erred in its belief that a pro-communist conspiracy was influencing the Court.[63]

Understanding the change in the Court's majority view on Red Scare issues requires an analysis of Chief Justice Warren's Red Scare opinions. Another transition, personal to him but of major significance to the Court, was to take place beginning in 1955.

Warren's championing of integration did not necessarily lead him to join with Justices Black and Douglas on Red Scare issues. To the contrary, from 1953 until 1955 Warren voted with the conservative majority in Red Scare cases. For example, he voted with the majority in 1953 to deny certiorari in the IWO case.[64] He also voted against Dr. Barsky in his battle to avoid suspension of his license to practice medicine because of his involvement with the Joint Anti-Fascist Refugee Committee.[65]

Also in 1954, Warren had joined the majority in *Galvan v. Press*.[66] In this case, a Mexican alien who had come to in the United States in 1918 at the age of seven admitted to the Immigration and Naturalization Service (INS) that he had been a member of the Communist Party from 1944 to 1946. In 1950 he was ordered deported under the Internal Security Act of 1950, which made an alien's membership in the Party grounds for deportation. Frankfurter, writing for the majority, recognized the harshness of the deportation but deferred to Congress, citing its power over aliens. Black and Douglas dissented, pointing out that Galvan had lived in the country for thirty-six years, had a family, was law abiding, and had joined a lawful organization. There were no accusations of disloyalty. Said Black, "For joining a lawful political group years ago—an act which he had no possible reason to believe would subject him to the slightest penalty—petitioner now loses his job, his friends, his home, and maybe even his children, who must choose between their father and their native country."[67]

Scholars of the Court have recognized the "implicit struggle going on between Justices Black and Frankfurter for the judicial soul of their new colleague."[68] During Warren's first two years on the Court, he appeared to have been under Frankfurter's influence, thereafter moving to concordance with Justice Black, with whom he became close personally, as well as in his decision making.

That Warren did change is evidenced by his modified opinions on Red Scare issues. Anthony Lewis found that "after *Barsky*, it's impossible to cite a case in which the Chief Justice was unresponsive to a claim by someone suffering for his political beliefs or associations."[69] Walter Murphy, another Court scholar, wrote, "One fact of strategic importance clearly emerged from the statistics of the 1955 term. Warren had shifted his position at the center of the Court and had solidly established himself in the left wing with Black and Douglas." He notes that the chief justice had moved to join the two liberals and particularly had reached a higher level of internal agreement with Black than Black had reached with Douglas.[70]

By virtue of his position as chief justice and because of his strong leadership of the brethren, this transition carried all the more weight. How is this change in Warren's position to be explained? Lewis stated that Warren, unlike most men, became more adventurous as he aged, "more liberated from conventional views, and [that] the same was to happen on the Supreme Court."[71] He added that the decisions reflecting Warren's changed position have to be read in a pragmatic way, "as an effort to mitigate, by whatever means available, the excesses of American anti-communism in the 1950's and 1960's."[72]

In a very real sense, Warren's transition reflects that which seems to have grounded his actions both on and off the bench: to ask what is fair and to protect the underdog from superior or tyrannical powers.[73]

In 1955, Warren was concerned about the growing resistance to the *Brown* decision in the South; he was also deeply troubled by the continued intolerant, hysterical passions on which McCarthyism had fed and which were still very much alive in the land. He felt, as did others, the need to speak out in defense of the Bill of Rights. That spring Warren delivered a number of speeches on college campuses dedicated to one theme: the need to tolerate dissent. Without directly mentioning McCarthy, he clearly indicated the dangers of the voices of conformity and their tendency to erode American liberties.[74]

This approach is confirmed by Leo Katcher in his biography of Warren, where he found explanation and evidence for this changed position in Warren's speeches and writings. Warren ended his college tour at the University of Wisconsin in June 1955, where he spoke at a centennial celebration for Robert M. LaFollette, Sr., saying:

[H]e [LaFollette] suffered the same treatment that courageous men of vision in all ages have suffered. He was called a radical, a disrupter, a Socialist, a subverter, and perhaps the only reason he was not called a Communist was because that term had not yet been popularized as a term of opprobrium.[75]

Probably the closest Warren got to explaining in writing why he aligned himself as he did in 1955 was in an article he wrote for *Fortune* magazine in November of that year. There he stated, "Our judges are not monks or scientists, but participate in the living stream of our national life," thus acknowledging that what happens in the life of the nation affects and influences the justices.[76]

Warren's central theme was the necessity of not losing sight that the nation's greatest strength in facing the challenge of communism was in preserving traditional freedoms. He wrote:

[A] challenge confronts the Constitution: Must a nation which is now the strongest in the world demand, for its own further strength and security, a sacrifice by its own citizens of their ancient liberties? This problem haunts the work of all our courts these days. But the Constitution exists for the individual as well as for the nation. I believe it will prove itself adaptable to this challenge. . . .

In the present struggle between our world and communism, the temptation to imitate totalitarian security methods is a subtle temptation that must be resisted day by day, for it will be with us as long as totalitarianism.[77]

His words were equally applicable to Red Scare issues as to civil rights for blacks:

When the rights of any individual or group are chipped away, the freedom of all erodes.

The moral is that if each minority, each professional group, and each citizen would imagine himself in the other's shoes, everybody's rights would have firmer support. The beginning of justice is the capacity to generalize and make objective one's private sense of wrong, thus turning it to public account. The pursuit of justice is not the vain pursuit of a remote abstraction; it is a continuing direction for our daily conduct.[78]

These remarks indicate what Warren feared by late 1955: that the Red Scare had gone too far and that the important principles of freedom that were at the foundation of the nation were being jeopardized. He was afraid that what was happening was no longer "fair," and he believed that the legal system must respond "to free men from the error and unpredictability of arbitrary forces." By also emphasizing that judges are "participants in the living stream of national life," he was stating that changes in the times affected the role and responses of the judiciary. He said, "Our system faces no theoretical dilemma but a single continuous problem: how to apply to ever changing conditions the never changing principles of freedom."[79] Thus by 1955, there were three votes in the liberal bloc. Because Warren was chief justice, the addition of Warren's vote was more important than a change by any other justice.

Justice Jackson died in October 1954 and was replaced by John Marshall Harlan II; he took his seat on March 28, 1955. Harlan was the grandson of the first John Marshall Harlan, whose fame had been secured by his dissent in *Plessy v. Ferguson*, in which he declared that the constitution was color-blind. However, the decision the grandson wrote for the three-judge panel of the Second Circuit Federal Court in *United States v. Flynn* upholding the Smith Act convictions of the second major trial of Party members endeared him to Eisenhower, already disappointed in Warren's work on the Court.[80] Nevertheless, Harlan's appointment resulted in a difficult confirmation process. It was used by segregationists and others who did not condone the direction of the Court to ventilate their views as they probed Harlan through extensive questioning. Harlan had spoken out against McCarthyism and had joined an organization that some held suspect. The confirmation process dragged on for five months, but the result was never in doubt.[81]

Some leading cases from the 1954 through 1956 Court terms demonstrate the shifting views of the Court and the reshuffling majority on Red Scare cases.

One such case was *Quinn v. United States*, where the issue was whether a union leader, on being called upon to testify before HUAC, could be properly found to have been in contempt of Congress if he failed to use the proper words to invoke his Fifth Amendment rights against self-incrimination.[82] The issue was raised when he refused to answer a question about his alleged membership in the Communist Party. He was cited for contempt, indicted, sentenced to six months in jail, and fined $500 by the district court.

Writing for a majority of the Court, Warren stated that since answering the question might have tended to incriminate Quinn, the issue was whether Quinn had indeed claimed the privilege when he stated his refusal to answer. With only Justice Reed in dissent, the justices stated that a person did not have to use a special combination of words or formula to properly invoke the right against self-incrimination. Furthermore, the decision required proof of the defendant's criminal intent, that is, proof beyond a reasonable doubt that he intentionally refused to answer. The majority, excepting Reed and Harlan, who joined him in dissent on this point, found that the government had not proved that Quinn's intent was criminal in nature.

Two companion cases decided the same day dealt with issues similar to *Quinn*.[83] As Chief Justice Warren wrote in a "Preliminary Statement" (apparently a guide for him in the conference of justices held on these cases), Julius Emspak had been convicted of sixty-eight counts of contempt and, like Quinn, fined $500 and sentenced to serve six months in prison for contempt of Congress. Fifty-eight questions were put to him demanding that he name names, eight on his own membership in the Communist Party, and two on whether he was affiliated "with alleged 'Communist front' organizations."[84]

Once again, Warren called for reversal of Emspak's conviction because the questions asked of him were incriminating in character, and although Emspak failed to invoke the Fifth Amendment privilege in "an ideal manner," what he did say was sufficient.[85]

The result was that the chief justice carried six of the nine justices with him; Reed dissented and Minton joined in his dissent, while Harlan once again agreed with the majority that the attempt to invoke the constitutional privilege was unartful but sufficient. However, Harlan dissented on whether all the questions required answers that were self-incriminating. He, for one, did not think so.

The third case involved Philip Bart, general manager of the Communist Party newspaper, the *Daily Worker*. Bart was similarly brought before HUAC and similarly refused to answer questions. This time, the witness did adequately present the constitutional privilege. The committee, however, departed from proper procedure when it failed to overrule his objections to questions and failed to instruct him to answer, as required for prosecution for criminal contempt.[86] The dissenters were Reed (with whom Minton joined) and Harlan.

Apparently, Chief Justice Warren circulated a preliminary statement on all three cases because some of the justices wrote to him about his views. Harlan wrote on May 4, 1954:

Dear Chief:
I have read with much interest your opinions in these cases, but regret to say that I still remain unconvinced as to (a) the "incriminating" character of some of the questions in *Emspak* and (b) the "willfulness" point, involved in the three opinions.
I am working on a dissent, which I hope to circulate next week.[87]
J. M. H.

A week before, both Douglas and Black had written to Warren. Douglas said he agreed with him on all three, adding:

I think your opinion in *Quinn* is magnificent, one of the very best in all the annals of the Court. I congratulate you for the wonderful job.[88]

Justice Black wrote:

As previously indicated to you, I agree with these opinions and think this is an excellent way to handle the cases. Congratulations.
H. H. B.[89]

The changed mood of these two justices, so long in the minority, was palpable. Not only did they have the chief justice on their side but, significantly, Frankfurter had moved to their position. Justice Reed became the consistent dissenter in the Red Scare cases of 1955–56, with Minton tagging along, always attaching himself to Reed's or Clark's dissenting opinions. Reed dissented from the majority on every Red Scare case beginning with *Quinn* until he left the bench in 1957. Justices Burton, Clark, and Harlan moved in and out of the newly developing majority.

Segments of the liberal press picked up the message of these three cases, recognizing a liberalization by the Court on the right to invoke Fifth Amendment protections. Acknowledging that the Court itself was changing on Red Scare issues, the *Nation* stated:

It appears, moreover, that the Chief Justice has succeeded in fashioning a new majority on civil liberties cases; he was joined in this instance by Justices Burton and Clark, as well as by Black, Douglas, and Frankfurter. The majority decision breathes a strong, confident spirit that is in refreshing contrast to the fear-ridden "crisis" tone that characterizes the court's unfortunate concessions to the hateful spirit of the cold war in the Dennis case and those related to it. It may well mark, therefore, an end to the court's retreat on civil liberties issues.[90]

Two liberal Catholic periodicals joined in praising these decisions. One pointed out that Julius Emspak and Thomas Quinn were officials of the "Red-dominated" United Electrical, Radio and Machine Workers Union and that Philip Bart was general manager of the Communist *Daily Worker*; nevertheless, they were entitled to the protection of the Fifth Amendment, an entitlement "vindicated by the highest judicial authority in the land."[91]

Yet the most significant case—the leading case of the Red Monday four—was yet to come. On October 17, 1955 the Supreme Court granted certiorari for nineteen petitioners, all of whom were state functionaries of the Communist Party from California, and all of whom had been found guilty of violating the Smith Act. The case was *Yates v. United States*.[92] J. Edgar Hoover realized what it foreshadowed: four justices had voted to review these Smith Act convictions, and it was plain that the new majority on the Court, reflecting Warren's leadership and the changed times, would emasculate, if not reverse, the *Dennis* decision, thus crippling or destroying the major legal weapon in the fight against domestic dissent, subversion, and the Communist Party.

Hoover understood that four votes plus one made up a new Court majority, and, given the decisions of 1955, it was reasonable to assume that the fifth vote was available. There could be no other plausible reason why the Court would agree to hear a Smith Act case after years of turning down appeals of Smith Act convictions except to revisit the basis for prosecutions under it. Understanding the Court's direction, Hoover turned away from the courts and initiated the COINTELPRO concept as his answer to a Court he could no longer depend on.

On March 8, 1956 Hoover made his appearance at the National Security Council for the purpose of getting tacit consent for his program of hard-hitting—and illegal—actions against the American Communist Party. Never fully stating what he intended (he had already been using some of these methods) and grossly exaggerating the menace of the Party, Hoover walked out of the meeting with President Eisenhower and major heads of the executive branch with the apparent authority to proceed.

Just one week later, on March 15, 1956, it became evident that the Justice Department was also aware of the meaning of granting certiorari in the *Yates* case. Having been on the losing end of the contempt cases in 1955, as well as having lost the fight to keep the *Yates* defendants from being granted review of their convictions, the department notified the FBI that future Smith Act prosecutions would have to include evidence of "an actual plan for a violent revolution" or the Justice Department would not prosecute.[93] But Hoover was ahead of his nominal boss; he was already pushing plans to make his first COINTELPRO operational. In August 1956, he succeeded.

Pennsylvania v. Nelson was argued orally before the Court in late 1955 and decided on April 2, 1956.[94] The importance of this case lay not only in what was at issue but also in the reaction it created in conjunction with two other cases decided that April. At issue was the appeal of the state of Pennsylvania against Steve Nelson (his real name was Steve Mesarosh), secretary of the Communist Party in that state, who had been convicted in a Pennsylvania state court for advocating the overthrow of U.S. government. The Pennsylvania Supreme Court had reversed the case on the grounds that the federal Smith Act preempted any state prosecution under state sedition laws where the alleged sedition was against the national government. Pennsylvania state prosecutors appealed this decision, and the Court took the case. The issue was whether the Smith Act superseded the enforceability of state sedition laws addressing the same conduct.

At the initial Court conference following oral argument, Warren stated his view that the Smith Act and federal regulation occupied the entire field on the subject of subversion and that prosecution could only be pursued by the federal government. Sedition against the United States government, he argued, was not a local matter. Initially, there appeared to be a stalemate as the justices expressed their views, but thereafter Warren was able to obtain a six-to-three majority, with only Reed, Minton, and Burton in dissent. Knowing that the decision would, in some quarters, generate an unfavorable reaction, Warren himself wrote the majority decision, incorporating in it none other than the views of Hoover and his FBI. Hoover was against states endangering the work of federal prosecutors, taking the spotlight away from the FBI and letting loose those whom he considered amateurs to prosecute Reds.

The developing uproar over the *Nelson* case took on another dimension when, one week later, the Court's decision in *Slochower v. Board of Education of New York City* was announced.[95] The case involved a tenured professor who was dismissed because he invoked his Fifth Amendment privilege when he was brought before the Internal Security Subcommittee of the Senate Judiciary Committee. When Professor Slochower was asked whether he had been a Communist Party member in 1940 or 1941 (he had admitted that he had been a decade later), he exercised his constitutional privilege against self-incrimination. Under New York City law, he could be dismissed for refusing to answer. Thus the issue before the Court was whether the city's law violated the due process clause of the Fourteenth Amendment by permitting Slochower's dismissal without notice, without a showing of cause by the city, and without a hearing. The Court, by the close vote of five to four, said yes. Justices Black and Douglas would have gone farther in striking down such laws; they concurred in the Court's judgment and opinion but referred to their dissents and concurrences in earlier cases in which they had objected to the basic validity of such laws.

Significantly, the majority opinion was written by Justice Clark, who had so often been with the majority on the other side of cases involving the use of the Fifth Amendment or concerning loyalty issues. This time he wrote, "At the outset we must condemn the practice of imputing a sinister meaning to the exercise of a person's constitutional right under the Fifth Amendment." [96] A reading of this majority opinion, combined with the *Quinn, Emspak,* and *Bart* cases, clearly indicated that the Court's endorsement of convictions for contempt and unconcern with lost jobs in earlier years had given way to changed attitudes and changed times. The First, Fifth, and Fourteenth Amendments as shields for individual liberty were being refurbished, if not resurrected.

In order to gain an appreciation of the scope, depth, and virulence of the reaction to Supreme Court decisions announced during the 1956 term, one must examine two additional cases on Red Scare issues. On April 30, 1956 the case of *The Communist Party of the United States v. Subversive Activities Control Board* was announced. This case represented the first time that the Party itself had come before the Court. [97]

One of the anti-Communist laws Congress had passed at the height of the Cold War-Red Scare was the Subversive Activities Control Act of 1950. President Truman had vetoed it because he felt it was a stupid (the outlaws had to register with the sheriff), ill-conceived attempt to control the Party and other communist organizations, [98] but his veto was overridden. In effect, the act called on the Party and all other communist organizations to register with the attorney general. If they did not register voluntarily, the attorney general could initiate a proceeding before the Subversive Activities Control Board to hold hearings on the matter. If the Board found that an organization was a "Communist-action organization," the Board could order it to register and to open its financial and membership records. The consequences for the organization and all its members were dire, but since Justice Frankfurter was writing an opinion for the majority that would delay the implementation of the act, these consequences were never felt.

The case was the kind Frankfurter dealt with best, one where the constitutional issues could be avoided because there were other relevant grounds, usually procedural in nature, for deciding the case without reference to constitutional questions. Frankfurter firmly believed in this guiding principle, and here was an opportunity to exercise it.

On appeal to the District of Columbia Court of Appeals from a Board finding that the Communist Party had to register, Party attorneys provided undisputed evidence that three witnesses for the government were paid political informers who had perjured themselves. The appeals court had nonetheless confirmed the Board's decision. The government's position, supported by an amicus curiae brief from the American Bar Association, was that there was ample evidence apart from these three witnesses to support the Board's and the court of appeals's finding. (The National Lawyers Guild and the American Civil Liberties Union wrote amicus curiae briefs on behalf of the Party.)

Frankfurter wrote for the majority in the six-to-three decision explaining that the appeals court should have returned the case to the Subversive Activities Control Board for the purpose of hearing the issue of false testimony. In his typical detailed, analytical fashion, Frankfurter pointed out that almost 750 pages of the record involved the testimony of these three witnesses, who the Court felt must have played a role in the Board's findings. Stopping short of any broad constitutional analysis, the Supreme Court majority remanded the case "to make certain that the Board bases its finding on untainted evidence," thus reversing the finding of the court of appeals.[99] Justice Clark wrote a dissent, joined in by Minton and Reed, arguing that the constitutional issues involved should have been decided, that there was ample untainted evidence to support the Board's finding, and that the allegations of perjury were too flimsy to support what was simply a delaying tactic by the Communist Party.

This case was one of the earliest Supreme Court cases in which a recording of oral arguments was made; an edited version may be heard and read.[100] On first reading the decision and then comparing the oral argument, the reader is left with some apparent contradictions. Not one word is present on the subject of the perjured testimony. The entire focus is on the applicability of First and Fifth Amendment rights. Justice Black, exhibiting his absolutist concept of the First Amendment, argued frequently with the government's attorney on those constitutional issues.

There is also an unmistakable quality exhibited in the arguments. When the act was enacted in 1950, the Cold War had been very hot and Red Scare legislation was the natural outgrowth of the times. By 1956, the reader senses, Red Scare arguments had lost their edge because they were made during different times and under different priorities. The solicitor general, representing the United States, made his arguments essentially in the past tense when he defended the act's aims and provisions. This tactic not only was the result of litigating a case that had dragged on for years but also indicated a convergence of the faded intensity of purpose, justification, and Red Scare rhetoric in the years since the Party had first been brought before the Board.

It is in the power of an appellate-level court, such as the Supreme

Court in this case, to reshape the issues in the light of the justices' own vision of the case, and this is what the majority under Frankfurter did in choosing to avoid the constitutional issues, even though they were the core of the oral argument.

The final Red Scare decision of 1956 concerned a civil service employee who had held the position of a food and drug inspector in the Food and Drug Administration under the Secretary of Health, Education and Welfare (HEW). The government acknowledged that he did not have access to government secrets or classified materials, and he was not in a position to influence policy.[101] Yet he was summarily suspended without pay from his position in November 1953 pending a loyalty investigation. Written charges against him stated that he had "a close association with individuals reliably reported to be Communists" and that he was a member of an organization that was allegedly subversive.[102] The authority for firing him came from a piece of Red Scare legislation from 1950 giving the secretaries of certain executive departments unreviewable dismissal powers over civilian employees when deemed necessary in the interest of national security. Initially, this power had not included HEW, but it was later extended by President Eisenhower to all departments and agencies.

At issue was whether employees of the government, regardless of whether they held nonsensitive positions, could be terminated for alleged disloyalty. Justice Harlan wrote for the same majority of six as in the last case, with the same three dissenters; Clark again wrote the dissent, joined by Reed and Minton. The majority found that the intent of the act was to allow the greatest latitude for the government when there was a risk to national security, but that the power to dismiss did not apply to employees who merely dealt with the national well-being. Thus the Court held that, unless the employee was in a position where he or she could affect national security, dismissal was not authorized under the Act of August 26, 1950, even though the employee may have been of dubious loyalty. In his dissent, Clark argued that such an interpretation might "leave the government honeycombed with subversive employees." However, the new Court majority no longer accepted this kind of Red Scare argument, one that had been so persuasive in earlier years.[103]

One reaction to the Red Scare decisions of 1955 and 1956 was to cement the opposition of southern segregationists and ultraconservatives to what the Supreme Court was doing in both Red Scare and segregation cases: continuing to strike down racial segregation laws and moving away from judicial endorsement of the Red Scare.

Strengthening this alliance were business organizations fearful of Supreme Court decisions favorable to organized labor. States had enacted right-to-work laws, and there was fear that the Court might, as it did in *Nelson* (where it had annulled state subversive regulations), invalidate state labor legislation on the same grounds.[104]

That unification, raising cries of "stop the Court" or even "stop Court treachery," was recognized by members of the Court. Chief Justice Warren and Justice Douglas understood what was afoot and later wrote about this development in their respective memoirs.[105] Warren was also aware of the personal attacks on him. He quoted from a speech of Senator McCarthy: "I will not say that Earl Warren is a Communist, but I will say he is the best friend Communists have in America," and he cited a speaker who went beyond the "Impeach Earl Warren" movement to call for lynching Warren as a more effective means of turning back the Court.[106]

The first and most important volley fired against the Court came on January 5, 1955, when Representative Howard Smith of Virginia, the Smith of Smith Act fame, apparently sensed well ahead of the event that the Supreme Court might interfere with state prosecutions of Reds. He introduced H.R. 3, which would have directed that, under most circumstances, no act of Congress could be construed by the courts as preempting state laws on the same subject matter. This proposed legislation actually cut across the desires of all three elements of the anti-Court coalition and became a rallying point for action against the Court.

The battle over this bill pitted Smith against Representative Emanuel Celler (D-N.Y.), chairman of the House Judiciary Committee. These two were ideological and personal enemies. Celler used delaying tactics for more than eighteen months but was then forced to hold hearings. With the *Nelson* decision confirming what Smith and Court opponents had foreseen, organizations lined up to be heard on H.R. 3. Ultimately the bill was shelved when, against Smith's wishes, its effect was limited to legislatively reversing the *Nelson* case. Smith could not get the broader bill he wanted, so he got none at all.

Another notable area of support for Smith and other anti-Court forces came from the American Bar Association (ABA), whose board of governors in 1956 adopted a resolution that was not only critical of the *Nelson* decision but also (without mentioning H.R. 3) supportive of the bill's purposes and principles:

Members of this Conference are gravely concerned by decisions of the Supreme Court of the United States which have held that Congressional enactments supersede state laws on the matters involved and thereby pre-empt those fields for the federal government alone. Judicial interpretations of this character seriously handicap the states in the regulation and administration of their internal affairs. . . . [The] Governors' Conference recommends to the Congress that federal laws should be framed that will not be construed to pre-empt any field against state action unless this intent is stated, and that the exercise of national power on any subject should not bar state action on the same subject unless there is positive inconsistence.[107]

This was not the first nor the last time that the ABA would break with its traditional role of supporting the work of the Court. Much more criticism relating to Red Monday cases was to follow in 1957, leading Chief Justice Warren to resign from the organization.

Those opposing the Court's work on Red Scare issues in 1955 and 1956 saw the results in this light. The Court had aided Communists and communism by curtailing the power of HUAC to send the Fifth Amendment Reds to jail, the Court had destroyed the work of those states (there had been forty-two with antisubversion laws) seeking to jail Communists, the Court had prevented the Subversive Activities Control Board from destroying the Party, and the Court had allowed a suspected Red sympathizer to keep his job with the U.S. government.

Because of its impact on all constituents of the anti-Court group, the *Nelson* decision generated the strongest reaction and H.R. 3 came the closest to enactment of all the anti-Court bills. There were, however, more than seventy anti-Court proposals introduced in the Eighty-Fourth Congress. Justice Douglas had this reaction to the *Nelson* decision:

The resulting uproar was loud and incessant. About seventy bills were introduced to change the result in the *Nelson* case; all but four died in committee. The others were debated on the floor of the Senate and the House and failed of passage. The gist of these bills was that nothing but an express provision in a federal law should prevent a state from prosecuting acts of subversion or sedition against the federal government.[108]

Former Supreme Court Associate Justice James Byrnes warned, "Power intoxicates men. It is never voluntarily surrendered. The Supreme Court must be curbed." Thereafter, the Georgia legislature passed a resolution in support of Byrnes and demanded impeachment of all justices who had joined in the *Nelson* decision.[109]

The language in the halls of Congress was harsh and bitter as members of the anti-Court group grew more strident with each decision. McCarthy declared that the Court's decision in the *Nelson* case was "the most outrageous instance of judicial legislation that has ever come to my attention."[110] Representative L. Mendel Rivers (D-S.C.) on the same day said that "something has to be done to stop the Supreme Court. They are a greater threat to this Union than the entire confines of Soviet Russia. If some way is not found to stop them, God help us."[111] It was not lost on southern segregationists that new northern anti-Court sentiments strengthened their cause. William M. Colmer (D-Miss.), having heard colleagues attack the Court, said, "What I wanted to say to the gentleman [Noah M. Mason (R-Ill.)] is this, that it is most refreshing to see that the gentleman, from one of our so-called northern States, has so much in common with so many from the so-called southern states here today."[112]

Three weeks later, George W. Andrews (D-Ala.) spoke in the House in response to the *Communist Party v. Subversive Activities Control Board* decision, declaring that because of that decision the Board had suspended all pending cases. He added, "Mr. Chairman, how much longer will this Congress continue to permit the Supreme Court to usurp the powers of Congress, write the laws of this land, destroy States' rights, and protect the Communist Party?"[113] On the Senate side, Karl E. Mundt (R-S.D.), in support of a bill he was introducing to reverse the *Cole v. Young* case, said,

What a travesty on our judicial procedure when in the joint efforts of Congress and the Executive to safeguard our fellow citizens against the clear and present dangers of communism, six men in black robes can nullify our every effort and expose the internal workings of our Government to the stealthy espionage and sabotage of Communist agents whose services the Government cannot now terminate unless the agency in which they work be designated "sensitive" or unless their individual positions are classified as "sensitive."[114]

In press reactions and evaluations, liberals were pleased with these decisions. *America* found the result in *Nelson* to be a happy one.[115] the *New Republic* saw *Nelson* as "another token of judicial thaw," but believed that since so many states had had sedition laws (42) and since so many state attorneys general had joined in opposing the position the Court had reached, Congress would probably pass legislation reversing the Court.[116]

The *New York Times* responded positively to the *Cole v. Young* decision, calling it a "common-sense limitation" imposed by the Court in limiting summary suspension and unreviewable dismissal powers to those employees working where national security is involved. The editorial also warned Congress to move "with the most extreme caution" in limiting the power of the Court and not let the "passions of the moment cloud its judgment."[117] The *Christian Century* warned that "utmost vigilance is necessary" to keep a "weird assortment" of anti-Court opponents from overturning valid Court decisions through legislation.[118] The magazine *Science* reported favorably on the *Cole v. Young* decision, quoting at length from an editorial in the *Washington Post* that said, "By making the national security program somewhat less arbitrary and capricious, the Supreme Court has made the Nation more secure."[119]

At the end of 1956, certain developments in the life of the nation and the Court come into focus. Despite the dramatic language and dire accusations against the Court, despite the formation of an anti-Court coalition, despite the power of Congress to reverse the flow of the new Court majority decisions on Red Scare issues, not one of the many proposals became law. None even passed both houses of Congress. But why?

With all the exhortations against the Court, with Warren as its chief justice and the leader of the new liberal majority, the Court persisted as the most sacrosanct government institution to those in and out of Congress. Franklin D. Roosevelt's failure to get legislation that would change the Court in 1937 was—and still is—the prime example of respect for an institution that most people feel must remain inviolate. McCarthy would say that there was something "radically wrong" with Warren, and Senator Eastland would suggest that Warren followed the Communist Party line and took "the same position that the Communists take when they attempt to protect themselves," but the vast majority of Americans did not succumb to such opinions.

The three threads making up the anti-Court coalition—segregationists, ultramilitant anti-Communists and big business organizations—were still a minority in their attacks on the Court. Most people endorsed the *Brown* decision and the promise of equality. Many Americans, if not most, were tiring of the persistent search for Reds. Most citizens appreciated and endorsed the pro-union stance of the New Deal and Fair Deal and expected the national government to play an active role in the economy.

One indication of changed times by 1956 can be seen in the waning appearance of articles on communism and related Red Scare news in the indexes of the *Readers' Guide to Periodical Literature* for the years 1949 through 1960. There was a substantial slackening in the numbers of such articles, with the exception of hard-core anti-communist publications such as the *American Mercury*. With the passing years, the tone of most articles seemed to reflect less fright and less outrage, yielding, after 1953 (perhaps tied to the end of the Korean War and the Eisenhower presidency), a more reflective, calm, and confident tone.[120] After McCarthy's fall, one senses that large segments of the population were bored by, or at least losing interest in, Red Scare disclosures. Stalin was dead, Ike was in charge, and the nation seemed to have regained its self-confidence. In the 1954 congressional elections, Redbaiting did not work well for Republicans. Ex-Communist informers were now under suspicion; Harvey Matusow admitted that he had fabricated testimony in a number of government cases. (He was tried for perjury and sent to jail.) The false testimony of other informers was also disclosed.[121] Even Senator Harry Cain (R-Wash.), appointed to the Subversive Activities Control Board, came out against the loyalty programs and the attorney general's Subversive Organizations List.[122]

When Eisenhower ran for president in 1952, he had asked the Republican Party to join him in a "crusade" to clean the crooks and the Commies (really, the Democrats) out of Washington. Four years later he was easily reelected, having promoted an end to the Korean War and having kept world peace. With Eisenhower at the helm exuding confidence, adopting a moderate, middle-of-the-road course, and running the nation shrewdly and pragmatically, the paranoia that had gripped the nation in earlier years was allayed.

From January through March 1955, William R. Hearst, Jr., the son of the man who had built the huge Hearst media empire, did something his father would not have done, nor something he himself most likely would have done in prior years. Hearst, like his father an ardent anti-Communist Cold Warrior, through his nationwide chain of newspapers aided and abetted the Red Scare. But in 1955, Hearst and two of his top people traveled to post-Stalinist Russia. For weeks on end, Hearst extensively reported his impressions of Russia and particularly of Nikita Khrushchev, who was described to millions of readers as the "No. 2 Russ." The result was the dissemination of rational, nonbelligerent views of Soviet leaders and sympathetic views of the Soviet people. Said Hearst:

I came away from Moscow with the impression that the Soviet leaders are quite sincere about co-existence and improvement of relations with the United States. Not because of any humanitarian reasons. Not because they have abandoned hope of achieving Communist domination of the world one day. But simply because they have a healthy respect for America's strength and don't want to risk a military showdown with the U.S. in the near future.[123]

That he would go to the enemy camp, exchange views, and report that the Kremlin leaders were displaying flexibility on world issues such as armaments was another reflection of the changed times. Hearst and his aides won a Pulitzer Prize for their work.[124]

Also in 1955, the president, for first time in ten years, met with Allied and Russian leaders in Geneva and explored ways of lessening world tensions. He could do this because most of the nation felt safe with the general-president at the summit talking detente. That is not to say that there were no limits to the thaw in the Cold War or that anti-Communism was disappearing as a prime domestic concern, but the times had changed and the Cold War-Red Scare complex was not as before.

By the summer of 1956, with Congress and the Court in recess, public furor further diminished. Chief Justice and Mrs. Warren traveled extensively, visiting European countries and, at the specific request of Secretary of State John Foster Dulles, accepting an invitation to visit India, where Warren would receive an honorary degree from the University of Delhi. Wherever he went, Warren was feted as the leader in the effort to end racial discrimination. He became an international figure and was revered, particularly in new Asian and African nations, as a great humanitarian. Widely reported in the press, the celebrations of Warren as a fine representative of the best of America further muted the anti-Court critics, or at least balanced their continued jeremiads.[125]

That same summer, in its July 14, 1956, edition, the *Nation* carried a lead article by C. Hermann Pritchett, a political scientist whose work on the Vinson Court is still well recognized and highly regarded. In his article, "The Warren Court: Turn Toward Liberalism," Pritchett stated, "As the third term of the Supreme Court under Chief Justice Warren closes, its growing support for civil liberties makes clear that the Court has turned one of its historic corners." Pritchett argued that not only the segregation cases, but Red Scare issues as well, demonstrated substantial change from the Vinson Court. His view of the Vinson Court on the subject of civil liberties meant that "any shift in direction had to be for the better," that is, more favorable to judicial protection of individual liberties.

Pritchett also noted that the impact of a liberal shift in the Court was apparently influencing lower federal courts to take positions that tended to restrict the abuses of congressional committees and to question the right of the State Department to deny passports.

Asking "Who speaks for civil liberties on the present Court?" his answer was Justices Douglas and Black, with Frankfurter moving more boldly to express and vote his "genuine devotion to the basic freedoms." The fourth vote was Warren; the fifth was, surprisingly, Clark in some instances, but clearly not in others. Harlan and Burton both moved in and out of the new majorities on civil rights issues.

Pritchett ended his analysis by warning that "the original Smith Act decision is still in place" and that "it would take a confirmed optimist to predict that the *Dennis* decision will be reversed." However, he also noted that the Court had accepted for review new Smith Act convictions and other Red Scare issues, which would be decided in 1957. While Pritchett was not without misgivings as to further evidence of liberalism by the Court, he recognized that "part of the Court's more favorable record in civil liberties may be due to the somewhat improved climate of opinion in the country at large. Nevertheless, a corner has been turned and the Warren Court is entitled to some of the credit."[126] In fact, his views suggested that the "improved climate" was of greater significance than changes in Court personnel.

His perceptions were correct: the Court had changed in membership and in decision making, with further changes about to occur. The times in which the Court was working had changed and, reflecting the constant dynamics of a nation's life, would continue to change.

Chapter 8
The Red Monday Cases

Our opinion is that June 17, 1957, will go down in the history books as the day on which the Supreme Court irreparably crippled the witch hunt.

I. F. Stone, *The Haunted Fifties*, 1963

[T]he cases decided in June, 1957, indicate that all anti-Communist laws may be so restricted as to lose their effectiveness.

Frank B. Ober, *American Bar Journal*, January 1958

After a summer recess, a Supreme Court term opens in October of each year. The four Red Monday decisions came near the close of the 1956–57 term on June 17, 1957, and were preceded by the usual steps of appeal: a petition for a writ of certiorari, followed by consideration of those petitions by the justices, usually over the summer. The responding party (usually the federal or state government) files its petition opposing a grant of any relief. As the fall session of the Court commences, the justices meet and vote on these petitions and objections to them. If four justices vote to hear the case, it is set for oral argument. Thereafter the brethren meet, voice their positions and commence the decision-making process. All four Red Monday cases had been granted certiorari: *Yates* in October 1955, *Watkins* and *Sweezy* in October 1956, and *Service* in November 1956.

But before certiorari was granted for these cases, a spate of Red Scare cases similarly had been in the certiorari pipeline. Some would be decided prior to Red Monday; others would be decided later during the fall 1957 to summer 1958 term.

When the Court granted certiorari in the *Yates* case, because it involved Communist Party members whose trials had followed in the wake of the *Dennis* decision, the signal was clear: the Supreme Court was willing to hear the arguments of Party members challenging the grounds for their convictions—arguments that it had refused to hear during the intervening years. When that became evident in October 1955, others caught up in the net of Red Scare cases also sought appeal. The result was a steady stream of civil rights-Red Scare petitioners seeking to open the door to the highest court of appeals.

Further changes in Court personnel were also to take place in 1957. Justice Sherman Minton resigned on doctor's orders in October 1956. While Minton and Warren had shared a love of baseball, Warren knew that Minton's resignation meant that a justice who had consistently opposed the new majority in every major Red Scare case decided in 1956 and who had written the majority decision in *Adler v. Board of Education* (upholding the New York law barring members of allegedly subversive organizations from teaching in public schools) would be gone. Minton had also been in the majority allowing the attorney general to hold communist aliens without bail if he thought them a danger to national security. Any replacement could hardly have been more supportive of the government's policies and actions than he.

Minton's successor, William J. Brennan, Jr., then on the New Jersey Supreme Court, was President Eisenhower's nominee. It still is a source of some amazement that Eisenhower nominated Brennan, who among other things was a Catholic and a Democrat. Apparently Brennan had impressed the attorney general of the United States, Herbert Brownell. Judge Brennan's decisions appeared to Brownell to be middle-of-the-road, and the president wanted someone who had judicial experience. By 1956 Eisenhower was attributing his disappointment in Warren to the chief justice's lack of experience as a jurist before his appointment. Furthermore, the Conference of Catholic Bishops had been relaying its dismay about the absence of a Catholic on the Court since 1949, and it pressed Eisenhower for the appointment of a Catholic justice. The year 1956 was also a presidential election year, and nominating the Irish Catholic Democrat from New Jersey appeared to be a wise political move.

It was only after Brennan was on the Court that the president understood that he had made another appointment error. Had he looked at Brennan's working-class background and noted that he had been a reformer and a liberal on the New Jersey Supreme Court, had he read Brennan's 1954 speech comparing McCarthyism to the Salem witch trials and his speech defending those who invoked the Fifth Amendment, Eisenhower might have realized something of the leanings of his nominee. At Brennan's confirmation hearing, McCarthy grilled him about his speeches for a full day, and when the voting took place McCarthy was the only senator who voted against confirmation.[1]

The Brennan appointment set off another tug of war, this time be-

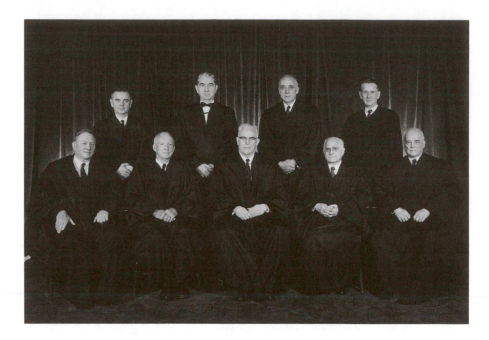

Figure 7. Justices of the Supreme Court of the United States. Official photograph, 1957. Collection of the Supreme Court of the United States. Photographer: Harris and Ewing.

tween Frankfurter, Brennan's former law professor, and Warren. This time the struggle was brief and ended promptly as Brennan aligned himself with Warren, Black, and Douglas. Reportedly, Frankfurter said, "I always encouraged my students to think for themselves, but Brennan goes too far." Yet Brennan was also to develop in the role of bridge builder between the liberal and conservative camps in these early years of his tenure, and increasingly so as the years passed.[2]

The other change was the retirement of Stanley F. Reed in 1957 after nineteen years on the high court. Justice Douglas's assessment of Reed was this:

Apart from Harold Burton, the kindest, friendliest, most polite and courteous Justice on the Court in my time was Stanley Reed. But like the [other] Truman appointees, Stanley [Reed] took a dim view of dissidents and revolutionaries, assuming a small-town stance when it came to the Bill of Rights. FDR probably named him because he felt that Stanley Reed would never strike down New Deal legislation. The difficulty with that kind of reasoning is that times change, and so do issues. The economic matters which seemed so overwhelmingly important to FDR were eclipsed in a year or two, and the country moved into new areas. It was in those areas that Reed was out of place. The Vinson Court almost always had his vote against a civil rights issue.[3]

Reed's replacement was Charles E. Whittaker, a federal appeals court judge who had been befriended by Attorney General Herbert Brownell. Eisenhower again reacted favorably to having a sitting judge move up to the Supreme Court. Additionally, Whittaker was, as earlier described, favored by J. Edgar Hoover.

In lists of "best/worst" justices of the Supreme Court, Whittaker always appears in the "worst" category.[4] The consensus was that he was intellectually over his head, unable to make up his mind, and unable to write opinions on his own. Justice Whittaker did not participate in any of the major Red Scare cases decided in 1957 up to Red Monday, with the exception of one in which he joined with every other judge.[5] In 1958 he dissented once, joining with Justice Clark.[6]

Thus Justice Reed, a consistent dissenter from the new majority, was replaced by a justice who most often chose not to participate in decisions or generally joined with the brethren in a unanimous decision. In effect, Justice Whittaker's vote did not change a single Red Scare decision in 1957 and 1958, with the exception of one in 1958.[7] By 1959 Whittaker was always casting his vote on the side of the government on any issue, and it mattered in some closely divided decisions. Whittaker never wrote an opinion or a dissent in a Red Scare case. The Court was apparently too strenuous for him; he retired a physically exhausted man in 1962.

On May 6, 1957 the Court decided two major Red Scare cases. These involved whether a state could bar a law school graduate from taking the bar exam and whether a state agency could prevent a person from practicing law because he refused to answer questions about his membership in the Communist Party or his political beliefs.[8] I. F. Stone said of these two cases, "While the Senate last week was burying McCarthy, the United States Supreme Court buried McCarthyism."[9]

When Rudolph Schware graduated from law school and filled out an application to take the bar examination, he candidly disclosed his background, including his past membership in the Communist Party (which he had quit more than fifteen years before), his use of aliases (to avoid anti-Semitism in employment and in his efforts to unionize workers), and his arrests in 1940 (although he was never tried or convicted) for taking part in labor protests and for violating the Neutrality Act of 1917 by urging men to go to Spain to aid the Loyalists in the Spanish Civil War.

Following a hearing held after his application was turned down, Schware was assessed as lacking the "requisite moral character for admission to the bar." [10] This was the finding of the Board of Bar Examiners, though there was overwhelming and uncontested evidence of his sterling moral character since 1940. On appeal to the New Mexico Supreme Court, the Board's decision, with one dissent, was upheld. It was understandable that the United States Supreme Court would be sensitive to matters involving the practice of law, and considering the Court's two earlier decisions on disbarment of lawyers and firings of public employees in academia, the granting of certiorari in this and the companion case was significant.

The issue before the Court was whether these activities—past Party membership, past arrests, and assumption of aliases—justified an inference of bad moral character that warranted keeping a candidate from taking the bar exam.

The chief justice assigned Justice Black to write for the majority in both cases after a justices' conference held on January 18, 1957. There apparently was little controversy over the *Schware* case because it was legal to be a Communist when Schware admittedly had been a Party member; the justices were also impressed with his army service record and "clean conduct" since ending his Party affiliation. [11] At the conference, only Clark had objected to the majority's approach, but then, in an undated handwritten note to Black, Clark changed his mind and wrote, "Dear Hugo—Brace yourself! Don't fall from your chair!—For in *#92 Schware*, I agree. T. C. C." [12]

On May 2, 1957, four days before the *Schware* decision was to be announced, Clark wrote Black again, this time backing off from joining in the majority opinion, but stating, "However, I have decided rather than being the sole dissenter on such a close question that I will join Frankfurter, J. His Concurrence comes closer to my views. Sorry, T. C. C." [13]

Frankfurter found that Schware's disqualification was based on a wholly arbitrary standard that offended the dictates of reason and the due process clause of the Fourteenth Amendment. Harlan also joined in Frankfurter's concurrence, and with Whittaker not participating *Schware* was essentially unanimous.

Black's writing in the *Schware* decision was notably different from majority decisions on Red Scare issues since the *Dennis* case. There was an absence of any deep discussion of the legal issues. Instead, most of the opinion reviewed the Schware's life and answered the charges against him by placing Schware's actions in the context of his life and times. In effect, Black and the other justices were stating: "We understand why he did what he did and when he did it. We also recognize the merit of his life over the past fifteen years and find no serious grounds to challenge his morality, or to see him as a danger to the legal profession." The approach and values expressed by the Court were distinctly different in tone from so many decisions that had preceded. I. F. Stone commented:

The words were those of Mr. Justice Black but no longer speaking in last-ditch isolation for Black and Douglas dissenting. Here he spoke for a majority which included not only Chief Justice Warren and our new (Catholic) Justice, Brennan, but even—*mirabile dictu*—Mr. Justice Burton. Indeed, the "right wing" of the Court, Justices Frankfurter, Clark, and Harlan, saw no reason to dispute the majority's judgment in respect to Schware. Their concurring opinion indicates the change in atmosphere as strongly as does the majority decision. . . . A few years ago, when McCarthy was riding high, it is difficult to imagine the Supreme Court even agreeing to hear the Schware and Konigsberg appeals.[14]

The companion case, *Konigsberg v. State Bar of California et al.*, was more hotly contested among the justices and yielded only a five-to-three majority reversing the Supreme Court of California's decision.[15] Raphael Konigsberg had graduated from law school in 1953 and had passed the bar examination. When the Committee of Bar Examiners of California refused to certify Konigsberg to practice law on the grounds that he had not proved he was of good moral character and that he had advocated forcible overthrow of the government, Konigsberg appealed to the California Supreme Court for review. That court refused (by a four-to-three decision) to hear the case, and Konigsberg obtained a writ of certiorari from the United States Supreme Court.

To Justice Black, writing for the majority, Konigsberg might have been (he had refused to answer whether he had been) a member of the Communist Party when it had been legal to belong, and he had written statements highly critical of government and the Court. However, such unorthodox beliefs were not evidence of bad moral character, Black wrote. There was no evidence that Konigsberg had engaged in or abetted unlawful or immoral activities. Black expressed the view that Konigsberg's writings criticizing the country's participation in the Korean War, the Supreme Court's decision in the *Dennis* case, and other political controversies were "not unusually extreme."[16]

Once again, Black delved into Konigsberg's background and his behavior, noting the number and variety of recommendations he had produced, and determined—which was disputable—that Konigsberg had not refused to answer certain questions that would have allowed the examiners to determine his moral character by drawing negative inferences from his refusals. I. F. Stone commented that for the past decade refusing to answer questions had been sufficient to show bad character and, therefore, sufficient reason to disqualify people from admission to the bar.[17]

With tongue-in-cheek comment, Stone reprinted some of the hyperbolic language used by *Konigsberg*, noting, "The majority seem to have regarded these brash utterances with a sense of humor that has been lacking here for some time." He further noted, "It has been a long time since the majority of the Supreme Court regarded radical utterances [including those directed against the Supreme Court] with such Hyde Park calm."[18]

Justice Frankfurter dissented; Harlan dissented separately, joined by Clark. Frankfurter wanted the case remanded to the California Supreme Court to make certain that proper procedures were followed in order to assure that the constitutional issue had been ruled upon. Harlan wrote a very long dissent, quoting extensively from the hearing record to prove that Konigsberg had not sustained his burden of proving good moral character because he had refused to answer questions relevant to his fitness for bar membership. Furthermore, the Court majority, Harlan felt, was intruding on the right of a state to administer its own bar admission standards.[19]

Behind the scenes, there was considerable bickering among the brethren as to the legal issues, the interpretation of the record, and the language used in the majority opinion, as well as in the dissent by Harlan. In an undated note from the chief justice to Black, Warren, who had assigned Black the task of writing for the majority, said, "I would be inclined to rest upon what you have [written]. Harlan's opinion is too long for anyone to read. And those who will attack us will do so anyway . . . E. W."[20]

I. F. Stone summed up his reaction to the *Schware* and *Konigsberg* decisions with the statement, "It looks as if the witch hunt is drawing to a close."[21] Agreeing with this sentiment was an article in the National Lawyers Guild publication, *Lawyers Guild Review*. National Lawyers Guild attorneys had represented Konigsberg, and three other members of the Guild had written an amicus curie brief in his support. The article, entitled, "Schware, Konigsberg, and Independence of the Bar: The Return to Reason," stated that these decisions offered "substantial grounds for the hope that the political test may be discarded as a qualification for obtaining or retaining a lawyer's license. . . . At the least we can say a new direction has definitely been set."[22]

As occasionally happens, the "new direction" set by these two cases did not ultimately help one of the individuals involved. At the end of the *Konigsberg* decision the majority stated, "A lifetime of good citizenship is worth very little if it is so frail that it cannot withstand the suspicions which apparently were the basis for the Committee's action. The judgment of the court below [California Supreme] is reversed and the case remanded for further proceedings not inconsistent with this opinion."[23]

With this decision in hand, Konigsberg asked the California Supreme Court for immediate admission to the bar. The court instead sent the matter back to the Bar Committee for further consideration. Another hearing was held in which Konigsberg introduced further evidence of his good character, but he again refused to answer questions about membership in the Communist Party, thus raising the issue of whether he was obstructing a full investigation of his qualifications. The Committee declined to certify him, and the California Supreme Court again refused review. In 1961 the case went back to the U.S. Supreme Court.

This time the majority shifted. Warren, Brennan, Black, and Douglas held for Konigsberg, but Frankfurter, Clark, Whittaker, Harlan, and a new justice, Potter Stewart (who had replaced Burton), held for the state on the grounds that the state's interest in ascertaining the fitness of those entering the bar outweighed the individual's rights to withhold answers to vital questions.[24]

To the anti-Court coalition in 1957, however, a new heresy was added to the litany of Court wrongs by these two 1957 decisions: Communists were allowed to enter the bar and to practice law. Once again, states' rights had been trampled on: the ability of states to control who became a lawyer had been invaded. Yet, whatever rancor these two decisions about entry into the legal profession caused, the Court's next major Red Scare decision would send shock waves of even greater magnitude.

Clinton Jencks had been president of a union local in New Mexico. Charged in 1950 with filing a false "Affidavit of Non-Communist Union Officer," he was convicted on largely circumstantial evidence provided by two paid FBI informers. One of them, Harvey Matusow, had already confessed to lying and inventing occurrences during his years as an informer. After a second perjury conviction, Matusow began serving a five-year jail sentence in June 1957. Matusow's subsequent recantation was raised as grounds for a new trial for Jencks, but the court refused to grant one. More important, however, both informers had testified that they had made written reports on Jencks to the FBI, and Jencks's lawyer had moved for "an order directing an inspection of reports" so that his counsel could use the reports in the cross-examination of these witnesses. Again, his motion was denied.

The majority opinion, written by Justice Brennan (the first he wrote involving Red Scare issues), emphasized what "[every experienced trial judge and trial lawyer knows [which is] the value for impeachment purposes of statements of the witness recording the events before time dulls treacherous memory."[25] By denying Jencks's request to inspect the reports, the district court judge had denied him his defense.

The implications of reversing the guilty verdict for failure to turn over the FBI reports were serious. At least five times the brethren met and discussed the case. Warren assigned Brennan to write for the majority. Brennan concluded that the demand for reports had to be a demand for a specific document and not a blind fishing expedition. But if the evidence were relevant and competent it had to be produced by the government and turned over to counsel for the defendant. The majority rejected an approach allowing the judge to first view the documents and determine their relevance before the accused got them. Instead, if the government decided not to produce the reports when ordered to do so, the criminal action had to be dismissed. Thus it was up to the government to decide "whether the public prejudice of allowing the crime to go unpunished is greater than that attendant on the possible exposure of state secrets and other confidential information in the government's possession."[26]

Justice Burton, with whom Harlan concurred, agreed with the majority, but he would have had the trial court retain discretion to examine and determine whether a document (report) was relevant or privileged. Frankfurter agreed with the majority and with Burton's concurrence. Only Clark, the former U.S. attorney general, dissented, citing his close friend J. Edgar Hoover on the need to keep FBI files "inviolate." Pointing directly to Congress to change the ruling announced by the majority (a highly unusual position for a justice to take), Clark warned that the Court had afforded to the criminal—and worse, to the subversive—"a Roman holiday for rummaging through confidential information as well as vital national secrets."[27]

Taking a calmer view, one scholar has noted that "read in its entirety, the *Jencks* opinion scarcely lived up to the nightmarish picture which Justice Clark's flamboyant dissent painted; it was not an invitation for a Communist 'Roman holiday' of rummaging through secret FBI files."[28] Yet Clark's dissent became a rallying cry for all who opposed the Court's ruling. They frequently cited Clark's language verbatim and used it to justify legislation designed to "correct" the Court's error. Behind the scenes, Justice Clark had, in conference with the brethren, agreed that the reports should have been made available, but he wanted the judge to screen them first, which was in line with Burton's concurrence. Later Clark apparently changed his mind, opting for dissent rather than joining Burton.

Frankfurter wrote to Brennan, taking the blame for the controversy that followed because he had not written a separate concurrence "sticking my pen into Tom's [Justice Clark's] hot air and puncturing his balloon." Unrealistically, he felt that his lone attack on Clark's dissent would have avoided the "rumpus" that followed and that [Attorney General] "Brownell & Co. . . . would not have made themselves the enslaved tools of Edgar Hoover."[29]

The seven-to-one (Whittaker did not participate) decision in favor of Jencks set off alarm bells at the Justice Department, in Congress, and with segments of the press. No one reacted more swiftly than J. Edgar Hoover himself. Until *Jencks*, "the Justice Department treated with disdain petitioners' contention that the government should have turned over to defense lawyers written statements furnished to the FBI by prosecution witnesses."[30] The *Jencks* decision forced it to reconsider its assessment when Jencks went free because of the government's failure to produce the statements.

Coming just two weeks before Red Monday, the *Jencks* case generated a reaction that combined with the reaction to Red Monday cases that followed soon after. But there was no confusion as to which of these decisions was the most alarming to J. Edgar Hoover. He had been preparing for the Red Monday cases with his COINTELPRO response since the Court had granted certiorari in *Yates v. United States* in October 1955, and his dirty tricks program against the American Communist Party had been operational for ten months prior to June 1957.

However, the *Jencks* decision was threatening to the FBI director because it would open to scrutiny the secret FBI files. To Hoover, this could not be allowed. The Supreme Court had proven sacrosanct against threats of reversing its Red Scare decisions of 1955–56; seventy attempts to change those earlier Court decisions may have failed. But this time, the Court would have to give way to the holy of holies—the files of J. Edgar Hoover's FBI.

In the press, and overwhelmingly in Congress, there resounded a call to reverse *Jencks*, which was then considered by some as a "dire threat to the American way of life." Senators and congressmen appeared to trip over each other in the rush to denounce the Court and to demand wide-ranging, immediate remedial legislation. To the litany of the anti-Court coalition was added the blasphemy of Communists and other criminals having access to FBI files.

A Hoover biographer explained why the FBI's reaction was so quick and hard hitting:

> Since 1949, Bureau reports identified informers by name or by category (and used the term "informant" to make such investigative techniques as break-ins, wiretaps, microphone surveillance, and mail openings) only on their administrative page. Within the body of FBI investigative reports, informants were identified by informant symbols (for example, "confidential informant T-2"). These procedures enabled the FBI to exercise total control over informers and to circumvent supervision by the Justice Department and by the courts.[31]

Judge Edward A. Tamm, a former FBI agent, called Hoover the day after the *Jencks* decision was announced to complain that the "potentials of such a ruling were tremendous." Hoover told Tamm that he had already gotten calls from various representatives and senators and that articles were to appear in the press attacking the decision. Hoover also let Tamm know that legislation was being prepared to correct the problem. Alexander Charns, who drew on recently available FBI files, has stated:

> Hoover considered the *Jencks* decision tantamount to a "burglary" of FBI offices; the day after the ruling another file was opened to track proposed legislation to remedy the problem. The Supreme Court was intruding upon the FBI's domain, and the bureau was going to enter the political fray to counteract the ruling.[32]

The day after the *Jencks* ruling, eleven House bills were introduced to deal with the decision. In all, a deluge of 101 anti-Court and anti-civil liberties bills came forth during the Eighty-Fourth Congress.[33] Louis Nichols, the number three man at the FBI, was assigned to lead the extensive FBI lobbying effort. Nichols was a good friend of Justice Clark; clearly, the Clark dissent was in tune with the position of the FBI.

Most of the published reaction reflected the FBI line: *Jencks* "has struck heavily at the effectiveness of the Federal Bureau of Investigation[34] and would "render impotent the most admired and efficient agency of the Federal government, the FBI."[35] Columnist David Lawrence called the decision "[t]reason's biggest victory," while columnist Constantine Brown asserted that the Communists had "tried every trick and subterfuge to deal a blow to our top investigative agency. . . . Now they appear to have succeeded."[36]

There were also calmer voices, both in the press and in Congress. These voices raised the issue of fair play in conducting a trial and questioned whether the ruling had realistically hampered the FBI. Typical of the liberal response was an editorial in *Commonweal*:

> We fail to see how this ruling imperils our national security, and we think the rights of an accused citizen takes primary inviolacy over the rules. . . .
> The government, and the F.B.I. as its agent, deserve respect but not unquestioning submission. The first ten amendments, let us remember, were designed to protect the citizen from the state, and not the other way around. Despite Tocqueville, we must not let the struggle against Communist tyranny lead us into tyranny of our own devising.[37]

Support for the *Jencks* decision brought together some strange bedfellows: it is rare that the *Wall Street Journal* and the *Commercial and Financial Chronicle* agree with the liberal press on civil liberties issues. In this instance, the business papers reflected the attitudes of businesses and individuals who had suffered from IRS, tariff commission, or antitrust investigations in which they were denied access to reports and documents for use in their defense.[38]

In Congress, there was no question that a bill would pass, given the power of Hoover and the anti-Court coalition and the support in the administration for corrective legislation. When Attorney General Brownell appeared before a subcommittee of the Senate Committee on the Judiciary on June 28, 1957, he opened his remarks in support of pending legislation by warning:

S. 2377 to amend the procedures for production of statements and reports in federal criminal cases is intended to correct a grave emergency in law enforcement which has resulted from the decision of the Supreme Court in Jencks v. United States in the field of federal law enforcement.[39]

Four days before, Brownell had sent a memorandum to Sherman Adams, a top assistant to the president, which recited that Brownell had met with the president on legislation "which would clarify" the *Jencks* case. He had gone on to say that the president "indicated that we should proceed and said he would like to be informed of our progress." Brownell had called it "an emergency situation" and said he was confident of "bipartisan sponsorship and support."[40]

Newspaper headlines demanding that Congress do something quickly to save the FBI, if not the country itself, hit responsive chords within the anti-Court coalition, the U.S. attorney general's office (and within it the FBI), and a broad spectrum of senators and congressmen. To gain the widest support possible, after the administration's bill was assigned to the Senate Judiciary Committee, Senator Eastland, the head of the Committee, sent it to the Subcommittee on Improvements in the Federal Criminal Code, to be chaired by Joseph C. O'Mahoney (D-Wyo.). Eastland's personal managing of the fate of the bill might well have been a kiss of death, given his white supremacist views and his history of Court bashing. O'Mahoney's liberal credentials, on the other hand, as well as his knowledge of and respect for Supreme Court decisions, helped build support for a legislative remedy.[41]

After the initial uproar had died down, calmer heads took over. Given the public outcry over the *Jencks* decision (whether justified or not) and given the power of J. Edgar Hoover's and the administration's backing, it was a foregone conclusion that a "Jencks Bill" would result. While the pressure was on, efforts to flatly overrule *Jencks* and to give the attorney general total control over inspection of documents failed. Slow-down warnings from liberals such as Wayne Morse (D-Ore.) and Joseph Clark (D-Penn.) seemed to have had an effect. Some newspapers echoed these warnings, citing Dean Erwin O. Griswold of Harvard Law School, who said that there was nothing in the *Jencks* ruling that gave the public access to FBI files.

It was clear that many of the Jencks Bill's supporters were simply on an anti-Court vendetta. Civil libertarians worried that the bill would do substantial harm to defendants. Arguments and counterarguments roiled as drafts of a variety of Jencks Bills were submitted, then debated and revised in the Senate Subcommittee. But the pressure to pass a bill was constant, and with the FBI mounting a campaign of less than subtle persuasion directed at members of Congress, in some instances, led by Hoover, it was probably irresistible.[42] After months of debate and drafting of versions, the fifth incarnation of a Jencks Bill passed the Senate on August 26, 1957, by voice vote.

In the House, the chairman of the Judiciary Committee, Emanuel Celler (D-N.Y.), was an outspoken civil libertarian: he had won the battle to stop H.R. 3 from becoming law after the *Nelson* decision. Celler argued that *Jencks* had been purposely and deliberately misinterpreted and misrepresented by the Justice Department because it disliked the ruling. But this time Celler could not stop the pressure to pass *Jencks* legislation as he had stopped H.R. 3. There was enough Red Scare leverage to effectively subdue the opposition. Hoover supplied a memorandum to the House that called the legislation "vital to the future ability of the Federal Bureau of Investigation to carry out its internal security and law enforcement responsibilities."[43]

The House, having passed a version differing from that of the Senate, required a committee to work out the differences. Compromises and changes were made; essentially, the final bill reflected the Senate version. The conference report version of the Jencks Bill was then passed in the Senate, 74–2 on August 29, 1957, and the next day in the House, 315–0. The president signed it into law as the "Demands for Production of Statements and Reports of Witnesses" act three days later.[44]

What, then, was the meaning and result of the Jencks Act? Walter F. Murphy, the leading scholar on the matter, has written:

The Warren Court's friends claimed that the Jencks law actually was no more than a codification of the High Bench's decision. The Court critics, on the other hand, claimed that they had slapped the Justices, lightly but meaningfully, across their robed wrists. Both sides were right to a degree.

The new statute did go a long way toward codifying the *Jencks* decision, although it followed more closely the procedures suggested in Burton's concurrence than in Brennan's majority opinion. With the exception of a few southerners and a handful of conservative Republicans in the House, almost all of the bill's supporters had taken great care to point out that they were not attacking the Warren Court. Mark Antony, of course, had disavowed criticizing Brutus, but the final bill would hardly have received the votes of almost every liberal

Court defender in both houses of Congress if such a legislative purpose had been widely accepted.[45]

An analysis by the *New Republic* found that "The legislation that emerged from the Jencks debate is not in our judgment the catastrophe for civil liberties that some liberals have claimed." The editorial went on to summarize the Jencks Act and concluded that the act did not gut the majority decision. Beyond following the Burton concurrence's choice of using the trial judge as the arbiter of what would be released to the defense, the most important provision of the act was to strike the testimony of any witness in the event that the government refused to produce that witness's statement, rather than having the indictment dismissed, as called for by the majority decision.[46]

Disregarding the actual details of the act, newspaper articles gave the public the impression that the Court had been rebuked and that the FBI had been rescued by quick action by Congress. Now FBI files were protected "from Earl Warren's Supreme Court's pro-communist decision."[47]

Yet passage of the Jencks Act only whetted the anti-Court coalition's appetite for more legislation. The southern segment of the coalition could never forgive the Court for *Brown* and its progeny. Fierce anti-Communists were angered by the what they saw as the Court's dismal record of wrongs and sensed the chance for further incursions against the Court. They similarly felt the urgency to act, given the waning public interest in Red Scare issues. It was noticeable, however, that a number of leading newspapers did not even feature the passage of the Jencks Act. If even the ultraconservative *Chicago Tribune* failed to include the act in its list of principal achievements of the first session of the Eighty-Fifth Congress, anti-Court forces realized that there was less public interest in Red Scare issues, resulting in greater difficulty in obtaining further legislation.

Red Monday: The Service Decision

June 17, 1957 came exactly two Mondays after the announcement of *Jencks*. Mondays, when the Court was in session, were always the days it announced its rulings on pending cases. This near end-of-term Monday was, for the anti-Court coalition, Red Monday—the day the Reds won—because of four decisions: *Service, Watkins, Sweezy,* and *Yates.* It was a long-awaited day; one of these cases, *Yates,* had been pending for a year and a half. While J. Edgar Hoover had been anticipating the Court's changed position, he was nevertheless bitter about it. Particularly after the *Jencks* decision, Hoover encouraged media attacks against the Warren Court.

The least controversial of the four decisions was *Service v. Dulles et al.*,[48] which involved a career foreign service officer, John Stewart Service, who had been discharged by order of Secretary of State Dean Acheson. Service had been a foreign service officer in China between 1935 and 1945. When he returned to the United States he gave some foreign service reports to the editor of *Amerasia* magazine. The editor, Service, and others were arrested and charged with violating the Espionage Act of 1917. However, the grand jury refused to indict Service and he was restored to active duty.

After President Harry S Truman ordered the establishment of a loyalty program, Service was subjected to loyalty investigations over many years; each time he was cleared as not a security risk and not disloyal, often after extensive hearings. These rounds of investigations, hearings, and "post-audit" reviews continued until December 1951, when a Loyalty Review Board on a "further post-audit" of the Loyalty Security Board (which had found favorably for him) advised the secretary of state to fire him. This Dean Acheson did under authority of the McCarran Rider, which gave the secretary "absolute discretion." The issues generated by the case involved whether regulations governing loyalty and security cases were applicable to someone discharged under the McCarran Rider and, if so, whether those regulations were violated by Service's discharge.

At the conference on April 5, 1957, after oral argument, the chief justice was troubled by the "absolute discretion" given to the secretary; he thought it was intended to mean "final," not absolutely arbitrary. Justice Black convinced him to reverse the lower court's decision on the narrower grounds that a government agency was bound by its own regulations and that those regulations had not been followed. All agreed with this approach except Burton and Whittaker, who would have affirmed. Clark stated that he would not participate unless there was a four-to-four tie. The chief justice assigned the opinion to Harlan, who wrote so convincingly that Benton and Whittaker joined him, leaving Clark simply not participating.[49]

Writing for a unanimous Court, Justice Harlan found that the regulations had been written to protect employees from unfounded accusations of disloyalty. Those regulations were applicable despite the McCarran Rider; therefore, the Service discharge had been improper.

To appreciate the *Service* decision is, however, to understand its broader Red Scare implications. Service had been caught up in the controversy over the "loss" of China to the Chinese Communists. The Nationalist lobby in Congress was very strong. After the fall of China to Communist control in 1949, the question was how it could have happened after all the money and effort expended to keep China allied to the United States. The China Lobby's answer was subversion by pro-

Communists. Service had written reports critical of the Chinese Nationalists during World War II. (The fact that they were truthful was beside the point.) Because of these reports, and because Louis Budenz, former Communist, former general manager of the Communist *Daily Worker*, and highly prized and paid informer, labeled Service as "pro-Communist," Service fell under attack.

Having lost his job in 1951, Service spent his next years, until the Supreme Court decision, working in a factory. Although he later got his State Department job back, he had only a limited security clearance and remained in low-level positions until he retired.[50]

Ed Cray, in the latest biography of Justice Warren, relates what was happening at the time: that Service was scapegoated by supporters of Chiang Kai-shek for the fall of China and that political pressure from the pro-Chiang China Lobby was involved in the Loyalty Review Board's decision.[51] That was in 1951. In 1957, under a new Supreme Court majority and with the Korean War (which had brought U.S. troops into confrontation with the Communist Chinese) fading from national memory, the response was different. The changed times were further demonstrated by the China Lobby's failure to get President Eisenhower to "unleash" Chiang to fight in Korea or to obtain the president's support for a Nationalist return to the mainland from the island of Formosa.

Red Monday: The Watkins Decision

"We approach the questions presented [in *Watkins v. United States*] with conscious awareness of the far-reaching ramifications that can follow from a decision of this nature."[52] With these thoughts, Chief Justice Warren, writing the majority opinion, moved the Supreme Court into an area of Red Scare issues that was highly controversial: the extent of the powers of the House Committee on Un-American Activities and, implicitly, the powers of all similar congressional investigating committees.

The case that brought this issue to the Court involved John T. Watkins, a union vice president who had been subpoenaed to appear before HUAC in Chicago in 1954. His case was perhaps unique in that he had readily answered Committee questions. He had said that although he had never joined the Communist Party, he could understand why informers would think that he had. That was because "from approximately 1942 to 1947, [he] cooperated with the Communist Party and participated in Communist activities to such a degree that some persons may [have] honestly believe[d] [he] was a member of the party."[53] Watkins's candor was so engrossing to Warren that his opinion extensively set forth Watkins's testimony. The Court noted that *Watkins* was not "the case of a truculent or contumacious witness who refuses to answer all questions or who, by boisterous or discourteous conduct, disturbs the decorum of the committee room."[54]

Furthermore, Watkins had refused to shield himself with the Fifth Amendment, but he did draw a line beyond which he would not go:

> I will not, however, answer any questions with respect to others with whom I associated in the past. I do not believe that any law in this country requires me to testify about persons who may in the past have been Communist Party members or otherwise engaged in Communist Party activity but who to my best knowledge and belief have long since removed themselves from the Communist movement.
>
> I do not believe that such questions are relevant to the work of this committee nor do I believe that this committee has the right to undertake the public exposure of persons because of their past activities. I may be wrong, and the committee may have this power, but until and unless a court of law so holds and directs me to answer, I most firmly refuse to discuss the political activities of my past associates.[55]

Even the government's brief noted Watkins's complete and candid statement about his political associations and activities. But because Watkins had drawn a line with his principled statement (framed by his attorney, Joseph Rauh[56]), he was cited for contempt of Congress, found guilty, and given the minimum fine under the statute, $100. He was also sentenced to one year in prison, but the sentence was suspended and he was placed on probation. The light sentence appeared to have been a response to how Watkins and his counsel had handled themselves before the Committee. When viewed in the context of prior contempt cases, *Watkins* appeared to be a well-orchestrated test case for the new Supreme Court majority.

When *Watkins* came to the Court on certiorari, only Justices Reed and Minton voted against hearing the case, and they were both off the Court by the time the case came up for conference discussion on March 8, 1957. Justice Burton, who most probably would have been with the majority, disqualified himself because his nephew had been the government's chief trial counsel.[57] At the conference, all but Justice Clark agreed with the chief justice that Watkins's conviction should be reversed. Thereafter, memorandums circulated among the justices as they worked out agreements on the legal focus and language of the majority opinion. This process continued until early June, by which time all the justices subscribed to the Warren opinion except for Frankfurter, who wrote a concurrence, and Clark, who wrote a dissent. Whittaker and Burton did not participate.

Both the Warren opinion and Clark's dissent were long and quite elaborate. The chief justice gave an extended history of contempt as it had been used by the English Parliament and then the U.S. Congress. He focused on the legislature's exercise of the contempt power and the fact that it was subject to judicial review. Warren confirmed that witnesses indicted for contempt of Congress were to be afforded the same rights as defendants in criminal cases. After his historical review, Warren's focus shifted to the explosion of contempt cases during the Cold War-Red Scare years and then to the *Watkins* case.

In line with suggestions the chief justice had received from other justices, the *Watkins* ruling stated that the power of inquiry by a committee performing an investigation was broad but not unlimited. A legislative purpose had to be demonstrable (not a mere semblance of purpose) in order to justify probing into private affairs. The legitimate interest of Congress as it related to legislating had to be evident. Exposure for exposure's sake—even if the goal was the "education" of the public—was insufficient to force the unwilling witness to answer questions when the alternative was to face contempt proceedings.

Because the Bill of Rights applied to congressional committee investigations, private rights had to be protected from unjustifiable encroachment by the legislature. Finding that the authorizing resolution for HUAC had been too vague and that the committee chairman had not reasonably defined what the inquiry was about, Watkins, the majority stated, had had the right to refuse to answer. The Court found that the explanation the committee chairman had given Watkins as to why he had to answer was "woefully inadequate to convey sufficient information as to the pertinency of the questions to the subject under inquiry." "Fundamental fairness" was at the heart of Warren's approach and reasoning.[58]

What was perhaps of greatest significance, however, was the short concurrence written by Justice Frankfurter. Frankfurter, the leading proponent of judicial restraint, sensitivity, and deference with respect to the powers of Congress and the limited role of the Court, joining in the majority, held that a witness must have "awareness of the pertinency of the information that he has denied to Congress." In other words, the questions asked of Watkins had not been pertinent to the committee's inquiry. The concurrence reflected Frankfurter's willingness to vote with the new chief justice and the former dissenting minority on Red Scare cases.

Almost equally important, to the extent that his vote solidified a new majority for Red Scare cases, was the position taken by Justice Harlan. With the exception of the *Konigsberg* case, Harlan had either joined in concurring opinions supporting the majority or voted with the majority in all Red Scare cases from the time he had joined the Court through the Red Monday cases. That he often did so reluctantly, preferring the narrower reasoning of Frankfurter or Burton, was apparent.[59] It was not until later that Harlan began dissenting from the position of the chief justice, Douglas, Brennan, and Black. In the 1956–57 term, with its Red

Monday cases, Harlan not only was with the new majority, he authored two of the Red Monday decisions.

Justice Clark's dissent was consistent with his dissenting position in the *Jencks* case. There he had held that protection of FBI files was superior to the rights of the accused. In *Watkins* the majority held that congressional investigating powers took precedence over any individual's right to resist answering questions so long as those questions were clearly pertinent to the legislative inquiry. In his *Watkins* dissent, Clark admitted that the "rules of conduct placed upon the Committee (HUAC) by the House admit of individual abuse and unfairness. But that is none of [the Court's] affair." His deferential defense of the powers of Congress in establishing and broadly authorizing investigating committees sounded much like the voice, if not the sophisticated theories and writings, of an earlier Justice Frankfurter.

Watkins v. United States was the first articulation of the broad constitutional principles that placed limits on congressional powers of investigation. That it was a Red Scare case involving HUAC made it all the more significant and controversial. In the eyes of the anti-Court coalition, it added to the list of "wrongs" committed by the Court. However, the controversy engendered by the ruling combined with the change in Court membership and the shifting views of some justices to limit these principles in the years that followed.

Red Monday: The *Sweezy* Decision

Paul M. Sweezy was a university professor who had been the subject of an investigation conducted by Louis C. Wyman, attorney general of New Hampshire. Under that state's laws, the legislature had appointed the attorney general as a one-person committee to ferret out violations of the state's 1951 Subversive Activities Act, including determining "whether subversive persons . . . [were] presently located within this state."[60] Wyman was simply to identify such persons and label them as "subversives."

Sweezy had been summoned twice to appear before Wyman, once in January 1954 and again in June of that year. Calling himself a "classical Marxist," Sweezy denied that he had ever been a Communist Party member or that he had been part of any program to overthrow the government by force or violence. The initial interrogation covered much of Sweezy's life. He answered most questions, but he refused to answer questions about the Progressive Party of New Hampshire or about persons with whom he had been acquainted in that organization.[61]

Behind the initial interrogation and the subsequent one was Louis C. Wyman. It was Wyman who had persuaded the New Hampshire legislature to pass the Subversive Activities Act of 1951, which was modeled after a similar statute in Maryland. Wyman had eagerly sought the authority the act gave him, and he used the investigative powers conferred on him to hammer at all perceived Red enemies. The fact that the FBI had identified only forty-three members of the Communist Party in the entire state of New Hampshire or that in 1948 the Progressive Party got only 1,970 votes there (0.84 percent of the votes cast) did not deter Wyman's anti-Red crusade.[62]

The fervor of the man was exemplified by his willingness to label dissident groups and individuals as "subversive" or communist "dupes" in shotgun fashion. Less than three months after the *Sweezy* ruling, Wyman spoke as president of the National Association of Attorneys General before the District of Columbia Bar Association. His speech not only attacked the Supreme Court decision in *Sweezy* and the other Red Monday cases as "quite literally offer[ing] real encouragement to increased Communist activity the length and breadth of the United States," but concluded, "It is a tragedy of the highest order that at this time in history, the door should be opened wider to Communism in the United States. These [Supreme Court] decisions do just that."[63] For this Cold War–Red Scare warrior, the times had not changed.

It was Wyman's June 1954 questioning of Sweezy that led to Sweezy's contempt conviction and appeal. He was questioned about his former wife's political associations, about the politics of others, and about a lecture he had given in a humanities course at the University of New Hampshire. The lecture was only the third Sweezy had been invited to give in three years. Maintaining that the questions about his beliefs and the contents of his lectures were protected by the First Amendment, Sweezy refused to answer.

In the Supreme Court, Chief Justice Warren again, as in *Watkins*, took the lead. He sensed an essentially unfair quality to the state proceeding and sought to impose broad constitutional constraints on the state legislature and its one-person investigating committee. Warren's position was that Sweezy's conviction wrongfully reflected "an invasion of petitioner's liberties in the area of academic freedom and political expression— areas in which government should be extremely reticent to tread."[64]

What troubled Frankfurter and Harlan was that the Court was moving beyond its traditional scope of review. Though the *Watkins* and *Sweezy* cases had been combined in conference discussions and memorandums that circulated among the justices, Justice Frankfurter wrote Warren, saying, "For me there is a wide, wide gulf between the issues of judicial review raised by refusals to answer [questions] in a congressional investigation and refusals to answer in an investigation conducted by state authority."[65] To Frankfurter, "there remains only the limitation upon state power implied by the due process clause of the Fourteenth Amendment." He called on Warren to limit his majority opinion, adding, "I suppose I am influenced by the fact of a quarter-century of my life as a university teacher . . . [and] the relation of universities to the state has been a chief concern of mine." His argument also reflected his view of "[the Court's] very limited function of review over state action."[66]

Thus Justice Frankfurter agreed with Warren that the conviction should be reversed because Sweezy's First Amendment rights, applicable to the states through the Fourteenth Amendment's due process clause, had been violated. But he would go no further. To Frankfurter, Warren's opinion violated the separation of powers and the sovereignty of the state.

Justice Harlan essentially agreed with Frankfurter's approach and told Warren so; he said, "I am ready to join in your opinion in *Watkins*. I must confess, however, to having great difficulty with the *Sweezy* opinion."[67] Warren fought back with a three-page memorandum addressed to "Dear Felix" on June 5, 1957, in which he attempted to convince Frankfurter to adopt his position on the abuse of investigatory power by state legislatures. Warren argued:

In my judgment, the vital consideration in the field of legislative investigations is not to be found in a formula for the questions that may be asked. The cause of the problem is the abuse of power by investigators for a variety of reasons. We could go a long way toward eliminating those abuses by requiring a greater assumption of responsibility by the full legislature. The entire assembly will at least not be guided by the personal motives that frequently seem to lead to the most egregious cases. In short, the problem of the nature of judicial review of investigations by the Congress or State Legislatures can be enormously reduced, I feel sure, if we strip away a measure of the personal vendetta power that exists.[68]

Warren felt this reform could be accomplished without seriously interfering with a state's legislative function. Frankfurter and Harlan disagreed; thus, while Warren incorporated some changes that Frankfurter had suggested, the result was that a majority consisting of Warren, Brennan, Black, and Douglas reversed Sweezy's contempt conviction with Frankfurter and Harlan merely concurring in the result.

In his concurrence, Justice Frankfurter drew a sharp line in favor of academic, intellectual, and political autonomy for the individual under the Constitution. He wrote:

The inviolability of privacy belonging to a citizen's political loyalties has so overwhelming an importance to the well-being of our kind of society that it cannot be constitutionally encroached upon the basis of so meager a countervailing interest of the State as may be argumentatively found in the remote, shadowy threat to the security of New Hampshire allegedly presented in the origins and contributing elements of the Progressive Party and in petitioner's relations to these.[69]

Justice Clark's dissent, in which Justice Burton joined, was a stinging rebuke of the Warren opinion as a denial of the right of the state of New Hampshire to investigate subversion in its chosen manner. Clark agreed with Frankfurter and Harlan that the internal affairs of the state "are of no concern to us"—the same thought he had expressed on the investigative procedures used by congressional committees at the core of the *Watkins* case.[70] Clark's major thrust was that the Court had the right to intervene only if Sweezy's constitutional rights were superior to that of the state's interest in uncovering subversive activities. He believed that they were not.

Clark wrote that his intent when he had joined the majority in the *Nelson* case (where states were barred from prosecuting subversion against the nation) had been to leave the states a "wide field" for action in the anti-Red campaign so long as they dealt with areas other than that of federal jurisdiction. He also saw no First Amendment questions in *Sweezy*.

In stark contrast to Clark's interpretation of *Sweezy* was Warren's view on why Sweezy's conviction had to be reversed:

> Our form of government is built on the premise that every citizen shall have the right to engage in political expression and association. This right was enshrined in the First Amendment of the Bill of Rights. Exercise of these basic freedoms in America has traditionally been through the media of political associations. Any interference with the freedom of a party is simultaneously an interference with the freedom of its adherents.[71]

Clark, however, maintained, "I am not convinced that the State's interest in investigating subversive activities for the protection of its citizens is outweighed by any necessity for the protection of Sweezy."[72]

Justices Warren, Frankfurter, Harlan, and Brennan all expressed strong sentiments concerning the *Sweezy* case. Bernard Schwartz has written that the justices "clearly wanted to strike at McCarthyism's insidious assault on academic freedom."[73]

The liberal press celebrated the *Watkins* and *Sweezy* decisions in glowing terms. I. F. Stone wrote:

> We have come to the end of an era. . . .
> The *Watkins* and *Sweezy* decisions must be read together. They promise a new birth of freedom. They make the First Amendment a reality again. They reflect the steadily growing public misgiving and distaste for that weird collection of opportunists, clowns, ex-Communist crackpots, and poor sick souls who have

made America look foolish and even sinister during the last ten years with their perpetual searching under the national bed for little men who weren't there. The full measure of the agony and suffering they have inflicted will never be known. We are grateful to the Chief Justice and to the Court, and we may all be proud as Americans that the great traditions of our country had sufficient strength to overcome them at last.[74]

While Stone celebrated the changes attributable to the new Court majority and the changed times, two of his assumptions were incorrect: that these decisions would be acceptable to the conservative press and that the anti-Court coalition would not attempt a renewed attack on the Court in Congress. Impairing or limiting the power of congressional investigating committees and encroaching on states' powers were bound to create resistance, notwithstanding the status of the Supreme Court and despite changed times. Furthermore, the Court could retreat in the face of such pressures. The new majority was not molded of stone; it could change back to being a minority on Red Scare issues if the dangers of not doing so were evident enough to change justices' minds.

Red Monday: The *Yates* Decision

As anticipated, the Supreme Court's decision in *Dennis v. United States*[75] in 1951 sanctioned the prosecution of Communist Party members. In New York the most notable of the prosecutions that followed involved prominent Party leaders, headed by Elizabeth Gurley Flynn, a member of the Party's National Committee.[76] The entire group were found guilty, which was hardly remarkable given the times and the *Dennis* ruling. An appeal of their convictions to the U.S. Court of Appeals for the Second Circuit was upheld in October 1954 by a three-judge appeals panel. Judge John Marshall Harlan II, who was then on that court, wrote the opinion, which was completely deferential to the government; without doubt, it helped secure his endorsement by the Eisenhower administration for a Supreme Court seat in March 1955. Yet Harlan was the justice who would write the *Service* and *Yates* decisions for the Court majority in June 1957.

As a judge on the U.S. Court of Appeals, Harlan had accepted and approved of the reasoning behind the *Dennis* case, which had reflected Learned Hand's "gravity of the evil" extension of the "clear and present danger" test. Nevertheless, Harlan's clerks said that Harlan believed anti-Communist legislation was "McCarthyite garbage" and that Harlan even entertained doubts about the Smith Act's constitutionality.[77]

The explanation for Harlan's complete turnabout on the validity of Smith Act prosecutions was, and remains, elusive.[78] He knew that the Supreme Court had turned down the *Flynn* appeal for a writ of certiorari, in effect confirming the opinion he had authored as an appeals court judge. He would not, however, endorse the Black/Douglas view that the Smith Act should be declared unconstitutional, a ruling that would have resulted in the reversal of ninety prior convictions. Yet it was Harlan who wrote the majority's *Yates* decision, which pragmatically emasculated the government's chances for further Smith Act convictions.[79] A dramatic change in Harlan's view was involved.

In October 1955, Harlan was on the Court when the vote was taken on whether to grant certiorari in *Yates*. A year later, he heard the two-day oral argument given by the petitioners' and government's lawyers on the case. Harlan was to participate in a number of conferences concerning *Yates* and was apparently influenced by Justice Frankfurter, who was similarly changing his view on the Smith Act, and whose jurisprudential approach resonated with Harlan's. Furthermore, these were the "calmer times" that Justice Black had hoped for, when "pressures, passions and fears" had subsided enough so that a majority of the Court "would restore the First Amendment liberties to the high preferred place where they belong in a free society."[80]

Oleta O'Connor Yates had been a Communist Party leader in California for many years prior to her indictment for violation of the Smith Act. She and thirteen other Communists were tried before a judge who was a devoted member of the American Legion (which was vehemently anticommunist) and who apparently went out of his way to give the Smith Act defendants a hard time. Judge William Mathes set "reasonable" bail at $50,000 for each defendant for an offense involving a maximum sentence of only five years. Because of the high bail, the defendants remained in jail for more than one hundred days until the Supreme Court ruled that the amount was not reasonable for the charges being prosecuted. Judge Mathes, after taking almost a month to mull the matter over, then decided that, notwithstanding the Supreme Court's determination, $50,000 was indeed reasonable bail. It took further appeals to reduce the bail to a fraction of what the trial judge felt was reasonable.[81]

The hard time given the defendants by Judge Mathes had been preceded by ugliness and callousness in their arrest and arraignment. At their arraignment, one federal judge had described the defendants' alleged offense as "more serious than treason." The prejudice against the defendants was just as evident during the trial.

The *Yates* trial commenced in Los Angeles on February 1, 1952 and lasted until August 6, 1952. All fourteen defendants were found guilty. During the trial, most of the defendants did not take the stand. Yates did and was asked on cross-examination whether she had known certain persons in her role as secretary of the Communist Party for California. She refused to answer, and Judge Mathes promptly found her in contempt of court. Over pleas to allow Yates to stay out of jail until her testimony was finished, the judge had her confined every night for five hot weeks in July and August 1952. Thereafter the judge sentenced her to one year in prison for contempt. When he sentenced the other defendants he gave them each the maximum fine and jail sentence that the law allowed. For Yates, however, he added a further three-year contempt sentence because of her continued refusal to name names. All the contempt convictions were eventually reversed on appeal.[82]

Yet the California Communists were more fortunate than those who had been tried and convicted in the New York (the *Flynn* case) and Baltimore Smith Act trials. The defendants there were all in jail, while the California defendants (except Yates) were out on bail because the Supreme Court had issued a writ of certiorari, agreeing on October 17, 1955 to hear their case. All others found guilty in Smith Act trials across the country had lost their pleas to obtain review of their convictions by the Supreme Court.

After more than four years, the Court granted its first writ of certiorari to review a Smith Act case since the *Dennis* ruling. It can only be speculated why the needed votes were there in October 1955 and not before. The votes of Warren, Black, and Douglas had to be joined by Frankfurter or Harlan (if not both) to stem the tide of Communist prosecutions. Perhaps either Frankfurter or Harlan (if not both) was willing to take another look at the ongoing Smith Act prosecutions. The number of Communists behind bars was already impressive. Frankfurter and Harlan may have felt that continued jailing of these dissidents had gone too far.

The vote to take the *Yates* case may have been influenced by the number and stature of those requesting the right to file friend-of-the-court briefs on behalf of the California group. One was the California-Arizona Conference of the Methodist Church, which struck a note that must have produced sympathetic responses among some of the brethren. "In this area [*sic*] of relaxed international tensions, when an attempt is being made in a peaceful world atmosphere to foster a true appreciation of American ideals, it would be anomalous and harmful for this court to place its stamp of approval on constitutional encroachments in the area of human rights."[83] As had happened before and would happen again in the nation's legal history, the petition came at the right time, to the right Court, with a newly emerging majority.

Just a week short of one year after granting certiorari in *Yates*, the Court allowed two days of oral arguments, on October 8 and 9, 1956. The importance of the case was highlighted by the unusually long time allowed the lawyers to present their arguments. Another eight months were to pass before the justices were ready to announce their decision.

The first conference of the brethren to discuss the *Yates* case took place three days after the oral argument. The justices had the briefs of the parties and had heard their arguments on the issues. As was correct procedure, the chief justice spoke first. He believed that the government had not shown that the purpose of the Communist Party was to use force and violence and concluded that the government's case was "weak, not substantial." Warren stated that only the membership of the defendants in the Communist Party had been proved, not unlawful conduct or overt acts, and that "nothing was shown there to prove advocacy of force and violence." In addition, Warren stressed that the time when the *Yates* case was tried (1952) was a very hostile time for all Communists. He exemplified this by pointing out that a congressional committee had released an FBI report "at a crucial time [that contained] a series of lurid articles." Once again, Warren sensed unfairness.[84]

Black and Douglas not only agreed that reversal of all the guilty verdicts was necessary but also called these verdicts examples of political trials that the First Amendment was supposed to prevent. Reed, Minton, Clark, and Burton, however, said they would vote to affirm the convictions. But Minton and then Reed were soon to be gone from the Court, and Burton was to change his position.

The crucial views were those of Frankfurter and Harlan, both of whom said they were not then ready to vote. Frankfurter, however, expressed gratification for Warren's emphasis in his remarks on an atmosphere that "fouled the air of this trial." Harlan, significantly, stated that if teaching incitement was necessary, he felt that the jury instructions used in the trial had been faulty.[85]

With a fragmented response from the brethren on how they would vote, Warren put the case over until the November 2, 1956, conference. By then Minton had retired. Reed, Burton, and Clark again voted to affirm. Warren, Douglas, and Black were for reversal. This time Frankfurter, and Harlan voted to reverse, both citing confusing, inadequate jury instructions. The vote was thus five for reversal, three for affirming.

As was his prerogative, Chief Justice Warren chose Harlan to write for the majority. Warren's strategy was to win backing from other justices by focusing the opinion on issues that would garner the broadest support. An opinion by Warren, Black, or Douglas would not garner such backing. With Harlan at the helm, the decision would be on solid but narrow grounds and muted in tone. The Smith Act would not be declared unconstitutional, but the pragmatic result would be to cease the prosecutions of Communists on the basis of advocacy of violent overthrow of the government, which had been the linchpin of prosecutions to that time.

For all his caution, Justice Harlan was, at least temporarily, to find himself (like Black, Douglas, and Warren) anathema to a broad range of anti-Court voices that viewed his *Yates* opinion as an act of treachery. For the first time he was a target of anti-Communist hate mail. Only in subsequent cases, as he gained the status of the "Great Dissenter of the Warren Court," was he restored to the good graces of conservatives, including the president whose nomination had given him his seat on the Court.[86]

The *Yates* case contains many significant contrasts, demonstrating that defense lawyers in Smith Act prosecutions had changed their strategy in response to the changed times and the changed composition of the high court. From a reading of the appellate briefs and other documents used by the defending attorneys in *Dennis* and of those used by the defending attorneys in the *Yates* case, a marked contrast becomes clear. The *Dennis* lawyers continued their courtroom theme of political warfare in their appellate briefs, including those addressed to the Supreme Court. Thus the language condemned the federal government as a repressive agency attempting to hamper remedies for social and economic ills. The *Dennis* lawyers attacked the constitutionality of the Smith Act, even arguing that, since "fascist" elements favored the Smith Act, its avowed purpose of curbing both communism and fascism was defeated. Defense lawyers also averred that the true intent of the prosecutions had been to curb the liberal trade union movement led by the Congress of Industrial Organizations (CIO). Ultimately, they stated that the case was a political persecution of members of a political party. The government had failed to prove any conspiracy to advocate a violent revolution. Moreover, the defense argued, the good acts of the defendants outweighed any slight evidence of conspiracy.[87]

In the *Dennis* briefs were appeals to the importance of freedom of advocacy of ideas and of political doctrines in a democracy. The *Dennis* briefs argued that ideas have social value because they offer reasons to change society and that the Smith Act was imprecise, too sweeping, and could only serve to deter political discussion and to chill free speech.

The contrast to the argument in *Yates* is immediately evident. The tone in the *Yates* briefs was more restrained; there is much less overt condemnation of the government. The salient feature in the *Yates* briefs was that they were fact-specific. These attorneys were off the soapbox. They grounded their arguments on specific acts of their clients and the lack of requisite intent.

Even in their expositions on constitutionality, the defendants were again fact-specific, balancing the government's security interest against the need for free expression in a democracy. No arguments were directly addressed to the legitimacy of the Smith Act itself. Instead, the defendants essentially focused on the absence of evidence to convict, pointing out, for example, that proof of opportunity is not proof of conspiracy.

Clearly, the times and the opportunity militated that they put forth arguments in form and substance, in writing and orally, that would convince the new majority, which had granted certiorari, to aid their clients, and thereby end these and all other prosecutions under the Smith Act.

It is also evident that the *Yates* briefs were much more "traditional," that is, more lawyerlike, than the work of the *Dennis* lawyers. It takes little imagination to understand the excitement that must have surrounded the work of the *Yates* attorneys. Here was the first opportunity since *Dennis* to argue before the Supreme Court on Smith Act convictions.

The defendants in the *Yates* decision had been convicted of violating the Smith Act, and specifically of organizing the Communist Party to carry out the intent to advocate the overthrow of the government by force and violence as speedily as circumstance would permit.

Justice Harlan wrote for a majority that included Warren and Frankfurter. Black and Douglas wrote to affirm what the majority had done, but dissented by calling for a total reversal of all fourteen convictions. Harlan's ruling had exonerated only five of the defendants, allowing the government the right to retry the other nine if it chose to do so. Justice Brennan, having arrived on the bench a week after the oral argument on the case, did not participate in the decision. Burton switched from favoring affirming the convictions to writing a separate one-paragraph statement concurring with Harlan's opinions. Whittaker did not participate, leaving only Clark as a dissenter; it was Clark's third dissent in the four Red Monday cases.

The task before the brethren was daunting. The record generated by the *Yates* trial was 14,000 typewritten pages. The Harlan opinion was 43 printed pages long. Black's concurrence and dissent followed by Clark's dissent took another 12 pages.

The initial sections of the Harlan opinion focused on the use of the word "organize" in the Smith Act as a charge against all fourteen defendants. In 1944 the Communist Party had, under Earl Browder's leadership, disbanded as a formal political party. This was part of his strategy to make Communists appear willing to play a role within the existing political framework and therefore appear more acceptable. But in early 1946 Browder had been deposed and expelled from a newly reconstituted Communist Party. His statement, "We [Communists] are the Americans, and Communism is the Americanism of the twentieth century," was acceptable during the war years (after Russia was invaded). But with the end of the war and the development of the Cold War, Browder's leadership lost favor and the "political association," as it was called, was reorganized as a political party in 1945.[88]

The conspiracy to organize was alleged by the government to have originated in 1945 and continued down to the date of the indictment

Figure 8. Oleta Yates speaking before dockworkers on the San Francisco water-front. It was her appeal from her Smith Act conviction that became the *Yates* decision on Red Monday. UPI/Corbis-Bettmann photograph.

in 1951. All the *Yates* defendants had been accused and thereafter found guilty of organizing a party as part of the conspiracy to overthrow the government. All these convictions, Harlan held, were defective because the Smith Act had a three-year statute of limitations for prosecution.

The Court majority accepted the petitioners' claim that "organize" meant "establish," "found," or "bring into existence," which logically and plainly fitted with the 1945 event. It rejected the government's contrary interpretation. Digging deeply into American legal history, Harlan quoted Chief Justice John Marshall in an early nineteenth-century opinion establishing that penal laws such as the Smith Act were to be strictly construed. Without clear guidance as to what Congress intended in using the word "organize," and finding dictionaries of little help, Harlan wrote that, without a definition in the statute itself, the ruling had to favor the defendants. He concluded:

> We are thus left to determine for ourselves the meaning of this provision of the Smith Act, without any revealing guides as to the intent of Congress. In these circumstances we should follow the familiar rule that criminal statutes are to be strictly construed and give to "organize" its narrow meaning, that is, that the word refers only to acts entering into the creation of a new organization, and not to acts thereafter performed in carrying on its activities, even though such acts may loosely be termed "organizational."[89]

The government's response was to argue that this was, in any case, a harmless error, since both charges, of organizing and advocacy, had been before the jury; the judge's instructions had included both terms as grounds for guilt. Harlan rejected this reasoning because it was impossible to tell which ground the jury had selected as the basis for its verdict. Harlan stated that the "organizing" charge in the indictment should have been removed and never been before the jury. This fact alone was enough to call for a retrial by virtue of a substantial error.

While Harlan could have stopped there, he did not. He moved on to a more controversial issue: the meaning of advocacy of violent overthrow of the government as required by the Smith Act. He wrote:

> We are thus faced with the question whether the Smith Act prohibits advocacy and teaching of forcible overthrow as an abstract principle, divorced from any effort to instigate action to that end, so long as such advocacy or teaching is engaged in with evil intent. We hold that it does not.[90]

After revisiting the leading Espionage Act cases following World War I and examining the language and intent of the Smith Act, the Court stated that the form of advocacy required to convict was proof of acts demonstrating advocacy of action to forcibly overthrow the government.

Advocacy of action—not discussion, abstract advocacy, or mere advocacy in the realm of ideas—was needed. And here, unlike in the *Dennis* case, the jury had not been so instructed. The fact that the *Dennis* court held advocacy of action for future overthrow sufficient meant that "advocacy, irrespective of its tendency to generate action was punishable if uttered with a sufficient intent to accomplish overthrow."[91] Mere "doctrinal justification of forcible overthrow" had been interpreted by the trial judge in the *Yates* case as sufficient; the Harlan ruling was that this was not enough.[92]

Harlan's decision in *Yates* was thus grounded on ruling that the trial court, with the court of appeals affirming, had "misconceived" the *Dennis* case, resulting in improper instructions to the jury. It had led the jury to misunderstand that it could find the defendants guilty for believing in something without also urging that action be taken.[93] The Court recognized "that distinctions between advocacy or teaching of abstract doctrines, with evil intent, and that which is directed to stirring people to action, are often subtle and difficult to grasp. . . . But the very subtlety of these distinctions required the most clear and explicit instructions . . . [because] they went to the very heart of the charges against these petitioners."[94]

Given that the core of the Court's ruling was to state that incorrect jury instruction on advocacy was a serious enough error to reverse all *Yates* convictions, it is fair to ask whether the jury, given the *Dennis* instructions or some variation that would have been acceptable to the Court majority, would have found the defendants innocent. The Court acknowledged that only subtle distinctions of language were involved. Given the times when the *Yates* case was tried, which were not that different from those when the *Dennis* case was tried, it can be argued that the jury would have returned a guilty verdict notwithstanding the use of "correct" instructions. This is not to say that juries do not take their task seriously; in fact, they do. But in the highly charged Red Scare times, with a "hot" war against communists going on during both the *Dennis* and *Yates* trials, and with both the trial judges apparently prejudiced against the defendants, the use of correct but still complicated jury instructions seems hardly likely to have insured a different result.

In English as well as American legal history, appellate courts have used errors made at trials—especially jury instruction errors—to correct a trial result. Jury instructions are supposed to state the law pertinent to the case with exactitude, so that the jury, having heard the facts, will then reach the correct verdict by applying these instructions on the law to what they have heard as evidence.

The process by which an appellate-level court goes through a record, reviewing it for error, has, under certain circumstances, been described as record worship. A leading American legal historian has commented:

> Record worship was a disease that probably did not randomly infect every type of case. Courts are stickier, for example, about small errors in cases where life or liberty is at stake. It would be no surprise, then, to find that the law of criminal procedure outdid civil procedure in record worship and technical artifice. This branch of law had a special place in American jurisprudence. The Bill of Rights contained what amounted to a miniature code of criminal procedure. The basic rights of man turned out, in large part, to be rights to fair criminal trial. . . .
>
> In a number of cases, it seemed as if the high court searched the record with a fine-tooth comb, looking for faulty instructions, improper evidence, error in formal pleadings, or prejudicial actions by the judge. Sometimes the upper court quashed an indictment for a tiny slip of the pen or set aside a verdict for some microscopic error at the trial.[95]

Was this, then, a case of "record worship" utilized to signal an end to these prosecutions of Communists? Some members of Congress thought so. Though he expressed his views in flawed and hyperbolic terms, one representative stated:

> Our present Supreme Court has developed a hypercritical faculty for finding microscopic flaws in the cases of convicted Communists. No matter how carefully and meticulously a Communist case is passed with kid gloves through the lower courts, our present Supreme Court can be trusted to find what it is pleased to call a reversible error. This is accomplished, of course, by the pattern the Supreme Court has established of usurping legislative functions, and changing the law and amending the Constitution at will.[96]

In a lengthy section of the Harlan opinion entitled "The Evidence," the record is reviewed to determine whether "the way should be left open for a new trial of all or some of the petitioners."[97] The result of that review, in effect asking whether there was, as to any of the defendants, so little evidence that "acquittal [was] unequivocally demanded," resulted in five being freed. As to the other nine, the Court said that "we would not be justified in closing the way to their retrial."[98] But the Court went further in its analysis, stating that "mere membership or the holding of office in the Communist Party" could not amount to "the requisite specific intent to accomplish such an overthrow" of the government as to be criminal.[99]

Though the Court's ruling in *Yates* left the door open to retrial of the remaining nine defendants, a fair reading indicates that the Justice Department's decision to stop further prosecutions under the Smith Act advocacy or organizing clauses was realistic. The Court was setting an evidence standard for conviction that was beyond anything the FBI could meet in its role as the investigatory agency. There had to be a specific plan of action; theoretical advocacy was not sufficient. To be criminal, the advocacy had to be reasonably and ordinarily calculable to incite people to action. So while the court did not overrule *Dennis*, its interpretation in *Yates* pragmatically destroyed the potential for further prosecutions under the organizing or advocacy portions of the Smith Act.

It can be argued, however, that if in *Yates* the advocacy charge to the jury was found to be faulty, and the evidence to be presented in the *Yates* retrial (or any other Smith Act trial) was essentially the same as in *Dennis*, why did the Justice Department after reading *Yates* substantially shut down its factory-like prosecution of Communists? Why not simply hew more exactly to the *Dennis* instructions and be more careful in preparing the evidence and the instructions? In part it was because defense lawyers reading *Yates* would emphasize to juries just what the new standard was and insist that the juries hear instructions clearly demanding proof of incitement to act in order to justify a guilty verdict. In part it was also a reflection that the times could no longer insure that juries could be counted on to find defendants invariably guilty regardless of the instructions.

In reality, the chances were slim that acts or actions that would meet the Court's standard of advocacy could be proven after 1957. Besides, the Communist Party was an empty shell, particularly after Khrushchev's "secret" speech before the Twentieth Congress of the Communist Party in Moscow on February 24, 1956. His speech exposed some—but far from all—of the evils and misdeeds of Stalin, including the phony treason trials of 1937–38, and effectively labeled Stalin as a coward, killer, and sadist. The speech was first published by the *Daily Worker*, which reprinted it in its entirety without a word of comment. The smashed idol rent asunder the small cadre of Party members in the United States who were still attached to the Party, leaving only a skeleton of true believers by 1957.[100]

Could Communist Party members and communism really have threatened the safety of the nation in 1957? To almost everyone but the most hard-bitten in the anti-Communist crusade, the answer was no. The *Yates* majority was adding a most crucial judicial "no" to the continued prosecution of Communists and other dissidents with the Red Monday, *Jencks*, and other decisions.

Herbert Block, the liberal cartoonist ("Herblock"), wrote about the Red Scare in this manner after Red Monday:

In their efforts to overcome the law of diminishing returns, Mr. [Francis E.] Walter [D-Penn.] and Mr. Hoover have tried to proclaim a kind of basic law of their own invention—that the fewer the Communists and the less their influence, the more imminent the danger from them. . . . The business of hunting Americans guilty of no crimes and of finding "subversion" in such things as free speech and freedom of assembly is not yet played out. But the chases aren't what they used to be.

The pursuers are still willing, but the audience is getting tired. And, worst of all, the pursued aren't all co-operating in quite the old way. . . . [P]eople aren't dropping the way they used to—or falling for all the old charges. As for running, the Supreme Court just sits there, handing down judicial opinions. . . . instead of fleeing when a pursuer comes roaring up, they just stand and spit in his eye.[101]

The *Yates* case demonstrated that the Court itself contained diametrically opposite views concerning the underlying threat to the country. Justice Black (joined by Justice Douglas) wrote, "I would reverse every one of these convictions and direct that all the defendants be acquitted. In my judgment the statutory provisions [of the Smith Act] on which these prosecutions are based abridge freedom of speech, press and assembly in violation of the First Amendment to the United States Constitution."[102] Black found that even under the Court's refined language calling for proof of doing something rather than believing in something, "defendants could still be convicted simply for agreeing to talk as distinguished from agreeing to act."[103] Black and Douglas believed that nothing in the record justified retrying the remaining nine, described the evidence as "flimsy," and declared that the trial judge should have directed a verdict of acquittal.[104]

Harking back to the Founding Fathers, Black closed with these thoughts:

Unless there is complete freedom for expression of all ideas, whether we like them or not, concerning the way government should be run and who shall run it, I doubt if any views in the long run can be secured against the censor. The First Amendment provides the only kind of security system that can preserve a free government—one that leaves the way wide open for people to favor, discuss, advocate, or incite causes and doctrines however obnoxious and antagonistic such views may be to the rest of us.[105]

Justice Clark's dissent reflected just the opposite of Black's views. He believed all were proven guilty of criminal acts in violation of the Smith Act and in perfect conformity with *Dennis*. To Clark, the *Yates* defendants faced the same charge as did the *Dennis* defendants, and he asserted that the trial record demonstrated that they were directly in league with the *Dennis* conspiracy. In a lengthy footnote, he reviewed the evidence against the five that were freed by the Court (pointing out that he could find no prior case where the Court had ever ordered an acquittal solely on the facts) and satisfied himself, at least, that even these five were correctly found guilty.

Clark also disagreed with the majority's view on the statute of limitations issue and that the jury instructions given contained reversible error. Interestingly, perhaps reflecting the sarcasm of a loner, Clark held that the Court, by expressing its views on the instructions as they should have been given, had actually resolved that problem for use in the retrial of the nine defendants. Clark added that, in any event, he could not understand the difference between the jury instructions condoned by the Court in *Dennis* and the ones now required in any further Smith Act trial. Clark closed his argument with these thoughts:

However, in view of the fact that the case must be retried, regardless of the disposition made here on the charges, I see no reason to engage in what becomes nothing more than an exercise in semantics with the majority about this phase of the case. Certainly if I had been sitting at the trial I would have given the *Dennis* charge, not because I consider it any more correct, but simply because it had the stamp of approval of this Court. Perhaps this approach is too practical. But I am sure the trial judge realizes now that practicality often pays.[106]

If Clark was sincere about "practicality," he should have understood that the practical result of the majority's ruling was to make further attempts to convict defendants of violating major portions of the Smith Act impractical.

The *Jencks* decision on June 10 and the Red Monday cases of June 17, 1957, were before the American public. That there would be a range of reactions in Congress, in the Justice Department, in the FBI, and in the media was a given. The Court had acted in calmer times, but not so calm that its work would fail to incite storms over what it had done.

About the Cartoons

So much has changed about the way information is transmitted to us that it is unique that one medium—the political cartoon—has remained the same for some hundreds of years.

The technique has altered very little. Using a drawing with minimal written message, the cartoonist conveys his reaction to some event or personality by caricature and juxtaposition. It endures as a form of political comment because it is effective as well as appealing.

Supreme Court rulings have been excellent grist for the cartoonists' mill throughout the nation's history. The *Jencks* and Red Monday decisions were the subject of many political cartoons. Here follows a selection of cartoons showing different responses to the Court's decisions.

Figure 9. Ferman Martin, "Rewriting the Laws Again," *Houston Chronicle,* June 19, 1957. The Supreme Court is portrayed as protecting communists and knocking over Congress—a reference to the *Yates* decision on the Smith Act, as well as the *Watkins* decision limiting the powers of investigating committees. This cartoon was published two days after Red Monday. Copyright 1957 Houston Chronicle Publishing Company. Reprinted with permission.

Figure 10. Roy Justus, "Out of the Darkness," *Minneapolis Star Tribune*, June 24, 1957. This cartoon supporting the Supreme Court's work appeared with an article that praised the Red Monday decisions. Reprinted by permission of the *Star Tribune*, Minneapolis, Minnesota.

Figure 11. Edward D. Keukes, "It's actually happening and that's hard to believe," *Cleveland Plain Dealer*, June 27, 1957. The Supreme Court's Red Monday decisions are portrayed as reflecting ignorance of the threat to the "American Way of Life." Reprinted by permission of the *Plain Dealer*, Cleveland, Ohio.

Figure 12. Karl Hubenthal or John Patrick Maloney, "Green Light for Reds," King Features Syndicate, June 26, 1957. The speaker is Nikita Khrushchev (1894–1971), premier of the USSR, who said that communism would bury capitalism. Nine persons are in the car, an obvious reference to the nine justices of the Supreme Court. The cartoonist may have been attempting to separate Justice Tom C. Clark, the consistent dissenter, by putting him in the rear, separate from the other justices. Reprinted by permission of King Features Syndicate-North American Syndicate; the Hearst Corporation.

Figure 13. Burris Jenkins, Jr., "What's Wrong with This Picture?" *New York Journal-American*, June 19, 1957. A clever statement to the effect that the Supreme Court was wrongfully "left leaning." Reprinted by permission of Burris Jenkins, Jr.

ALL OF THOSE
DECISIONS ON
THE LEFT SIDE !

Figure 14. James J. Dobbins, "Tilt," June 1957. This cartoon was syndicated to a number of papers and widely reprinted. It succinctly stated the message that the decisions of the court were "left leaning." Reprinted by permission of James J. Dobbins, Jr.

Figure 15. Raymond Evans, "And They Call It 'Justice'!" *Columbus Dispatch*, June 27, 1957. A strong presentation to the effect that the Supreme Court's "ultra-liberal" rulings favor "Communists who want to destroy our country." Reprinted by permission of the *Columbus Dispatch*, Columbus, Ohio.

Figure 16. "Herblock" (Herbert Block), "Prayer Rug," *Washington Post*, July 10, 1957. Herblock's take on the *Jencks* decision clearly indicated his view that Congress was obeying Hoover's wishes to the detriment of the rights of individuals that the court's ruling sought to protect. Herblock was among the few cartoonists willing to portray Hoover in a negative light. Reprinted by permission of Herblock and Creators Syndicate.

Figure 17. Carmack, "Open—But Not to Him," *Christian Science Monitor*, July 3, 1957. The Supreme Court decision in the *Jencks* case generated a great deal of public concern and discussion because its critics, led by J. Edgar Hoover, claimed that the FBI would be compromised if defendants could get copies of reports to the Bureau from informants and agents. The *Jencks* ruling brought immediate congressional reaction in the form of legislation to keep defendants from having access to FBI files. This cartoon, unlike many others, did not attack the Court, but rather portrayed Congress in a positive light, protecting the files from "misuse." Reprinted by permission of *the Christian Science Monitor*.

6/18/57

Figure 18. "Herblock" (Herbert Block), "Can You See Me Now?" *Washington Post*, June 18, 1957. It took only one day for famed syndicated cartoonist Herblock to produce a cartoon responding in a positive fashion to the Red Monday Supreme Court decisions. Reprinted with permission of Herblock and Creators Syndicate.

Figure 19. Cartoonist unknown, "For Safer Driving," *Christian Science Monitor*, June 19, 1957. This positive and prompt reaction to the Red Monday decisions sees the essence of the Court's rulings as did Herblock and others: individual rights gaining protection from Red Scare abuses. Reprinted by permission of the *Christian Science Monitor*.

HERBLOCK
©1957 THE WASHINGTON POST CO.
6/19/57

Figure 20. "Herblock" (Herbert Block), "Boy, Am I Burning Up," *Washington Post*,
June 19, 1957. This Herblock syndicated cartoon appeared the day after "Can
You See Me Now?" The emphasis here was on the *Watkins* and *Sweezy* decisions
of Red Monday—decisions that attacked the right of investigating committees
to expose for the sake of exposure and their failure to carry out due process in
their hearings. Both involved reversing contempt convictions against witnesses,
one by the House Un-American Activities Committee (HUAC) and the other by
the attorney general of New Hampshire. Herblock may have gotten the idea for
"burning" from the unusually hot weather as well as from the torch of the Statue
of Liberty. Reprinted by permission of Herblock and Creators Syndicate.

Chapter 9
Red Monday: The Aftermath

Newspapers: Reporting the Decisions

Which news is deemed worthy of publication, as well as the play a story is given, depends on a number of factors, not the least of which is the absence of more dramatic events. For better or worse, the heat wave that gripped the nation in mid-June 1957 was for many newspapers the major story of the moment.

Yet, regardless of the heat, the announcement that the Supreme Court had set free five convicted Communists was front-page headline material. The controversial *Jencks* decision of just two weeks before, making FBI files available to defendants, followed by the four Red Scare cases of June 17, 1957, was major news. Also, after the *Brown* decision in 1954, the Supreme Court's activism in desegregation and race-related issues had focused serious attention on a Court whose decisions were touching, even altering, the fabric of American life.

Another story poignantly related to the Red Monday decisions appeared the same day. It was the story of William K. Sherwood, age 41, a prominent biochemist and father of four who had been working under a grant from the American Cancer Society. Subpoenaed to appear before the House Committee on Un-American Activities for a hearing that was to be televised, Sherwood chose to commit suicide rather than appear before HUAC and answer its questions. The particular HUAC session in which he was to have appeared was dedicated to Communist "intellectual infiltration."

In a suicide note, Sherwood stated that "the Committee's trail is strewn with blasted lives and the wreckage of youthful careers."[1] He also said he had a "fierce resentment of being televised." For some months before he was subpoenaed, Sherwood had been interrogated by FBI agents seeking names of past associates in alleged left-wing activities.

It can only be speculated whether, had Sherwood learned of the Red Monday decisions (particularly the *Watkins* ruling), they would have eased his mind. Reading of the Court's work on June 18, 1957 could certainly have strengthened his resolve.[2]

In reporting the Red Monday decisions, some newspapers, such as the *Washington Post, Chicago Daily Tribune,* and *Los Angeles Times,* announced the Court's rulings with headlines below those reporting the continued heat wave.[3] The drama of freeing five of the *Yates* defendants and reversing the convictions of the other nine attracted the most coverage. Some reports barely mentioned the other cases in their initial reactions.

The *New York Times* put the weather report ("Record 93 Degree Heat Taxes City's Power Supply") on the bottom of its front page and devoted in-depth coverage to all four Red Monday cases in four front-page columns.[4] With a photograph of the chief justice alongside the article, a banner headline declared, "Judiciary Seen as Setting Limits on Other Branches: Supreme Court Declares Rights of Individuals Must Be Protected." James Reston wrote:

> The Supreme Court today warned all branches of the Government that they must be more faithful to the Constitutional guarantees of individual freedom.
> Reasserting its ancient role as a defender of the Constitution and the Bill of Rights, the high court condemned the tendency to punish men for beliefs and associations, warned the Federal Executive to guard the constitutional freedoms of its employees, and sharply criticized the Congress for giving undefined and unlimited powers of investigation to Congressional committees.[5]

Reston also noted that *Jencks* and other decisions by the Supreme Court were pointing in the same direction. In its coverage, the *New York Times* devoted almost five full pages, reporting major portions of the texts of *Yates* and *Watkins,* including dissents by Justice Thomas C. Clark. Also in the *New York Times* (June 18, 1957), were the comments of the U.S. attorney at Los Angeles. He predicted that there would be "tremendous problems" in retrying the nine, noting that it had been five years since the original *Yates* trial. The attorney representing most of the defendants also reflected on the impact of the passage of time, stating, "Today's decision is a reflection of the changed atmosphere which Mr. Justice Black predicted would some day take place in his dissent in the *Dennis* case."[6]

The *Daily Worker* recited the good news that had for so long been absent from its reporting of Communist Party causes. The paper declared, "A wave of elation and relief broke over democratic-minded America yesterday with news of the battery of decisions that go far to cleanse the air of the smog of McCarthyism. . . . Friends of liberty—and its enemies, in and out of Congress—recognized at once that the Day of Decisions, Monday, June 17, is already a historic landmark."[7] The *Daily Worker* quoted spokespeople for the American Civil Liberties Union and the Lawyers Guild, as well as newspaper columnists commenting favorably on the Court rulings. But it also cited negative reactions in newspapers such as the *New York Daily News*, which had editorialized under the headline "Aid and Comfort to the Enemy," that "If a movement should start in Congress to impeach one or more of the learned justices, it might have much popular support."[8]

The audience of the *Daily Worker* was far greater than Party members and supporters; the FBI and constituents of the anti-Court coalition read the paper and quoted it often in support of the thesis that these Court decisions had brought cheer and comfort to the Reds. To this coalition, whatever found favor with the Reds must be wrong. On the other hand, it was ironic that Communists sought refuge in the American legal system and complimented the Supreme Court after years of vitriolic condemnation of the courts as a bastion of capitalist repression. Apparently, the *Daily Worker*'s outlook very much depended on whose foot was being stepped on.[9]

Newspapers: Editorial Responses

Editorial responses to Red Monday rulings appeared as early as the next two days, June 18–19. The decisions also stimulated the ingenuity of political cartoonists, whose creations exemplified the entire spectrum of reactions to the work of the Court. Editorials generally fell into three categories: those that argued the country had been betrayed by the Court majority, those that said the Court had done the nation a great service, and those that expressed appreciation for the Court's work in protecting the right to dissent while expressing fear of the consequential weakening of the war against subversion.

Typical of the editorials praising the work of the Court was one published by the *St. Louis Post-Dispatch*, which asserted, "The Bill of Rights . . . is stronger because of [these] four decisions."[10] The *Washington Post* highlighted that the Court had "reasserted its guardianship of individual liberty [which was] long overdue."[11] The *Atlanta Constitution* joined in by endorsing the work of the courts in their emphasis on "the rights of man . . . as guaranteed by our Bill of Rights. . . ."[12] The *New York Times* editorial on the Red Monday decisions complimented the Supreme Court by stating:

> Time and time again, and especially in recent years, the Supreme Court has shown itself to be by far the most courageous of our three branches of Government in standing up for these basic [civil rights] principles.[13]

Those who disagreed with the Red Monday decisions were just as adamant as they expressed their misgivings. Writing that the Court "has brazened forth [with] a group of decisions which have the effect of making the Communists superior to every other citizen of the country," The *New York Daily Mirror* called the decisions a "moment for weeping." [14] The ultra-conservative *Chicago Tribune* headlined its editorial response "Major Service for Reds," adding, "The boys in the Kremlin may wonder why they need a fifth column in the United States so long as the Supreme Court is determined to be so helpful." [15] Those who reacted against the Court's work typically characterized the decisions as victories for communists and did not engage in analysis of the implications in any broader sense. The *Cleveland Plain Dealer* carried out this approach with its editorial headline, "Comrades, Come and Get Us," stating, "Well, comrades, you've finally got what you wanted. The Supreme Court has handed it to you on a platter." [16] The *New York Journal American* called Red Monday Communists' "Greatest Victory." [17]

Other newspaper editorials reflected a more cautious response. The *Portland Oregonian* saw the decisions as having opened new controversies, which would spur arguments over the interpretation of the meaning and result of the rulings. [18] Others felt that changes were perhaps needed in the Constitution and in federal law to cope with the impact of Red Monday, but the *New York World Telegram and Sun* added that the "worst apprehensions may prove unjustified." [19]

Columnists

Newspaper columnists, some syndicated nationwide, weighed in with their views. As would be expected, liberals and moderates saw positive results flowing from Red Monday, while conservatives and anti-Red crusaders questioned the wisdom of the Court's work.

James Reston of the *New York Times* wrote, "In the series of opinions handed down this month, and particularly this week, the high court has simply been serving once more as the moral conscience of a people drugged by the uncertainty, perplexities, prosperity and diversions of the past two decades." [20]

The nation's preeminent columnist, Walter Lippmann, in his widely syndicated column, emphasized the changed times that were reflected in the Court's opinions:

> The Supreme Court has waited a long time—some 10 years—before it has intervened. . . . I do not think the long patience of the court shows that the Eisenhower court is more liberal than the Roosevelt-Truman court, but rather that the times have changed. The emergency—if there was one which could not be met by lawful means—is over.[21]

George Sokolsky, a Red Scare crusader, wrote, "Maybe the United States needs an American Supreme Court," implying that the Red Monday decisions were not "American" and adding that the Court had in effect destroyed the Smith Act. He saw the "mischief" of the Court in not only helping Communists but, perhaps worse, aiding other bands of criminals.[22]

Dorothy Thompson, another widely read syndicated columnist, wrote that the Red Monday cases were definitely linked to the changed times, pointing out:

> It is most unlikely that these decisions would have been given five years ago. The high court would hardly have so ruled during the Stalinist period and the Korean or Indo-Chinese wars. The Committee on Un-American Activities reached its zenith when America was genuinely afraid that communism might sweep the world and engulf the United States, and America was feverishly rebuilding its external and internal defenses. Then the security of the state took precedence over the rights of the individual, as it always does in war. War, hot or cold, is the perennial enemy of personal freedoms and invariably reduces the area of what is considered to be tolerable.
> These decisions are, therefore, a expression of restored confidence.[23]

One of the most perceptive analyses of what Red Monday decisions meant, how they fitted into the unfolding scheme of events, and why they generated such strife was written for the *Christian Science Monitor* by Richard L. Strout.[24] After acknowledging that the Court "is once again up to its black-robed neck in controversy," he pointed out that this was nothing new, except that in earlier times "attack came from the left; today it is from the right." Strout called it inevitable that a "troubled generation," having endured World War II, the Cold War, and the Korean War, would place "judicial emphasis . . . on the need for national security" rather than personal freedoms.

Strout then defined the turning point for the Court and the nation: the *Brown* decision. He believed that the negative reaction in parts of the South to *Brown* extended to subsequent Court decisions, including those of Red Monday. Most significantly, Strout stated, "Without the fire lit by the original unanimous desegregation decision in 1954, the heat over the 1957 decisions in subversive and Communist cases would have been less intense. All these emotional issues together have precipitated the court into the biggest controversy since the New Deal [Court packing] days." His conclusion was that the new direction the Court had taken "after a generation of rulings tending to favor the state as against the citizen" reflected the Court's anxiety "lest individual freedoms were in danger and was bent on shifting the balance."

Magazines

Red Monday decisions were also widely covered by the nation's magazines. News magazines, published weekly, generally gave short synopses of the decisions, most often featuring the *Yates* and *Watkins* cases. The *Service* and *Sweezy* cases were frequently treated as personal victories rather than as news of national importance.

Time put Chief Justice Warren on its July 1, 1957 cover with the title: "U.S. Supreme Court: The New Direction." The gist of its analysis was that to Warren, "the law was a temple and the Supreme Court a builder." To *Time*, "the blueprints were ready, the motor was flying, and the marble blocks were moving toward a new look in U.S. legal architecture." *Time*'s view was that the "new look" was chiefly the result of Warren's leadership and that the path to the Red Monday decisions was traceable to his leadership in the *Brown* desegregation case. After briefly reviewing the 1955–56 Red Scare cases, it commented that "these were early indications of the new look. Judges in lower courts across the land duly took note and began slowing up consideration of pending Communist cases, since no judge likes to be reversed." The article summarized the effects of the new Court's decisions, stating that they would broaden civil liberties "in the best tradition of U.S. constitutional law," along with slowing down the "prosecution of Communists to a crawl." It was in this latter area that *Time* found fault.[25]

Newsweek's coverage was dedicated to explaining the decisions and succinctly stating the meaning of each. Early reactions from senators and the Justice Department were given. The article concluded that a period of adjustment was in store for all, stating that "it may be so difficult to convict a man under the Smith Act, [that] the law could become a dead letter."[26] As to the Justice Department, "the prevailing mood was sheer bafflement. That department had not yet recovered from the *Jencks* case ruling when it was hit over the head by last week's Smith Act decree. Said one haggard Justice lawyer: 'never but never has the government taken so many shellackings from the Supreme Court in one period.'"[27]

Under the heading, "The Supreme Court's New Line-Up," *Business Week* took an in-depth look at the justices and the realignment of the Court, noting that "there is one definite characteristic of the Warren court that makes it different from recent courts: its willingness to seek out big issues on which to take a forward stand of its own choosing"; in these cases, the result was "a strong reaffirmation of basic liberties."[28]

U.S. News & World Report carried a three-page editorial statement by its editor, arch-conservative David Lawrence. Outmatched by few in his use of strong language, Lawrence titled his statement, "Treason's Biggest Victory," excoriating the Court for decisions that he felt made the "path of traitors easier" and adding that "today it is the coward [those duped by the Communist line] who is extolled." After reciting his view of the results of each Red Monday decision, he repeated, "Treason has won its biggest victory."[29]

On the other side, liberal magazines extolled the new Court majority and its decisions of June 17, 1957. The *Atlantic Monthly* said the Court's resurgence after the McCarthy era was "one of the most heartening events of the year."[30] The *Nation* and the *New Republic* also championed the Court. The *Nation* wrote, "Monday, June 17, 1957, is still a day to remember, for on this day the Supreme Court rejected some of its own doubts and misgivings of the last decade and reaffirmed its confidence in freedom as a way of life."[31]

Under the title, "The Supreme Court's June 17th Opinions," Alan Barth wrote in The *New Republic* that "Civil liberties have come back into fashion. In an extraordinary quartet of opinions handed down on Monday, June 17, the Supreme Court reaffirmed and revitalized its traditional role as the guardian of individual rights against arbitrary governmental authority."[32] And David Reisman, in a subsequent issue of the *New Republic*, called the Red Monday decisions "[m]ore courageous even than the admirable school desegregation cases (especially coming as they do in the wake of the fury stirred up by the latter)."[33]

The *Reporter* reprinted a portion of a broadcast over CBS Radio in which Eric Sevareid had commented on the rulings by the Court. Addressing the *Watkins* case and applauding the work of the majority in finally curbing the abuses of the Un-American Activities Committee (which he believed had created much of the Red Scare), Sevareid said:

> Only a short time ago, the best students of the problem were convinced that the Supreme Court never would, and perhaps never should, checkmate this committee.
> Times change, men change. Today, in the Eisenhower era, the Supreme Court is coming full circle, after its relative immobility in the Truman era, to an active role as the leading champion of civil liberties in the endless contest between the individual and the state he has created.[34]

Religious periodicals followed the Court's decisions closely. The *Christian Science Monitor* wrote that the decisions marked "an emphatic return to constitutional guarantees of liberty."[35] The liberal Catholic magazine *Commonweal* expressed a similar view:

> All of these decisions favor the individual rather than the State, freedom rather than security, and liberty rather than authority. In ruling in favor of these undoubted values, the Court has fulfilled its historic function.[36]

Letters to the Editor

Judging by the number of letters to the editor in the aftermath of Red Monday, readers were following the story with interest. Their views ranged from calls for impeachment of the justices to expressions of admiration for the Court. Charles A. Walsh, of Concordia, Kansas, wrote, "The applause for the court is now directed by communist cheerleaders. Applause of this body by those who approve treachery, treason, and conspiracy, is a bitter drink for patriots and Americans." [37]

Nathan B. Forrest wrote to the *Chattanooga News-Free Press*, "Not one Communist who has appealed to the Supreme Court has lost. In fact, the czars in the Kremlin couldn't have helped the Communist Party more than the Supreme Court has in its decision freeing the Communists who were indicted for teaching overthrow of the United States by force." [38]

But many Americans praised the Court's decisions of June 17 and called for an end to Redbaiting. Julian Jack, of New York City, wrote, "The Supreme Court has finally put an end to the era of McCarthyism. They have shown wisdom, patriotism and a decent respect for the Constitution." [39]

Congressional Reaction

Those in Congress who reacted against the Supreme Court decisions would have summarized what the Court had done in this manner: it freed five Communists and gave nine others probable freedom, it gave two suspected Communists the right to practice law, it reinstated a security risk in the State Department, it frustrated the investigatory proceedings of state and federal committees, and it exposed FBI files to criminals. As the leading historian of the relationship of the courts to Congress has written, "These results, played up by newspaper headlines which were often as exaggerated as Justice Clark's dissents, provided ready ammunition for the Court's enemies." [40]

The Red Monday cases served to pour more gasoline on the flames already burning from the results of the *Jencks* case of just two weeks before. Once again there was a rush to the podium to excoriate the Court and demand further remedial legislation. Articles attacking the decisions as well as suggesting everything from the lack of judicial expertise to treasonous conduct or the work of communist agents within the Court appeared in the *Congressional Record*. Frequently the *Congressional Record*, by request of a member of Congress, reprinted an article so that it would be read by other members who might not otherwise have been exposed to its message.

Those supporting the Court's work and defending the justices also spoke out and similarly had articles and speeches they collected reprinted. Thus, on June 19, 1957, Representative James Roosevelt (D-Calif.) described himself as having been vilified as part of the "pseudo-left wing liberals, Communist apologists and other terms to discredit our views" but celebrated the fact that the Court had "sustained our viewpoint" and hoped that "instead of interpretation, the fundamental correctness of the Supreme Court's position will be accepted and followed." He then had two newspaper articles supportive of the Court's work inserted in the *Record.*[41]

He was immediately followed by Representative Donald L. Jackson (R-Calif.), who said, "Monday, June 17, was truly black Monday for the American people. That day culminated in the Supreme Court of the United States a long series of events which served to completely nullify and vitiate the efforts of the Congress of the United States and of the FBI to seek out American agents of the conspiracy and to legislate on findings for and on behalf of the people of the United States and our security against the acts of traitors."[42] He promised that he would be back with more comments and a call for action by Congress.

While the *Jencks* case (FBI files) provoked the most urgent calls for action and in some respects was the most frequently referenced "error" of the Court (undoubtedly reflecting the power and influence of J. Edgar Hoover), the *Yates* and *Watkins* rulings were to receive their share of special attention. For Court critics, Justice Clark was the hero who alone spoke the truth. His dissents (but not the majority opinions) were reprinted in full in the *Congressional Record,*[43] bracketed by comments such as these by James C. Davis (D-Ga.): "It seems that if there is one thing that is well settled, it is that a Communist cannot lose a case in the United States Supreme Court.[44] After inserting into the *Record* portions of the London *Communist Daily Worker* praising the Red Monday decisions and particularly the work of Justice Black, George W. Andrews (D-Ala.) spoke: "Mr. Speaker and Members of the House, let me appeal to you to take action before the Supreme Court destroys this nation."[45]

Besides those urging remedial legislation, particularly to "correct" the *Jencks* decision, others stood to recommend impeachment of justices, citing as grounds that the Court was "attempting to overthrow the government through fallacious reasoning."[46] Still others sought to prescribe a new method for recommending candidates to the president for Supreme Court appointments.[47]

While momentum gained in support of a bill to correct the *Jencks* decision, voices were heard in both houses of Congress calling for calmness and proper respect for the role of the Court. One was that of Alexander Wiley (R-Wis.), the senior Republican on the Senate Judiciary Committee. He rose to speak against the angry denouncements of the Court, calling on his colleagues to "stop, look, and listen, before criticizing [the] Supreme Court of the United States," adding:

> Let there be no abuse of the highest tribunal of our land. Let us respect the men who wear the honored robes of the highest judicial office which can be attained in the American system of government. The majority in each of these decisions rendered its verdict, I am sure, in good faith. The fact that any of us may differ with any of the decisions, should not lessen our respect for the sincerity with which the decisions were rendered.[48]

Despite the scattered voices of moderation, this was a field day for the anti-Court coalition. Most of the extreme language and demands for revolutionary measures came from avowed segregationists, joined by voices from the extreme right wing of the Republican Party. Most of what have been called "wild-haired radical schemes" came from this group. There was little or no chance for any of these proposals to get very far in terms of passing either house, but there was "a fear not only among conservatives but among moderates as well as some liberals that the Justices had gone too far in protecting individual rights and in so doing had moved into the legislative domain."[49]

Aside from the continued pressure for a *Jencks* bill, the most important legislative threat to the work of the Supreme Court came from William E. Jenner (R-Ind.). Jenner had been a sworn enemy of President Truman and an anti-Communist crusader. On July 16, 1957 a speech he had made outside of Congress was reprinted in the *Congressional Record*. It was his opening volley against the Court, followed by a speech to the Senate on July 26, 1957.[50] It has been described as "a verbal assault on the High Bench which could have competed in intensity with any made by his southern colleagues."[51] Only McCarthy, of all northern senators, had made similarly searing attacks on the Warren Court.

Jenner's speech was followed by the introduction of a bill, S.R. 2646, which attacked the Court by removing from its appellate jurisdiction five types of cases that covered all the areas of the Court's work on Red Scare issues except the *Yates* case. Other bills pending were designed to change the results in *Yates* in future prosecutions. Under Article III of the Constitution, Section 2, paragraph 2, the Supreme Court's original jurisdiction is very limited: this listing is followed by the words, "In all other Cases before mentioned, the supreme Court shall have appellate Jurisdiction, both as to Law and Fact, with such Exceptions, and under such Regulations as the Congress shall make." This plainly means that Congress can control which appeals the Supreme Court may hear.

From time to time, a Congress angry with Supreme Court decisions has threatened to end the Court's right to hear appeals of cases in a specific area. Here "Jenner's proposal was soon to grow into the most fundamental challenge to judicial power in twenty years."[52]

The push for the Jenner Bill commenced that summer and continued into the fall 1957 congressional sessions. The anti-Court coalition representatives were met head-on in public hearings by the pro-Court defenders, and Jenner sought a compromise. With the assistance of his fellow senator and McCarthy supporter, John Marshall Butler (R-Md.), a compromise bill was put together. While the Jenner-Butler Bill made slow headway in the Senate, the House passed five of the many anti-Court bills that had been introduced, all of which were designed to reverse specific decisions rather than slice into the appellate jurisdiction of the Court. Walter Murphy has written this assessment of the situation:

> They [the House measures] were symbols, symbols of congressional repudiation of the moral authority of the Warren Court to lead the nation. And lacking either means of physical coercion or control of money, the Court's power teeters on its moral authority far more precariously than that of either Congress or the President. If Jenner-Butler or all or most of the House bills were enacted into law the resurgence of judicial power would come crashing down.[53]

Murphy identifies three factors opposing the Jenner-Butler forces: the potential of a presidential veto, the Senate liberals, and Lyndon B. Johnson (D-Tex.), Senate majority leader. These factors, particularly the work of Johnson, finally defeated all these anti-Court bills. Except for the Jencks Act, which as a symbolic slap at the Court did not substantially change the majority ruling, all threats had been turned back, but barely, and only after exhausting everyone involved until the final maneuvers on Sunday, August 24, 1958. At certain points, more senators had voted for anti-Court bills than had voted against the Franklin D. Roosevelt "court-packing" plan.

The long, bitter struggle over anti-Court legislation can be argued as proof of the stubborn supporters of the Red Scare, despite the changed times. But it can also be understood as something more than a reaction against the Red Monday rulings; it was, in addition, an attack on the Court's desegregation and race decisions. Southern senators and representatives were the most vocal and most cohesive anti-Court group, not because they were more patriotic or more security-conscious, but because slamming at the Court, even by changing its appellate powers, would hurt the institution that had hurt them. Desegregating southern schools, ruling that blacks could no longer legally be relegated to second-class citizenship, was to them the gravest sin of the Warren Court. Undoubtedly most of these southerners also believed that the

Communist Party's platform and advocacy of racial equality "stirred up" blacks and therefore constituted a serious enemy.

Northern anti-Communist activists in Congress were a small but vocal and powerful minority that united with segregationists on the common ground of believing that the Court had hurt the war against subversion. Adding the power of certain big business groups, the resulting coalition blamed the messenger as well as the messages, the decisions as well as the deciders. After all, until 1954 the segregationists were reasonably content with the Court and its rulings; then the *Brown* case exploded on them. One year later they could welcome the other constituents of an anti-Court coalition to their fold as the results of the new Warren majority were announced. All now attacked a Court that had, until 1955, been on the "right side" of Red Scare issues.

The anti-Court coalition was willing to substantially alter the power of the Supreme Court either directly, as in the Jenner-Butler Bill, or indirectly, as in the House bills designed to reshape the law so as to effectively dismantle the Court's work in the field of civil liberties. To the segregationists, the potential payoff was to slow down, if not reverse, the desegregation movement. To northern anti-Communist crusaders, congressional action would take areas of jurisdiction away from a Court they could no longer trust not to intrude into the field of government action. That the Supreme Court justices watched what was happening and knew of the jeopardy to their institution, as well as to their rulings in sensitive areas of civil rights, is certain. The next sessions of the Court would indicate how greatly these threats affected them.

The Supreme Court

Judges, too, are exposed to their enveloping atmosphere. It is their special responsibility to be on guard against the influence of prevailing popular agitation calculated to disturb, however subtly, the exercise of a serene and just judicial judgment. An important safeguard in enforcing a Constitutional principle is to stand on the formulation made in times of calm and not attempt its reformation when the air is charged with conflict and tension.

Justice Felix Frankfurter[54]

The thoughts of Justice Frankfurter have relevance throughout the Red Scare cases, but they are perhaps particularly significant regarding the conflicts and tensions that followed the *Jencks* and Red Monday decisions. The justices felt the heat of Congress as opinions were voiced and legislation of serious impact was debated. The threat of the Jenner-Butler Bill was real. Would the majority crack under this pressure as further Red Scare cases were scheduled for the new fall 1957–58 session?

Would the applause for the Court's work balance the condemnations and threats?

Clearly, most of the justices felt that the attacks in Congress and in the press were unwarranted, and they were especially sensitive to those critics who were not otherwise considered fringe characters.[55] The reviews of the Court's work also appear to have exacerbated the growing rift between Warren and Frankfurter, which spilled over from behind-the-door case conferences to bitter confrontations at oral arguments.[56] There was also a continuing and deepening enmity between Frankfurter and the other members of the new majority: Douglas, Black, and Brennan.[57] These tensions and attacks held the potential of denying further new majority decisions if Frankfurter departed and no other justice joined the four.

The fall 1957 Court decisions showed that the new majority's alliance was still intact on Red Scare issues. In *Rowoldt v. Perfetto*,[58] an alien who had lived in the United States for forty years but who was briefly a member of the Communist Party in 1935 fought an order for deportation brought under the Internal Security Act of 1950. There was no evidence that his membership reflected any attachment to the concept of violent overthrow of the government.

In a five-to-four decision, with Frankfurter writing the majority opinion, the Court held that Party membership unconnected with a meaningful association did not supply grounds for deportation. Frankfurter asserted a distinction between the membership that supported the 1954 deportation order the Court affirmed in the *Galvan v. Press* case[59] (in which Frankfurter had also written the majority opinion) from that of this case. Douglas and Black, who had been the only dissenters in *Galvan*, sided with Frankfurter, who now had switched sides to the liberal majority.

Harlan broke with the liberal majority and was joined by Clark, Burton, and Whittaker, finding that membership was membership—in *Galvan* and in this case—and that the Court, just to alleviate the rigors of a harsh statute, had taken impermissible liberties.

The same five-to-four split, with the same justices on the same sides, decided another important Red Scare issue about passports in June 1958; this time, Justice Douglas wrote for the five and Justice Clark wrote for the four. By the end of the 1957 term in June 1958, it was apparent that Harlan had moved away from the liberal majority and that Frankfurter's vote would be the deciding one.

Rockwell Kent, an artist and political activist, applied for a passport. Kent was the former president of the IWO, which was defunct by 1954, a casualty of the Red Scare. Kent sought his passport to allow him to travel to England and to attend a meeting of an organization known as the World Council of Peace in Helsinki, Finland.

His request was denied under a 1952 law that forbade issuance of a passport to a member of the Communist Party or to one who supported the Communist movement or was reasonably believed to be going abroad to advance the Communist cause. Though Kent was entitled to a hearing on this denial, he was advised that regardless of the outcome of a hearing he also had to submit an affidavit as to whether he was then or ever had been a member of the Communist Party. Kent refused to provide the affidavit on the grounds that only his citizenship was relevant to the issuance of a passport.[60] He took his case to court after the State Department refused his request without the affidavit and ultimately gained entry to the Supreme Court for review.

Douglas's opinion pointed out that "A passport is not only of great value—indeed necessary—abroad; it is also an aid in establishing citizenship for purposes of re-entry into the United States."[61] This was followed by an extensive history of passport laws in American history. Then, examining the 1952 law, he concluded that the power of the secretary of state to issue passports was couched in broad terms by Congress but had always been exercised narrowly. There were two categories of cases where refusal to issue a passport was traditionally permitted: when the applicant was proved not to owe allegiance to the United States, or when the applicant was participating in illegal conduct or trying to escape the law. Douglas found no reason to impute that Congress meant to give the secretary of state unbridled discretion to grant or withhold a passport for any other reason he might choose. Moreover, he wrote, this was not a wartime restriction, which might thereby be justified. Douglas wrote that when crucial liberties are involved the Court narrowly construes all delegated powers that curtail or dilute such liberties. As Kent fell into neither of the two categories for denial, the secretary of state was held to have no statutory authority to deny him his passport.

The majority did not challenge the constitutionality of the law; it held only that Congress had not intended to delegate the authority to deny freedom of travel to a citizen who refused to be subjected to inquiry about beliefs and associations. Justice Clark's minority opinion sought to place a broader construction on the law so that the secretary of state could lawfully prevent anyone from traveling if there was a need to protect the country's internal security. Notwithstanding that five years had passed since the Korean War armistice, the dissenters believed that a state of emergency still existed, an emergency involving attempted world conquest by communist imperialism.[62]

Meanwhile, as the Court continued its work, the pragmatic effect of the Red Monday decisions was being felt. Hearings were suspended while the *Watkins* and *Sweezy* decisions were being evaluated. Claims were made that congressional committees were rendered "innocuous as two kittens in a cage full of rabid dogs." [63] Realistically, since the heart of the *Watkins* decision was procedural, greater care was mandated by this ruling—not an end to the kind of investigative work carried on by HUAC and the Senate Internal Security Committee. *Watkins* and *Sweezy* had the important effect of admonishing committees about the rules and limits of their work. The fact that the Supreme Court (and thus lower federal courts) would no longer invariably approve of Red Scare committees' procedures and contempt citations was very meaningful.

As to the *Yates* ruling, for those Communists whose appeal time had expired or who had exhausted the appeal process, it was of no benefit. The *Dennis* defendants remained in jail after two of them had their petitions for rehearing rejected by the Supreme Court. The result was that those already in jail remained there, but all who were not were saved from prison by the *Yates* decision.[64]

In his annual report for the fiscal year ending June 30, 1958, the attorney general began, "The impact of the *Yates* case on other Smith Act conspiracy prosecutions was immediately felt." [65] The report went on to detail the remanding of cases by the Supreme Court to lower courts for consideration of convictions in the light of the *Yates* ruling. Almost two pages were devoted to the reversals and remands the government suffered in its Smith Act prosecutions. Underlying all those reversals, remands, and dropped prosecutions was the admission that the *Yates* standard could not be met. On this basis and because the case was so old (witnesses missing or dead), the nine *Yates* defendants were not retried.[66] Similarly, when the Pittsburgh Smith Act case, *United States v. Mesarosh* (Steve Nelson), came before the Court in its fall 1957 term, the convictions were reversed and the government dismissed the indictment rather than retry the case because "of death and unavailability of a number of witnesses and the effect of the *Yates* decision." [67] One appeals court judge stated with apparent bitterness that *Yates* had left "the Smith Act, as to any further prosecution under it, a virtual shambles." [68] But, as it turned out, that was not quite true.

What the Supreme Court had not ruled on was another section of the Smith Act, the membership provision, which had not been present in the *Yates* case. The Smith Act made it unlawful to be a knowing and actively participating member of an organization (here the Communist Party) that advocated the violent overthrow of the government. As early as the *Dennis* case, Justice Department prosecutors had been considering, and in a sense experimenting with, pursuing Party membership as a grounds for indictment. By 1954, the government was ready to act;

without public fanfare, an indictment was obtained against Illinois Party Secretary Claude Lightfoot. More indictments were obtained and convictions followed in 1955–56,[69] particularly aimed at fulfilling Republican Party platform promises of more Communist indictments.

Though grounded on a different portion of the Smith Act, the trials basically trod the same path, using much the same evidence and even the same witnesses; similarly, the high bail amounts often could not be raised by the defendants. Michal Belknap has pointed out that, although the bare fact of membership alone was not a crime,

the government conducted these proceedings as though the prisoner in the dock were an organization rather than an individual and, as in the conspiracy cases, offered irrelevant but inflammatory evidence, intended to discredit the CPUSA. During the *Scales* trial, for instance, the government had Barbara Hartle testify at length about Communist opposition to the American role in Korea.[70]

Belknap added, "The most obvious similarity between the membership and conspiracy cases was their outcome." Four major membership trials ended in guilty verdicts, but, unlike earlier Smith Act trials, at least one required numerous ballots, which Belknap thought "was a good indication of the extent to which emotional anti-communism was losing its grip on the country."[71]

Both Junius Scales and Claude Lightfoot lost their appeals in their respective courts of appeal, but the Supreme Court granted certiorari in early 1956. As a result of the *Jencks* decision, the fact that reports to the FBI by informers testifying at the trial were not produced caused the Court on October 14, 1957 to reverse and remand the membership cases before it.[72]

The government moved to retry Scales and then waited for the Supreme Court's further ruling on the membership provision. The irony involved was that when Scales—who favored a faction of the Communist Party that quit rather than accept Party control by an "old-guard" Party group—was tried again, it was after he had left the Party.

Though the second *Scales* trial came after the *Yates* decision, the verdict of guilty was rendered and the trial court sentenced Scales to six years in prison. By December 1958 the *Scales* case was back in the lap of the Supreme Court, which had agreed to review it. Another membership clause case was also on its way to the Court, the case of John Noto.

Though oral argument was held in early 1959, no decision was forthcoming until another oral argument. The rulings for both *Scales* and *Noto* were issued on June 5, 1961. The long delay in deciding the two cases was extraordinary. According to Justice Clark, the delay was probably deliberate. Justice Frankfurter, apparently in response to congressional attacks and wishing to avoid any Communist cases for awhile, sought, in effect, to bury the cases for as long as he could; his colleagues, with the exception of Clark, went along with his plan.[73]

The delays that lasted for years in reaching a decision in these membership cases not only were a response to the reactions following Red Monday but more ominously indicated that the liberal majority on Red Scare issues since 1955 was coming apart. Statistics have shown that in Court terms following the 1956–57 session, the number of certiorari petitions involving civil liberties claims that the Court rejected (thus refusing to hear these cases) rose dramatically.[74] An important link between cooling down on favoring civil rights in Red Scare cases and the adoption of a go slow attitude toward racial integration can be seen in Court rulings on cases in both areas in the 1958 and subsequent Court terms.

The decision in the *Scales* case, finally announced on June 5, 1961, involved Junius Irving Scales, who was the chairman of the Carolina District Communist Party. Justice Harlan, who had written the *Yates* decision for the majority, now wrote for a new majority that included Potter Stewart, a justice appointed in October 1958 by President Eisenhower to replace the retiring Justice Burton.

Stewart had been on the Sixth Circuit Court of Appeals for only four years and, at age forty-three, became the second youngest justice on the Court since the Civil War. While considered a swing vote, Stewart's record on Red Scare issues placed him almost invariably with Frankfurter and Harlan. Since Harlan and Frankfurter had by then moved out of alliance with Warren, Black, Douglas, and Brennan, Stewart's vote did swing the results in *Scales* to favoring the government.

The Harlan opinion upheld the conviction of Scales because the government had proven that Scales was more than a mere member, that he was "active" as against "passive" or "nominal" in his membership; he was obviously a Party leader.[75] Thus, if the provision making such "active" and "knowing" membership grounds for conviction passed constitutional muster, the guilty verdict was correct. Turning back all constitutional challenges and finding that the evidence was adequate in identifying Scales with a knowing membership firmly tied to Party goals, the five–four ruling said that no error had been committed.

Justices Black, Douglas, and Brennan (who was joined by Warren) each wrote dissents, finding that the First Amendment had been violated and that the Subversive Activities Control Act (McCarran Act) barred prosecutions under the membership clause of the Smith Act. Douglas was apparently very upset with this decision, stating, "Even the Alien and Sedition Laws—shameful reminders of an early chapter of intolerance—never went so far as we go today. . . . We legalize today guilt by association, sending a man to prison when he committed no unlawful act. . . . It borrows from the totalitarian philosophy."[76]

That same day, June 5, 1961, the Court handed down its ruling in a companion case, *Noto v. United States.*[77] By a unanimous vote, the Court reversed the judgment of the court of appeals, which had confirmed Noto's conviction at trial based on the membership clause of the Smith Act. Justice Harlan again wrote the decision, finding that a conviction under that clause could not stand in this or any other membership case without "substantial or circumstantial evidence of a call to violence now or in the future which is both sufficiently strong and sufficiently pervasive to lend color to the otherwise ambiguous theoretical material regarding Communist Party teaching, and to justify the inference that such a call to violence may fairly be imputed to the Party as a whole, and not merely to some narrow segment of it."[78]

In effect, the standard set by *Noto* was so severe in terms of what had to be shown in each case that it appeared to take away the power to prosecute Communists that had been recognized in the *Scales* decision. Douglas, Brennan (with Warren joining him), and Black would have gone further as expressed in their concurrences. Even Justice Clark agreed with the *Noto* result. In a letter to Justice Harlan dated February 21, 1961, Clark said, "Being a captive [since the majority was against him] of *Yates*—which I continue to believe wrong—I see no alternative but to join your analysis of the facts in *Noto* and reluctantly in your opinion. I, of course, still join in your *Scales* opinion."[79]

Instead of reopening grounds for attacks on Party members, the result of *Scales* and *Noto* was the dismissal of membership clause indictments and reversal by a court of appeals of a prior conviction because of the insufficiency of the government's evidence.[80] Belknap has written that the gloom of the dissenting justices in *Scales* was hardly warranted, since, while that ruling was potentially dangerous, Harlan's *Noto* decision "drastically restricted its impact. In that case [*Noto*] the crafty conservative [Harlan], having made his bow to the legislature by validating the statute [in *Scales*] focused on the evidence," establishing a standard that was very difficult for the government to meet. Thus Belknap concurs that membership prosecutions while "theoretically possible [were] practically difficult."[81]

While the *Scales* decision demonstrated the loss of majority status for the Court liberals in this particular area of Red Scare cases and sent Scales to jail,[82] the *Noto* decision imposed so narrow a window of opportunity that the government never initiated another membership prosecution. It was also true that there were few Communists left for prosecution on any bases.

By 1961 *Yates* had been the law for four years. By that time, the nation took much less interest in Red Scare cases. Even a reading of the Justice Department's annual reports for the late 1950s and early 1960s indicated a lack of the enthusiasm that had been so prevalent in the reports covering earlier years. *Yates* had done its work, and that work had not been undone by the membership decisions.

Michal Belknap concludes his study with the summation that "As a weapon with which to wage war on the CPUSA [Communist Party USA], the Smith Act had lost its utility. *Yates* had made conspiracy prosecutions impossible, and now the membership clause too was a spent bullet. . . . The Smith Act had reached the end of its anti-Communist career."[83]

Justice Harlan's biographer confirms that

the surgery Justice Harlan performed on the Smith Act's membership clause, like that inflicted in *Yates* on its advocacy provisions, made successful prosecution under the act exceedingly difficult. Thus, although Junius Scales became a sacrificial lamb in the Court's effort to avoid a direct challenge to Congress' authority in a very controversial field, Smith Act prosecutions ceased altogether.[84]

While the Court kept delaying for years deciding the Smith Act membership issues, in the interim between Red Monday and the *Scales/Noto* decisions of 1961 the Court did revisit the *Watkins* decision (limiting HUAC's powers) and the *Sweezy* ruling (circumscribing a state's investigative powers). Two years almost to the day prior to *Scales* and *Noto* rulings came two Court decisions, on June 8, 1959. Those cases were *Barenblatt v. U.S.*[85] and *Uphaus v. Wyman.*[86]

Red Scare crusader Louis C. Wyman, attorney general of New Hampshire, was a consistent activist who was apparently not deterred by his loss in the *Sweezy* case on Red Monday. He continued his battle against "subversive persons" in New Hampshire, demanding that Willard Uphaus, executive director of World Fellowship, Inc., turn over to him, as a one-man investigating committee, the names of all those who attended the summer camp run by the organization during 1954 and 1955. When Uphaus failed to provide the names, he was brought before a state court where he denied that the state had the right to obtain that information because its demand violated his First Amendment rights.

Before the Supreme Court of New Hampshire, Wyman offered proof that some speakers at the camp were members of the Communist Party or were members of organizations on the attorney general's list. From a finding that Uphaus was in contempt until he turned over the list of names, an appeal was taken to the Supreme Court.[87] There Chief Justice Warren called for reversal because he believed the state failed to show that a legitimate interest was endangered or being subverted, and that not to reverse would deter people from speaking freely.[88] He was, however, outvoted, with the new justice, Potter Stewart, joining with Clark, Frankfurter, Whittaker, and Harlan to constitute a majority. Clark's opinion rejected all Uphaus's arguments, most of which were based on the *Nelson* and *Sweezy* cases. The majority found that the interest of the state in protecting itself by determining whether "subversive persons" had attended the camp outweighed any conflicting interests of guests to associational privacy; unlike *Sweezy*, they found no infringement of academic or political freedom.

Justice Brennan wrote an impassioned dissent, joined by Warren, Black, and Douglas. Black and Douglas would have decided the issues on First and Fourteenth Amendment bases, but also joined in endorsing Justice Brennan's analysis. Brennan argued that the entire proceeding was one of exposure for exposure's sake, proscribed by the *Watkins* decision. He could find no "requisite legislative purpose" that would subordinate Uphaus's constitutional protections. After an extensive review of Wyman's report to the state legislature, Brennan concluded:

> The emphasis of the entire report is on individual guilt, individual near-guilt, and individual questionable behavior. Its flavor and tone, regardless of its introductory disclaimers, cannot help but stimulate readers to attach a "badge of infamy," *Wieman v. Updegraff*, 344 U.S. 183, 190–191, to the persons named in it.[89]

Just as *Sweezy* was in tandem with *Uphaus*, so another decision announced on June 8, 1959, two years after Red Monday, was related to the *Watkins* ruling. Lloyd Barenblatt was a young psychology instructor who had taught for a term at Vassar College and was under subpoena to come before HUAC in June 1954, during a session devoted to "Communist Methods of Infiltration (Education)." There he was asked the usual questions that almost invariably began with "Are you now a member of the Communist Party; have you ever been a member of the Communist Party?"[90] Barenblatt refused to answer these or any other questions that might implicate others or detail his activities as a graduate student and teaching fellow at the University of Michigan; instead, he submitted a prepared statement. Quickly indicted for refusing to answer, he was convicted of contempt, sentenced to six months' imprisonment, and fined $250.

Harlan's opinion for the majority had the opportunity, not present in *Watkins*, to rule directly on Barenblatt's First Amendment claims. Harlan did not accept what Vinson had done in the *Dennis* case as that decision dealt with these same First Amendment claims; Vinson had used Learned Hand's "gravity of the evil" variation of the "clear and present danger" test. Instead, Harlan expressed his preference for a balancing of the interests approach: which weighed heavier, the needs of government to expose Communists and for self-preservation or Barenblatt's right to refuse to answer on the grounds of his First Amendment freedoms? In adopting this test, and in his willingness to favor the government, Harlan was apparently following the lead of Frankfurter, though his biographer points out that Harlan clearly embraced the test in his own right.[91] The majority opinion also rejected all due process issues, in effect stating this case would not be governed by *Watkins*. Here, Harlan said, the questions posed by Barenblatt were pertinent and education was a legitimate area for inquiry. The majority did not, however, overrule or make *Watkins* ineffective.

Justice Black wrote for the minority, consisting of himself, Douglas, the chief justice, and Brennan. At the certiorari conference these four voted for granting the writ, with Clark, Whittaker, Frankfurter, and Harlan against the grant. With those four votes favoring review, certiorari was granted. The deciding in terms of ruling on the case was thus in the hands of Stewart, who came to the Court after this certiorari vote. By joining with Clark and the others, this final Eisenhower nominee assured the majority would favor the government so long as the position of the others did not shift.

In one paragraph, the essence of the dissenting minority was expressed by Justice Brennan:

I would reverse this conviction. It is sufficient that I state my complete agreement with my Brother Black that no purpose for the investigation of Barenblatt is revealed by the record except exposure purely for the sake of exposure. This is not a purpose to which Barenblatt's rights under the First Amendment can validly be subordinated.[92]

From the pen of a writer whose work on HUAC was intensely critical and clearly disappointed with the *Barenblatt* ruling, came this balanced assessment:

The rebuff of the Watkins case, the close decision on Barenblatt, the powerful dissent, the criticism implicit in the Harlan ruling—these had a chastening effect, at least to the extent of bringing more order into its [HUAC's] proceedings during the late fifties and into the present [1960s] decade.[93]

These two decisions demonstrated the shift in the balance taking place in the Court, realigning majority and minority status on Red Scare issues among the justices. In both decisions the four liberals held together. While Harlan moved farther from the four liberals, it was the desertion by Frankfurter that most effected the change. For Frankfurter, the reaction to Red Monday in Congress and in all the expression of anti-Court sentiments may have been particularly difficult. He was a jurist who deeply believed in judicial restraint and respect for the rights and powers of the other branches of government, to which the Court must show deference. Yet he was also deeply concerned with the protection of individual rights and civil liberties. So, for example, in a letter to Justice Brennan, Frankfurter attempted to defend in *Uphaus v. Wyman* New Hampshire's right to exercise its judgment "regarding the purposes for which a legislative investigation is conducted." He added his personal list of abuses and abusers (including J. Edgar Hoover) who he felt were similarly not within the Court's scope of review. Frankfurter closed by stating, "Need I add another word, namely, that there isn't a man on the Court who personally disapproves more than I do of the activities of all the un-American Committees, of all the Smith prosecutions, of the Attorney General's list, etc., etc." [94]

Yet, despite his apparently genuine dislike of those manifestations of the Red Scare, he changed and voted with Clark and Harlan in support of the state and federal government, its agencies and committees.

The explanations for Frankfurter's and Harlan's shift in these two cases, as well as in a number that followed, have been varied. Professor Murphy attributed it to a motif traceable throughout the Court's history, which he described as a "well-worn pattern": decisions are made on important aspects of public policy, then criticism of those decisions is followed by a "judicial retreat." [95] The retreat in 1958–61 was, however, no rout. [96] The impact of the 1955–58 decisions in favor of civil liberties were significant and enduring, even when narrowed by later decisions.

Perhaps the new majority of 1955–58 was highly unstable, containing Harlan and Frankfurter, justices who were more deferential to Congress and the executive branch on constitutional issues raised by political dissenters. It can also be seen as an adjustment to the times: the worst of the Red Scare was over; why not defer to Congress and avoid more *Jencks* laws or statutes even more dangerous to the power of the Court? Frankfurter would have been personally devastated if a significant diminution of the appellate jurisdiction of the Court took place and was in any measure attributable to his work.

Furthermore, the old Communist Left and its fellow travelers were so insignificant by the 1960s (in part, replaced by the New Left) that perhaps there was little apparent need to protect them from the government. The reality was that Whittaker, Stewart, Clark, Harlan, and Frankfurter were a new majority, which was to be changed again with the arrival of Arthur Goldberg—who replaced Frankfurter in 1962 and was himself replaced by Abe Fortas in 1965—and changed still again when Thurgood Marshall replaced Clark in 1967. It was during the 1960s that those other liberal landmark Warren Court cases were to be decided, reflecting the return to yet another new majority.

The shift to a conservative majority in the 1959 Court term may also have been the result of such additional factors as the error of Chief Justice Warren in not granting Frankfurter a greater role by assigning more decision writing to him or otherwise placating Frankfurter's needs by employing aspects of his legal approach and his choice of language in writing opinions. Professor Murphy has also criticized the Warren Court for "poor craftsmanship in cases like *Nelson, Jencks, Watkins* and *Sweezy*." [97]

Important, Congress did not statutorily change any liberal decision on Red Scare issues except the *Jencks* case, and even there the Jencks Act did not substantially alter the essence of the Court's decision. Nor was the appellate jurisdiction of the Supreme Court altered. Thus it can be said that this shift in the Court's majority did not pragmatically reverse the impact of Red Monday and related decisions. The effect of these 1955–58 decisions was felt by Congress, the executive, and the nation: the Supreme Court no longer endorsed the unqualified use of the court system to further the aims of the Red Scare.

Chapter 10
In Retrospect

More than forty years have elapsed since Red Monday. Nevertheless, the era of the second Red Scare itself has, in many respects, remained a subject of continued and intense controversy. The overarching issue is perhaps the most hotly debated: Were the anti-communists right, even in their excesses? Was paranoia a valid response? Focusing on the Communist Party, a new and vigorous defense of militant anti-communism has been voiced, declaring that the Party and its so-called fellow travelers and sympathizers were indeed overtly dangerous to the country. Thus the trials of leading Communists, Party influence in Hollywood, in unions, with farmers, and among minorities and intellectuals, the work of HUAC and Senator McCarthy, as well as continuing battles over the guilt or innocence of Alger Hiss and of the Rosenbergs as atomic bomb spies—all have come under new and continuing scrutiny.

In large measure this has been a result of the opening of some of the heretofore inaccessible files in Soviet Russia's agencies and revelations by former Soviet agents, as well as the release of some U.S. government documents from what are known as the Venona files. The latter reflect the work of the U.S. Army Signals Intelligence Agency in the mid-1940s, which partially broke the Soviet diplomatic codes used at that time. The disclosures from those sources name names and describe activities of American communists that, in the assessment of some historians of the era, call for a radical departure from past views about people, events, and even trials held during the Red Scare era.

In essence, what is being called for is nothing less than a reevaluation of basic attitudes about the Red Scare. Some of those considered to have been martyred (e.g., the Rosenbergs, Alger Hiss, Cedric Belfrage, Harry Dexter White) were, it is asserted, really spies for Russia, and others who were not prosecuted should have been. As to those who escaped prosecution, it has been argued that "passage of time should not relieve them of the responsibility to account for their acts. Nor should their countrymen—journalists and historians in particular—ignore the dishonorable and villainous conduct of the spies still among us."[1]

The other side of the coin being argued by these revisionists is that admitted communist spy Elizabeth Bentley and former Soviet spy Whittaker Chambers, both of whom have been vilified as Red Scare hysteria mongers and liars, were in fact correct in their accusations against those whom they believed were in the service of Russia. Having unjustifiably been made villains, they should, the argument goes, be totally exonerated.

What, then, is being overtly argued is that the Red Scare was a necessary adjunct to the Cold War and that, notwithstanding the wrongs that were perpetuated, it was ultimately justified. As John Earl Haynes has written, "For all its sporadic ugliness, excesses, and silliness, the anticommunism of the 1940s and 1950s was an understandable and rational response to a real danger to American democracy." Richard Gid Powers argues that anti-communists were not all irrational people seeking to destroy the lives of others and denigrate civil liberties but were principled people, sincerely involved in defending the nation from a real and quite dangerous internal menace.[2]

Thus the battle over the meaning and validity of the Red Scare, sorting out the heroes from the villains, continues. Recently one of the leaders of the revisionist camp, Ronald Radosh, whose coauthored book about the *Rosenberg* atomic bomb spy case presented "compelling" evidence that Julius Rosenberg was a spy, claims that liberal academics who dislike his views on the Red Scare derailed his candidacy for an academic position.[3] Such are the passions involved in evaluating the what, why, and how of the Red Scare.

Rebuttals to these arguments are certain to be forthcoming. The Soviet archives have yielded some important information and proofs, but there are justifiable issues about the reliability of these records and serious questions as to what is being shown as against what is not. It is also to be noted that prior to the collapse of the Soviet Union and the opening up of these wellsprings, it was vociferously argued that little or nothing coming out of any Russian source was to be trusted or believed. Some of these same people now hold forth that everything out of these same sources is to be accepted as truthful and reliable.

Soviet agents were certainly active during the entire Red Scare era; the same was and is true of American agents operating in Russia and other former Soviet states. The declarations of "turned" agents have always been suspect, as well they should be. It is known that Soviet agents, to protect themselves and serve their masters, invented reports of having secured the cooperation or participation of Americans in supplying information. Now to take such reports as filed in Moscow or as recited by these former agents as truthful is clearly suspect as a means of substantiating a charge. There is and will be much to be gained from these personal and archival sources, but only careful sifting and further substantiation will establish where the truth lies. The same is true of the Venona intercepts. How much is guesswork, connecting names given by code with real persons, is an open issue; yet, again, this is undoubtedly a valuable and heretofore unavailable source that should yield answers to continuing disputes.

What is the relevance of these continuing controversies to this work, which examines the history of dissent and focuses on the important Supreme Court cases and impact of shifts in the views of the Court? In large measure these cases stand apart from the tug of war over Red Scare personalities and their involvement with espionage against the United States. Most of the leading cases that are the focus here were the result of prosecutions brought under the 1940 Smith Act: prosecutions for advocacy, for belief, for organizing, for teaching the duty, the necessity, the desirability or the propriety of overthrowing the government—not for committing espionage.

Prosecutions were also undertaken for perjury: lying under oath about Communist Party membership or on non-communist affidavits. Still other grounds for prosecution were for contempt of Congress for refusing to answer questions and name names. Some cases focused on arguments over rules of evidence: to what is an accused entitled by way of confronting accusing witnesses? All essentially presented questions regarding freedom of speech, press, and assembly—of dissent, not espionage.

The *Amerasia*, *Rosenberg*, and *Coplon* cases presented questions of espionage. According to some recent views, the *Amerasia* case was mishandled by the Justice Department. It involved the unlawful publication of classified documents in a small-circulation journal dealing with foreign policy debates. Six persons were arrested in June 1945 and accused of espionage on behalf of the Chinese Communists, thereby opposing the American-backed leadership of Chiang Kai-shek and his Kuomintang party. Two persons were found guilty of possessing documents they should not have had. Most of the documents turned out to be of little secret value and, in fact, were embarrassing to the government. No trial was held; the two defendants paid a nominal fine. The case was for the most part forgotten until later in the Red Scare era, when it was alleged by Senator McCarthy that there had been a cover-up, which led to and fed on the concept of a conspiracy to "lose" China to the Communists. As Stanley I. Kutler said in his review of a recent book on the case, "The Amerasia affair reminds us of how little it took to ferment hysteria in the 1940s and 1950s. Any support for an idea or policy that deviated from hard-line anti-communism was suspect and a cause for patriotic parades."[4]

The *Coplon* case involved accusations of passing counterintelligence data to Soviet agents. Judith Coplon worked for the U.S. Department of Justice and had access to FBI secrets. Twice she was found guilty; twice the conviction was reversed for serious trial errors. According to Haynes and Klehr, Venona intercepts proved she was a Soviet agent.[5] Even assuming they are correct, the significance of the *Coplon* cases was that they were used to "prove" that the Truman administration was unfit to protect the nation against communist penetration (an argument advanced by Representative Richard M. Nixon) and that there were, as Senator McCarthy charged, Soviet agents in the government.[6]

The most serious espionage case, the *Rosenberg* prosecution, resulted in convictions and death sentences for both husband and wife in 1951; they were quickly executed in 1953 without a full review of this important case by the U.S. Supreme Court. Once again, archival and Venona intercepts are cited as proof of Julius Rosenberg's guilt. Yet the *Rosenberg* case persists as troubling primarily because of the death sentence for both, which the Justice Department demanded with the intent to extract confessions from either or both of them.

Even J. Edgar Hoover had misgivings about executing Ethel Rosenberg, given her minimal role in the matter and the fact that her execution might make her a martyr, particularly because she left two small children as orphans. Though there were and still are protests concerning the case and the rapid executions, the general mood of the country at the time (1953), which was then at the peak of the Red Scare phenomenon, was profoundly unsympathetic to the Rosenbergs.

These espionage prosecutions were not Smith Act cases, nor did they otherwise involve First Amendment issues. In the media and apparently in the minds of Americans, this was too fine a distinction. It was all one: spying for Russia, belonging to the Communist Party, belonging to or supporting civil rights groups, contributing to liberal causes, reading left-wing or liberal papers, associating with nonconformists, refusing as a matter of conscience to sign a loyalty oath, refusing to name names— all were lumped together as subversive, un-American, and thus a danger to the nation. When I was in college during the Red Scare era, a professor with a nervous laugh one day commented that he would not come to class wearing a red tie. He laughed, but neither he nor the class regarded this as just a joke.

That there were Soviet spies seeking U.S. secrets is unquestionable. That Russia gave financial support to the American Communist Party seems proven. That some few Party members were used to gain secret intelligence for Russia seems evident. Yet these acts did not generate either the Cold War or the Red Scare. They did, however, play a role in inflaming hysteria, paranoia, and passion that escalated far beyond the genuine security interests of the nation. Politics also played a vital role, because being a fervent anti-communist became (as Senator McCarthy and others realized) a source of power and safety, as well as the most fertile grounds for attacking the Democratic Party's control of the presidency and Congress.

The courts as an institution played a key role throughout the Red Scare. This was particularly true on the appellate level of the federal system as it was brought into dealing with Red Scare issues through reviewing the results of prosecutions, particularly alleged violations of the Smith Act. J. Edgar Hoover not only wanted to destroy the Communist Party through prosecuting its leaders and their beliefs under the Smith Act, but he wanted to educate the American public as to the need to search for "Reds" in any and every shade.[7] He wanted the public to join in his passion, elevated to the status of a national crusade, in which no "enemies" were to be spared.

But would the courts, and particularly the highest court in the land, approve? Clearly, the signals sent in the form of its decisions would place an incontrovertible stamp of approval on the Red Scare by finding convictions to have been proper and justified. Just as clearly, if the Court placed stumbling blocks in the way of prosecutions by requiring a high threshold of proof, demanding evidence of acts beyond mere beliefs, allowing a wide measure of dissent and favoring broad interpretations of First Amendment rights, the message would be that the most prestigious court in the world was placing its weight against the use of law and courts to further the Red Scare. In fact, during the 1950s the Court did both; therein lies the tale. It is a tale of how the Supreme Court mirrored society in the hottest years of the Red Scare (1946–54) and why, in calmer times, the justices substantially dismantled the use of the courts to further the aims of the Red Scare, epitomized by the Red Monday decisions.

What is the relevance of this today? Even as the United States has seen a new wave of antigovernment groups enter the national scene in the 1990s, and even as terrorist attacks have been carried out sporadically, the Smith Act has not been resurrected. Yet these factions have been to some extent demonized by the American public as communists were at the height of the Red Scare.

Tied to the radical right, these groups often carry components of racism, xenophobia, and anti-Semitism in their programs. Some have sought to isolate themselves from normal community life, while others have posed as armed protectors from a federal government which they believe has been secretly taken over by foreign elements. All are heavily involved in accepting numerous conspiracy theories, in turn leading some to declare their independence from U.S. government control or to call for overthrowing the corrupt, alien-controlled national government.

Violence has broken out with attacks on government agents and agencies and armed challenges to the authority of the federal government. Violence has been used to gain funds to finance these movements and to purchase weapons of war.

The Posse Comitatus, Christian Patriot Defense League, White Patriot Party, Police Against the New World Order, and Branch Davidians are groups that have armed themselves, that believe in force, and that have demonized the federal government and often called for its overthrow.[8] A "militia movement" operating in a number of states has armed, trained, and drilled its members, teaching them how to conduct terrorist acts and to intimidate federal judges and marshals. When the government has acted in response to these developments, the indictments and trials that follow usually charge defendants with illegally obtaining, possessing, or using weapons or means of mass destruction (TNT, bombs) or with conspiracy to commit federal crimes.

Yet the Smith Act has not been used in prosecuting any person or group charged with violence or conspiracy against the government. Thus, when the World Trade Center building in New York City was bombed on February 26, 1993, numerous charges were filed against Omar Abdel-Rahman (also known as "Sheik Omar") and more than a dozen other defendants, with one of the charges being that of Seditious Conspiracy under Section 2384 of Title 18 of the United States Code. This law comes close to the Smith Act in content, and it appears in the same chapter as the Smith Act (Chapter 115, Treason, Sedition, and Subversive Activities).

The emphasis in the Smith Act is advocating or teaching the duty of overthrowing or destroying the government of the United States or any state. The section used in these prosecutions and in other 1990s prosecutions makes it a federal crime to conspire to overthrow the government. The two sections are so close that they in fact overlap in concept and content. However, the Smith Act section was not used against Abdel-Rahman, nor against any other defendant or group.

The same was true in the aftermath of the Waco, Texas incident in April 1993 involving David Koresh and his Branch Davidian group. Charges filed by the United States, which Koresh called "The Beast," included ten counts involving federal law, but not the Smith Act. Had Koresh survived, he might have been charged with the same seditious conspiracy charge as in the World Trade Center bombing.

Timothy McVeigh, found guilty in 1997 of eleven counts charging various violations of federal laws involving the Oklahoma City bombing case, was not charged with violating the Smith Act or with seditious conspiracy, even though his act in blowing up a federal building on April 19, 1995 was characterized by the prosecuting attorney as the hoped-for "first shot in a violent, bloody revolution."[9]

There have been numerous other trials during the 1990s that did not achieve high-profile status. Usually these cases involved illegal weapons and bomb devices. Conspiracies have been alleged, but the Smith Act has not been invoked. The reticence to use the act that provided so many government victories in the 1950s is probably to avoid comparisons with Red Scare times. It certainly is not because the words and deeds would fail to fit what the Smith Act prohibits.

Under the last major interpretation of the Smith Act by the Supreme Court in 1969, the restrictive test requiring "imminent lawless action" could have been easily met as the standard in these 1990s cases. Though this 1969 standard was more demanding than *Yates* and other Red Monday cases required, it can nevertheless be argued that the government could easily have proved violation of the Smith Act in those cases, if it had chosen to do so.[10] Instead, as explained, government authorities have chosen to use another criminal statute dating back to the Civil War where they have sought to prove a seditious conspiracy rather than use the Smith Act of 1940.

It requires little imagination to realize the elation of J. Edgar Hoover if he could have presented the kind of evidence that a Senate subcommittee recently heard when investigating militia activities: that weapons, gas masks, and military hardware had been seized from these groups, along with documents that revealed plans to destroy bridges, radio stations, and other targets, as well as plans to use a lethal poison to kill federal employees and law enforcement agents.[11] Imagine if he could have accused any of the Communist Party members of holding shootouts with federal agents, making bombs, holding up banks to get funds, committing sabotage, or blowing up a federal building. Unfortunately for his cause, Hoover was unable to find any link between acts of sabotage during the Korean War and communists. He admitted in March 1951 that, after full investigation, none of the sabotage complaints, which had increased by 600 percent in the previous year, could be characterized as "Red-directed."[12]

But indeed, in the 1950s, evidence of such acts was unnecessary to secure convictions. On the other hand, in the 1990s, there have been many instances where, even with such evidence, the government has still lost in trial courts, particularly in low-profile cases.[13]

Because the law has changed since the 1950s, a defendant charged with a serious crime has the right to obtain counsel, assigned and paid for by the federal government. Two major problems are thus avoided by all current defendants as against Red Scare times. For example, it was estimated that the attorneys assigned to the McVeigh defense cost taxpayers more than ten million dollars.

In the 1990s there is a level of skepticism concerning government and its leadership that was not present in the Red Scare era. Then, for most people, the idea that the government would fabricate or withhold evidence or that the word of the FBI might be questioned was simply not believable. Such accusations were, in effect, outside the normal ambit of otherwise justifiable criticism.[14] Clearly, the times have changed.

Yet the Smith Act is still part of the living law of the United States, and the high standard of proof required to punish abstract advocacy stated by the Supreme Court in 1969 can be overturned or modified so as to once again open the door to prosecutions for dissent.[15]

When "calmer times" change to times of internal tensions, anxiety, and even paranoia, will the lessons of the Red Scare influence the nation and its courts to avoid the abuses that befell those clinging to the protections of the Bill of Rights? The answer is in the nation, as well as its courts, because ultimately the law, the courts, and all the judges mirror society. The answer, then, is up to all of us.

Notes

Chapter 1. Red Monday and J. Edgar Hoover

1. *Washington Post*, June 18, 1957.

2. *Watkins v. United States*, 354 U.S. 178 (1957); *Sweezy v. New Hampshire*, 354 U.S. 234 (1957); *Yates v. United States*, 354 U.S. 298 (1957); *Service v. Dulles*, 354 U.S. 363 (1957).

3. Alexander Charns, *Cloak and Gavel: FBI Wiretaps, Bugs, Informers, and the Supreme Court* (Urbana: University of Illinois Press, 1992), p. 9. Charns also edited collections of FBI records, which have been published on microfilm by University Publications of America (Bethesda, Md., 1991). Primarily since Hoover's death in 1972, he, his tactics, and the FBI under his leadership have been the subject of intensive biographical study. The result has been to demolish much of the edifice he built about himself and the FBI, particularly his anti-communist, anti-dissident crusades. Among books examining Hoover are Kenneth O'Reilly, *Hoover and the Un-Americans: The FBI, HUAC, and the Red Menace* (Philadelphia: Temple University Press, 1983); Athan G. Theoharis, ed., *Beyond the Hiss Case: The FBI, Congress, and the Cold War* (Philadelphia: Temple University Press, 1982); Athan G. Theoharis and John Stuart Cox, *The Boss: J. Edgar Hoover and the Great American Inquisition* (Philadelphia: Temple University Press, 1988); Anthony Summers, *Official and Confidential: The Secret Life of J. Edgar Hoover* (New York: Putnam, 1993); Ovid Demaris, *The Director* (New York: Harper's Magazine Press, 1975); Sanford J. Ungar, *FBI* (Boston: Little, Brown, 1976); and Richard G. Powers, *Secrecy and Power: The Life of J. Edgar Hoover* (New York: Free Press, 1987).

4. Powers, pp. 338, 567 n. 54. Quotes taken from Hoover to Seaton, June 26, 1957, FBI, Seaton Papers, Dwight D. Eisenhower Presidential Library, Abeline, Kans.

5. Charns, p. 3; see also Roger V. Newman, *Hugo Black* (New York: Pantheon Books, 1994), pp. 422–23. On the matter of law clerks, see Athan G. Theoharis, *From the Secret Files of J. Edgar Hoover* (Chicago: Ivan R. Dee, 1991), pp. 265–67.

6. Summers, pp. 204–5.

7. James J. Kelley, Special Agent in Charge of the New York Office, to Hoover, "Personal and Confidential" memorandum, April 5, 1954, 37356-NR, FBI Records. Quoted by Charns, p. 5.

8. *Dennis v. United States*, 341 U.S. 494 (1951); Charns, pp. 45–46; Smith Act, 18 U.S.C. 2385 (1940).

9. Charns, pp. 64–68, 112–19. Douglas firmly believed that the FBI was out to

destroy him and get him off the Court as well as prevent him from participating in deciding a case in which the Bureau had a particular interest. Douglas to Parvin, October 18, 1966. Cited by Charns, p. 167.

10. Newman, pp. 424–25; see also Samuel Walker, *In Defense of American Liberties: A History of the ACLU* (New York: Oxford University Press, 1989).

11. Charns, pp. 11–13; Theoharis and Cox, pp. 302–3.

12. Quoted in Stephen J. Wermlel, "Writing Supreme Court Biography: A Single Lens View of a Nine-Sided Image," *Journal of Supreme Court History, 1994 Yearbook of the Supreme Court Historical Society*, p. 15. There have been numerous comments about President Eisenhower's views, particularly of his Warren appointment. The leading recent biographer of the president, Stephen E. Ambrose, in *Eisenhower*, vol. 2, *The President* (New York: Simon and Schuster, 1984), takes the position that, at least during his presidency, Eisenhower remained convinced that Warren was the right choice; see pp. 129, 191. Nevertheless, Ambrose is the source of the "S.O.B." response of Eisenhower, given in the 1965 interviews. See "The Ike Age," *New Republic*, May 9, 1981, p. 30; and Bernard Schwartz with Stephan Lesher, *Inside the Warren Court* (New York: Doubleday, 1983), p. 92, where Eisenhower is quoted as saying his appointment of Warren was "the biggest damn-fool mistake I ever made."

13. Charns, pp. 13–15. Federal judges below the Supreme Court level had been subject to politicized FBI background checks since 1930; Theoharis and Cox, pp. 302–3.

14. Kevin Gotham, "Domestic Security for the American State: The FBI Covert Repression, and Democratic Legitimacy," *Journal of Political and Military Sociology* 22 (winter 1994): 216.

15. Quoted in Curt Gentry, *J. Edgar Hoover: The Man and the Secrets* (New York: Penguin Group, 1992), p. 442; Gotham, p. 208. See Charns, pp. 118, 134–35 n. 20, and Powers, pp. 338–40.

16. Summers, p. 393. The identity of this group has never been determined. They were probably Vietnam protesters.

17. *Supplementary Detailed Staff Reports on Intelligence Activities and the Rights of Americans*, Book 3, Final Report of Select Committee to Study Governmental Operations with respect to Intelligence Activities/United States Senate, April 23, 1976 (Washington, D.C.: GPO, 1976), p. 3. Hereinafter cited as *Report*.

18. Ibid., p. 3; See also Nelson Blackstock, *COINTELPRO: The FBI's Secret War on Political Freedom* (New York: Random House, 1976), p. xi; and Ward Churchill and Jim Vander Wall, *The COINTELPRO Papers, Documents from the FBI's Secret Wars Against Domestic Dissent* (Boston: South End Press, 1990), p. 40.

19. *Socialist Workers Party v. the Attorney General of the United States*, 73 Civ. 3160; 642 F. Supp. 1357 (S.D.N.Y. 1986).

20. *Report*, pp. 7–8.

21. Ibid. p. 9.

22. Ibid. p. 10.

23. Ibid. p. 10.

24. Ibid., p. 449.

25. Hoover, Top Secret [now unclassified], Memorandum, SUBJECT: Discussion at the 279th Meeting of the National Security Council, Thursday, March 8, 1956; Eisenhower Library.

26. Robert Mollan, "Smith Act Prosecutions: The Effects of the *Dennis* and *Yates* Decisions," *University of Pittsburgh Law Review* 26 (1965): 735.

27. Powers, p. 338; Michal R. Belknap, *Cold War Political Justice: The Smith Act,*

the Communist Party and American Civil Liberties (Westport, Conn.: Greenwood Press, 1977), pp. 156, 178 n. 13. These last Smith Act prosecutions were dismissed in the fall of 1957 by the government, so no conviction resulted. Mollan, p. 705.

28. Powers, pp. 339–43; Churchill and Vanderwall, pp. 41–48.

29. *Report*, p. 77.

30. Mollan, pp. 705ff.

31. As a result of a report by the House Un-American Activities Committee, the Mundt-Nixon Bill was introduced into Congress. Debates took place over whether the Smith Act was adequate in view of perceived threats, with vigorous arguments on both sides. Mundt-Nixon passed in the House but not in the Senate. See *Congressional Record*, 91st Cong., 1948, pp. 5860–66, 5876–77 for debate in the House.

32. Peter L. Steinberg, *The Great "Red Menace": United States Prosecution of American Communists, 1947–1952* (Westport, Conn.: Greenwood Press, 1984), pp. 103–4. Quotation from Clark to Steinberg, March 28, 1975.

33. Ibid., p. 111.

34. Mollan, pp. 705ff. 129 convictions were based on the "advocacy" clause of the Smith Act; 8 were prosecuted under the "membership" clause.

35. Ibid.

36. Tom P. Brady, foreword to *Black Monday* (Winona, Miss.: Association of Citizens' Councils, 1954); *Brown v. Board of Education*, 347 U.S. 483 (1954).

37. Anthony Lewis, "This Is Not a Police State," reprinted from the *New York Times* in the *Chicago Daily Law Bulletin*, May 1, 1996.

Chapter 2. Historical Antecedents of the Second Red Scare

1. *An Act Concerning Aliens*; 1 Stat. 570, June 25, 1798; *An Act in addition to the act entitled An Act for the Punishment of Certain Crimes Against the United States* (Sedition Act), 1 Stat. 596, July 14, 1798.

2. Emerson, Thomas Irwin, David Haber, and Norman Dorsen, eds., *Political and Civil Rights in the United States* (Boston: Little, Brown, 1967), pp. 37–38.

3. David M. Rabban, *Free Speech in Its Forgotten Years* (New York: Cambridge University Press, 1997), makes the case that the free speech controversies during and after World War I did not "spring from a void" but were firmly rooted in controversies and debates that occurred in the 1870–1920 period, both inside and outside of courtrooms.

4. *Ex parte Milligan*, 71 U.S. 2 (1866). This concept has not been repudiated by the Court, but it certainly was not followed in the cases involving the internment of Japanese-Americans during World War II.

5. 65th Cong., 1st sess., 1917, Chap. 30 (Espionage Act); 65th Cong., 2d sess., 1918, Chap. 75 (Sedition Act, amending the Espionage Act).

6. Alfred H. Kelly and Winfred A. Harbison, *The American Constitution* (New York: Norton, 1970), pp. 674–75; William Preston, Jr., *Aliens and Dissenters: Federal Suppression of Radicals, 1903–1933* (New York: Harper and Row, 1963), p. 145ff.

7. Kermit L. Hall, editor in chief, *The Oxford Companion to the Supreme Court of the United States* (New York: Oxford University Press, 1992), p. 942.

8. The late nineteenth and early twentieth centuries witnessed a Red Scare responsive to attempts to organize unions and bring about strikes. Most attention was paid to legislating on the state and national level against the Industrial Workers of the World (the "Wobblies").

9. *Patterson v. Colorado*, 205 U.S. 454 (1907).

10. *Fox v. Washington*, 236 U.S. 273 (1915).

11. *Schenck v. United States*, 249 U.S. 48 (1919).

12. Ibid. at 52 (emphasis added).

13. *Abrams v. United States*, 250 U.S. 616 (1919).

14. *Debs v. United States*, 249 U.S. 211 (1919).

15. Ibid. at 215.

16. *Frohwerk v. United States*, 249 U.S. 204 (1919), quotation on pp. 208–9.

17. Hall, p. 6.

18. G. Edward White, "Looking at Holmes in the Mirror," *Law and History Review* 4 (Fall 1986): 458–59; David M. Rabban, "The First Amendment in Its Forgotten Years," *Yale Law Journal* 90 (1981): 514–80.

19. Richard Polenberg, *Fighting Faiths: The Abrams Case, the Supreme Court, and Free Speech* (New York: Viking Penguin, 1987), pp. 366–67.

20. Ibid.

21. William E. Leuchtenburg, *The Perils of Prosperity, 1914–1932* (Chicago: University of Chicago Press, 1958), pp. 66–77; Polenberg, pp. 164–67.

22. Leuchtenburg, p. 81.

23. *Gitlow v. New York*, 268 U.S. 652 (1925).

24. Ibid. at 673.

25. *Whitney v. California*, 274 U.S. 357 (1927).

26. Ibid. at 377. Note the use of the male gender, although Whitney was female.

27. *De Jonge v. Oregon*, 299 U.S. 353 (1937).

28. Emerson et al., p. 61.

29. Title 1 of the *Alien Registration Act.*, 54 Stat. 670; sec. 1, now incorporated in 18 U.S.C. sec. 2387, deals with impairing the morale of the armed services. Secs. 2 and 3, now incorporated into 18 U.S.C. sec. 2385, contains the antisubversive provisions. Michal R. Belknap, *Cold War Political Justice: The Smith Act, the Communist Party, and American Civil Liberties* (Westport, Conn.: Greenwood Press, 1977). Belknap offers an explanation as to why FDR signed the Smith Act, recognizing as he did what the legislation represented. The Smith Act was endorsed by major administrative departments and was a way of getting back at the Communist Party for its anti-Roosevelt stand during the period between the Hitler-Stalin Pact and the invasion of Russia.

30. The relationship between Smith and Hoover can be gained through biographies of Hoover; see Athan G. Theoharis and John Stuart Cox, *The Boss: J. Edgar Hoover and The Great American Inquisition* (Philadelphia: Temple University Press, 1988), p. 261; and Kenneth O'Reilly, *Hoover and the Un-Americans: The FBI, HUAC, and the Red Menace* (Philadelphia: Temple University Press, 1983), pp. 95, 312 n. 46.

31. *Hirabayashi v. United States*, 320 U.S. 81 (1943).

32. *Korematsu v. United States*, 323 U.S. 214 (1944).

33. David Caute, *The Great Fear: The Anti-Communist Purge Under Truman and Eisenhower* (New York: Simon and Schuster, 1978), p. 89, where the committee's authority is quoted.

34. Griffin Fariello, ed., *Red Scare: Memories of the American Inquisition, An Oral History* (New York: Norton, 1995), p. 17; Walter Bernstein, *Inside Out: A Memoir of the Blacklist* (New York: Knopf, 1996); Bernard Weinraub, "From the Days of McCarthy, a Lingering Chill," *New York Times*, January 16, 1997; Victor Rabino-

witz, *Unrepentant Leftist: A Lawyer's Memoir* (Urbana: University of Illinois Press, 1996).

35. O'Reilly, p. 74. Details can also be found in Theoharis and Cox, p. 250ff.

36. Richard G. Powers, *Secrecy and Power: The Life of J. Edgar Hoover* (New York: Free Press, 1987), pp. 286–90.

37. Peter Hamill, "In Defense of Honest Labor," *New York Times Magazine,* December 31, 1995, p. 19, quoting Walter J. Sheridan.

38. Mary Jo Buhle, Paul Buhle, and Dan Georgakas, eds., *Encyclopedia of the American Left* (New York: Garland, 1990), p. 335.

39. See Ellen W. Schrecker, *No Ivory Tower: McCarthyism and the Universities* (New York: Oxford University Press, 1986), for stories of academics; oral histories in Fariello; Williams for personal accounts; Bud Schultz and Ruth Schultz, eds., *It Did Happen Here: Recollections of Political Repression in America* (Berkeley: University of California Press, 1989); Richard M. Fried, *Nightmare in Red: The McCarthy Era in Perspective* (New York: Oxford University Press, 1990), who relates tales of those "caught in a nightmare from which there is no awakening" (p. 27); and Carl Bernstein, *Loyalties: A Son's Memoir* (New York: Simon and Schuster, 1989). Some sense of the volume of people involved in one manner or another may be gained by the reading the indexes in Buhle et al. and in William K. Klingaman, ed., *Encyclopedia of the McCarthy Era* (New York: Facts on File, 1996). While some of the names are well known, the hundreds contained reflect a much wider group than those who were, for one reason or another, brought into enough notoriety to be included in these works.

40. Schultz and Schultz, p. 101.

41. Edward Hoagland, "Drawing on a Daring Life," *Civilization* (January-February 1996): 50.

42. Peter H. Buckingham, *America Sees Red* (Claremont, Calif.: Regina Books, 1988), p. 216.

43. For example, see Michael F. Tigar's review of David Caute's *The Great Fear,* in *Harvard Civil Rights-Civil Liberties Review* 15: 507, where he directly contradicts this thesis. Tigar writes, "The hopes raised by *Yates, Watkins,* and *Sweezy* were soon dashed" (p. 519).

Chapter 3. Red Scare at High Tide: The *Dennis* Case

1. Michal R. Belknap, *Cold War Political Justice: The Smith Act, the Communist Party, and American Civil Liberties* (Westport, Conn.: Greenwood Press, 1977), pp. 41–42.

2. Belknap points out that an attempt by Republicans to label FDR and the Democratic Party as tools of the Communist Party failed in 1944. By 1948, according to Gallup Polls he cites, the communist question had become a major political issue (p. 43).

3. David Frumkin, *In the Time of the Americans* (New York: Knopf, 1995), p. 508.

4. Truman spoke out many times against Senator McCarthy's operation and methods, and in September 1950 he vetoed the Internal Security Act, known as the McCarran Act. Some Democrats, including liberals, tried to outdo Senator McCarran with their own legislation that was even "tougher"—really more violative of the Bill of Rights—than McCarran's. Truman's veto message pointed out that requiring communist organizations to register and divulge information

about themselves was "about as practical as requiring thieves to register with the sheriff." Quoted in William K. Klingaman, ed., *Encyclopedia of the McCarthy Era* (New York: Facts on File, 1996), p. 368.

5. *Annual Report of the Attorney General of the United States for the Fiscal Year Ending June 30, 1947*, p. 11.

6. *Annual Report of the Attorney General of the United States for the Fiscal Year Ending June 30, 1948*, pp. 11–12.

7. Klingaman, p. 240. For an exhaustive study of this subject, see Ralph S. Brown, Jr., *Loyalty and Security: Employment Tests in the United States* (New Haven, Conn.: Yale University Press, 1958). Also among his conclusions are "We [Americans] have acquiesced in extravagant demands to invade the pasts, the privacy, and the minds of millions of our fellows" (pp. 477–78). "Loyalty tests are supported by no valid arguments of necessity" (p. 478).

8. *Report of the U.S. Department of Justice, for the Fiscal Year Ending June 30, 1948*, pp. 12–16.

9. Ibid., pp. 20–21.

10. *Joint Anti-Fascist Refugee Committee v. McGrath*; *IWO v. McGrath*, 341 U.S. 123 (1951). The third organization was the National Council of Soviet-American Friendship.

11. U.S. Senate, 80th Cong., 2d sess., Judiciary Committee, Control of Subversive Activities Hearings, Washington, D.C., 1948, pp. 1–9.

12. Donal Prater, *Thomas Mann: A Life* (New York: Oxford University Press, 1995).

13. Klingaman, pp. 320–21.

14. "The Independence of the Bar," *Lawyers Guild Review* 13 (1953): 159–61; Benjamin Dreyfus and Doris Brin Walker, "Grounds for Discipline of Attorneys," *Lawyers Guild Review* 18 (1958): 67; "Weissman, Sacher, and Isserman in the Courts," *Lawyers Guild Review* 12 (1952): 39.

15. William O. Douglas, "The Black Silence of Fear," *New York Times Magazine*, January 13, 1952, p. 1.

16. Harper, "Loyalty and Lawyers," *Lawyers Guild Review* 11 (1951): 705.

17. House Committee on Un-American Activities, *Report on the National Lawyers Guild, Legal Bulwark of the Communist Party*, 81st Cong., 2d sess., 1950, H. Rept. 3123.

18. Proceedings of the House of Delegates, 1950. *A.B.A. Journal* 36 (1950): 948, 972; see also "The Lawyers Loyalty Oath," *A.B.A. Journal* 37 (1951): 128; and Proceedings of the House of Delegates, pp. 309ff. In 1951 an article argued that communists could not be good Americans and suggested that constitutional protections should not be afforded them. Frederick B. Wiener, "Freedom for the Thought That We Hate: Is It a Principle of the Constitution?" 37 *A.B.A. Journal* (1951): 177ff.

19. Lawrence M. Friedman, *A History of American Law*, 2d ed. (New York: Simon and Schuster, 1985), p. 457.

20. Arthur J. Sabin, *Red Scare in Court: New York Versus the International Workers Order* (Philadelphia: University of Pennsylvania Press, 1993). In this book the argument is made that the judge and the lead prosecuting attorney had political ambitions that would be enhanced by involvement in this case. While the judge was not promoted, apparently for political reasons not associated with this case, the prosecuting attorney moved up to a judgeship and then was appointed U.S. attorney for the Southern District of New York. President Eisenhower also offered him a federal judgeship, which he declined.

21. Gerald Gunther, *Learned Hand: The Man and the Judge* (New York: Knopf, 1994), pp. 152, 161, 259. The Hand decision was *Masses Pub. Co. v. Patten*, 244 Fed. 535 (S.D.N.Y. 1917), reversed, 246 Fed. 24 (2d Cir. 1917), where as a trial judge he had found in favor of the defendants whose publication was alleged to have violated the Espionage Act. This decision has been highlighted by Gunther and others as of significance in deterring his advancement to the appellate-level federal court and beyond.

22. The details of the movement to prosecute leaders of the Communist Party are contained in two studies: Michal R. Belknap, *Cold War Political Justice: The Smith Act, the Communist Party, and American Civil Liberties* (Westport, Conn.: Greenwood Press, 1977), and Peter J. Steinberg, *The Great "Red Menace": United States Prosecution of American Communists, 1947–1952* (Westport, Conn.: Greenwood Press, 1984).

23. Belknap, pp. 44–53; Steinberg, pp. 87–97; Richard G. Powers, *Secrecy and Power: The Life of J. Edgar Hoover* (New York: Free Press, 1987), pp. 292–94.

24. Powers, p. 294.

25. Steinberg, p. 97; see also Belknap, pp. 46–53.

26. Athan G. Theoharis and John S. Cox, *The Boss: J. Edgar Hoover and the Great American Inquisition* (Philadelphia: Temple University Press, 1988), pp. 248ff; quote on p. 249.

27. Steinberg, p. 97.

28. David Caute, *The Great Fear: The Anti-Communist Purge Under Truman and Eisenhower* (New York: Simon and Schuster, 1978), p. 187.

29. Powers, pp. 294–95.

30. Theoharis and Cox, pp. 250–55.

31. *Dennis v. United States*, 341 U.S. 494, 497 (1951).

32. Belknap, p. 69.

33. *Cramer v. United States*, 137 F.2d 888 (1943); 325 U.S. 1 (1945).

34. J. Woodford Howard, Jr., "The Cramer Treason Case," *Journal of Supreme Court History* 1 (1996): 48–59; quotes taken from text.

35. Ibid., p. 53.

36. Ibid., p. 57.

37. The attempt to wreck his health, like everything else the defense tried to accomplish, failed; Medina lived well into his nineties.

38. Ibid., pp. 68–69.

39. Ibid., p. 67.

40. Quoted in Caute, p. 189.

41. *New York Times*, September 24, 1949.

42. Melvin B. Lewis, "Judicial Forging of a Political Weapon: The Impact of the Cold War on the Law of Contempt," *John Marshall Law Review* 27 (1993): 14. Among the decisions other than the *Dennis* decision itself are *Sacher v. United States*, 343 U.S. 1 (1952) (affirming the contempt convictions based on trial misconduct); *In re Isserman*, 345 U.S. 286 (1953) (disbarring one of the *Dennis* lawyers for trial misconduct); *Sacher v. Association of the Bar of the City of New York*, 347 U.S. 388 (1954) (declining to disbar another *Dennis* lawyer); *Green v. United States*, 356 U.S. 165 (1957) (affirming contempt convictions based on failure to surrender to serve the Smith Act sentences); *Foster v. Medina*, 170 F.2d 632, 633 (2d Cir. 1949); and *United States v. Sacher*, 9 F.R.D. 394, 409, repeated at 182 F.2d 416, 444–45 (1950) (Contempt Count 27).

43. Belknap, pp. 13–15.

44. Lewis, p. 14.

45. *United States v. Green*, 1767 F.2d 169, 172 (2d Cir. 1949).

46. *Sacher v. United States*, 343 U.S. 1, 14 (1952) (Black, J. dissenting); *United States v. Sacher*, 182 F.2d 416, 418 (2d Cir. 1949).

47. Lewis, p. 16; he quotes Professor F. Rodell.

48. *Sacher v. United States*, 343 U.S. 1 (1952).

49. *Bloom v. Illinois*, 391 U.S. 194 (1968).

50. Belknap, pp. 219–21; Caute, pp. 97–99.

51. Caute, pp. 290–91; p. 613 n. 34.

52. Belknap, pp. 219–22. As early as September 1951, President Truman had urged the bar to recognize the obligation to offer defense counsel to those accused of Smith Act crimes, that is, those accused of conspiring to overthrow the government by force.

53. Jerold S. Auerbach, *Unequal Justice* (New York: Oxford University Press, 1976), pp. 234–36; quote from p. 235.

54. Belknap, p. 222.

55. Ibid., pp. 188–89.

56. Gerald Horne, *Communist Front? The Civil Rights Congress, 1946–1956* (Rutherford, N.J.: Fairleigh Dickinson University Press, 1987).

57. Belknap, pp. 172–73; Klingaman, pp. 141–42, 164–65, 178.

58. Caute, pp. 178–80.

Chapter 4. The Aftermath of the *Dennis* Trial

1. Mary Jo Buhle, Paul Buhle, and Dan Georgakas, eds., *Encyclopedia of the American Left* (New York: Garland, 1990), pp. 296–97.

2. Carl Smith, *Urban Disorder and the Shape of Belief: The Great Chicago Fire, the Haymarket Bomb, and the Model Town of Pullman* (Chicago: University of Chicago Press, 1995), p. 126.

3. *New York Times*, July 21, 1948.

4. On Judge Medina, see, for example, *New York Times*, November 6, 1948; January 16, 18, 23, 25, 1949. See also Sidney Shelt, "The Trial of the Eleven Communists," *Reader's Digest*, August 1950, pp. 57–72; "Communists—'The Field Day Is Over,'" *Time*, August 22, 1949; and "Communists," *Time*, September 26, 1949. Descriptions such as "long-suffering" were typical (*Time*, May 30, 1949). *Time*, April 11, 1949, noted that the judge had become the defendants' adversary: *Time*, April 11, 1949. In the "Religion" column of *Time*, March 19, 1951, Medina is quoted as having depended on divine guidance for the strength to get through the ordeal. In part, he stated:

> There came a time . . . when I did the most sincere and the most fervent praying that I have ever done in my life. I suddenly found myself in the midst of the trial of the Communists. It took me a long time to realize what they were trying to do to me. But as I got weaker and weaker, and found the burden difficult to bear, I sought strength from the one source that never fails.

5. *Time*, October 24, 1949.

6. *New Republic*, October 24, 1949. Similar views were stated in the *Nation*, October 22, 1949, where Robert Bendiner wrote that "the place to beat the Communists . . . is the political field and not in the courts." Interestingly, both articles hoped the U.S. Supreme Court would rectify the matter.

7. *Reader's Digest,* August 1950.

8. *Congressional Record,* Appendix, 1949, A6410, Remarks of Representative L. Gary Clemente (D-N.Y.), on October 17, 1949.

9. *Congressional Record,* House, 1949, 14600, Remarks of Representative Harold H. Velde (R-Ill.), on October 14, 1949. Velde was a former FBI agent who became chairman of HUAC and a consistent anti-communist crusader who saw "Reds" everywhere.

10. Jerold S. Auerbach, *Unequal Justice: Lawyers and Social Change in Modern America* (New York: Oxford University Press, 1976), p. 241.

11. See Melvin B. Lewis, "Judicial Forging of a Political Weapon: The Impact of the Cold War on the Law of Contempt," *John Marshall Law Review* 27 (1993): 3 (quoting letters obtained from the FBI through a Freedom of Information Act (FOIA) request).

12. Ibid., pp. 13–14.

13. Michal R. Belknap, *Cold War Political Justice: The Smith Act, the Communist Party, and American Civil Liberties* (Westport, Conn.: Greenwood Press, 1977), pp. 113–14.

14. The correspondence is contained in the files of the chief prosecutor in the case of the *People of the State of New York by Alfred J. Bohlinger, Superintendent of Insurance v. The International Workers Order, Inc.,* 199 Misc. 941, 106 N.Y.S. 2d 953 (N.Y. Supp., 1951), Williams Office Files, Correspondence for 1951. These files are now in the IWO Archives at the New York State School of Industrial and Labor Relations, Labor-Management Documentation Center, at Cornell University, Ithaca, N.Y. See also the Lewis article for more instances of a Hoover-Medina relationship.

15. Harold R. Medina, *The Anatomy of Freedom* (New York: Henry Holt, 1959); Hawthorne Daniel, *Judge Medina* (New York: W. Funk, 1952).

16. Belknap, p. 190.

17. Ibid., p. 191.

18. Ibid., pp. 192–97.

19. Peter L. Steinberg, *The Great "Red Menace": United States Prosecution of American Communists, 1947–1952* (Westport, Conn.: Greenwood Press, 1984), p. 177. Hoover's words and thoughts had not changed in their expression or concept since he began prosecuting "Reds" in 1919.

20. Quoted in ibid., p. 181.

21. Quoted in ibid., p. 182.

22. Ibid., pp. 182–83.

23. M. J. Heale, *American Anticommunism: Combating the Enemy Within* (Baltimore: Johns Hopkins University Press, 1990), pp. 146–55.

24. Geoffrey Wheatcroft, *Times Literary Supplement (London),* June 6, 1997, p. 10.

25. Internal Security Act of 1950; 64 Stat. 987; 50 U.S.L. secs. 781–826.

26. Stephen J. Whitfield, *The Culture of the Cold War* (Baltimore: Johns Hopkins University Press, 1991), pp. 49–50.

27. Heale, pp. 147–49; quotes on pp. 148 and 149.

28. Whitfield, p. 43.

29. *100 Things You Should Know About Communism* and *Guide to Subversive Organizations and Publications* (Washington, D.C.: GPO, 1951).

30. William K. Klingaman, *Encyclopedia of the McCarthy Era* (New York: Facts on File, 1996), p. 187.

31. Belknap, p. 157 and n. 16, explaining the figures and the difficulty summing up the results; see p. 178. See also David Caute, *The Great Fear: The Anti-*

Communist Purge Under Truman and Eisenhower (New York: Simon and Schuster, 1978), pp. 197–205. Caute's tally, including Membership Clause prosecutions by the end of 1956 is as follows: 145 indictments; 108 convictions, 5 severances; 10 acquittals, with others pending. The attorney general's *Report* for 1953 states:

> The affirmance by the Supreme Court of the conviction of the eleven members of the National Board of the Communist Party, USA, for conspiring to violate the Smith Act resulted in greatly increased activity in the enforcement of that Act during the past fiscal year. From the time of the first indictment returned against the Communists under the Smith Act in July, 1948, until the close of the fiscal year 1953, 85 persons had been indicted, 51 had been convicted, and 34 were awaiting trial. (p. 9)

32. Caute, pp. 206–9; Belknap, pp. 261–65. To be noted is that the first Communists to be arrested under the Membership Clause were the *Dennis* defendants themselves as they came out of prison. They had been indicted for membership but not tried for that offense. They were never brought to trial on the Membership Clause, because the Justice Department apparently chose not to do so.

33. Caute, p. 208.

34. Belknap, pp. 279–80.

35. For a sympathetic account of the physical suffering of imprisoned *Dennis* defendants, see Caute, pp. 209–12. See also Gilbert Green, *Cold War Fugitive* (New York: International Publishers, 1984); Victor Rabinowitz, *Unrepentant Leftist: A Lawyer's Memoirs* (Urbana: University of Illinois Press, 1996); Bud Schultz and Ruth Schultz, eds., *It Did Happen Here: Recollections of Political Repression in America* (Berkeley: University of California Press, 1989); Carl Bernstein, *Loyalties: A Son's Memoirs* (New York: Simon and Schuster, 1989); Selma R. Williams, *Red-Listed: Haunted by the Washington Witch Hunt* (Reading, Mass.: Addison-Wesley, 1993); and Griffin Fariello, ed., *Red Scare: Memoirs of the American Inquisition, an Oral History* (New York: Norton, 1995).

36. Caute, 181–84.

37. Arthur J. Sabin, *Red Scare in Court: New York Versus the International Workers Order* (Philadelphia: University of Pennsylvania Press, 1993). The details, facts and history of the IWO and its legal battles are given in this book.

38. Roger Keeran, "The International Workers Order and the Origins of the CIO," *Labor History* (Fall 1989).

39. Bernard DeVoto, "The Ex-Communists," *Atlantic Monthly*, February 1951, p. 61.

40. *Application of Bohlinger*, 106 N.Y.S 2d 953 (1951).

41. *In re International Workers Order, Inc.*, 113 N.Y.S 2d 755 (1952).

42. *In re People by Bohlinger, Superintendent of Insurance. Appeal of International Workers Order, Inc.*, 305 N.Y. 258 (1953).

43. *Petition for Writ of Certiorari to the Court of Appeals of the State of New York, by Alfred J. Bohlinger, Superintendent of Insurance of the State of New York; Petition* by the IWO dated July 22, 1953. *Brief for Respondent in Opposition* (the state's response to the *Petition*), dated September 17, 1953.

44. Statistics obtained from the office of the clerk of the Supreme Court of the United States.

45. Paul W. Williams interview.

Chapter 5. On Appeal

1. Lawrence M. Friedman, *A History of American Law*, 2d ed. (New York: Simon and Schuster, 1985), chaps. 7, 8; Hendrik Hartog, "Lawyering, Husbands' Rights, and the Unwritten Law in Nineteenth-Century America," *Journal of American History* 84, 1 (June 1997): 67–96.

2. *American Communications Assn., C.I.O., et al. v. Douds, Regional Director of the National Labor Relations Board*, 339 U.S. 382 (1950).

3. Ibid. at 396.

4. Ibid. at 388–89.

5. Ibid. at 384–85.

6. *Blau v. United States*, 340 U.S. 1959 (1950).

7. Certiorari is from the Latin: to be informed, or to be made certain in regard to. In essence, it is an order to review the work of a lower court—an order to send up the record. Four justices must favor issuing the writ for a case to be reviewed on appeal.

8. *Blau*, 340 U.S. at 161.

9. "Self Incrimination," *Washington Star*, December 13, 1950.

10. "Constitution and Communists," *New York Herald Tribune*, December 13, 1950.

11. *Nation*, December 23, 1950, pp. 666–67.

12. Joseph L. Hefferman to Black, December 22, 1950, Justice Hugo L. Black Papers, Manuscript Division, Library of Congress.

13. Ickes to Black, December 14, 1950, Black Papers.

14. *Joint Anti-Fascist Refugee Committee v. McGrath*, 341 U.S. 123 (1951).

15. *Dennis et al. v. United States*, 341 U.S. 494 (1951).

16. Arthur J. Sabin, *Red Scare In Court: New York Versus the International Workers Order* (Philadelphia: University of Pennsylvania Press, 1993), p. 208.

17. Felix Frankfurter Collection, pt. 1, no. 47—*Joint Anti-Fascist*. Harvard University has the Frankfurter Archives; the photocopy was taken from facilities of the Manuscript Division of the Library of Congress.

18. *Joint Anti-Fascist*, 341 U.S. at 139.

19. Michal R. Belknap, in Kermit L. Hall, editor in chief, *The Oxford Companion to the Supreme Court of the United States* (New York: Oxford University Press, 1992), p. 451.

20. *Bailey v. Richardson*, 341 U.S. 918 (1951).

21. *New York Times*, May 2, 1951.

22. David Caute, *The Great Fear: The Anti-Communist Purge Under Truman and Eisenhower* (New York: Simon and Schuster, 1978), p. 170.

23. Ibid., pp. 518–38. See also Belknap, who summarized the matter, stating, "Public officials and private citizens used the list extensively to pillory, intimidate, and ostracize radicals and other dissidents" (p. 452). This decision did not change the situation.

24. Caute, pp. 177–78; William K. Klingaman, ed., *Encyclopedia of the McCarthy Era* (New York: Facts on File, 1996), pp. 2089–90. J. Parnell Thomas himself went to jail after being exposed for accepting kickbacks and bribes. He served his sentence in the same federal penitentiary that held people who had been convicted of contempt of Congress because of refusing to testify or supply information or names to HUAC while he was chairman. Klingaman, pp. 363–64.

25. The contempt citations were confirmed in *United States v. Bryan*, 72 F. Supp. 58 (1947), and in *United States v. Barsky*, 72 F. Supp. 165 (1947).

26. *Barsky et al. v. United States*, 167 F.2d 241 (D.C. Ct. App. 1948); cert. denied, 68 S.Ct. 1511 (1948).

27. *United States v. Fleischman*, 339 U.S. 349 (1950).

28. *Barsky v. Board of Regents of the University of the State of New York*, 347 U.S. 442 (1954).

29. Ibid. at 461.

30. *Rogers v. United States*, 179 F.2d 559; 339 U.S. 956 (1951).

31. Ibid., p. 376. Justice Jackson switched sides; initially he voted with the dissenters; apparently Vinson then convinced him to go with the majority. Staying with the dissenters would not, however, have changed the result. Memorandum by Jackson, December 21, 1950, box 198, William O. Douglas Papers, Manuscript Division, Library of Congress.

32. William O. Douglas, *The Court Years, 1939–1975: The Autobiography of William O. Douglas* (New York: Random House, 1980), p. 388.

33. He has been described as "[t]he greatest judge never to be appointed to the Supreme Court. Learned Hand is widely considered the peer of Justices Holmes, Brandeis, and Cardozo." From the dust jacket of Gerald Gunther, *Learned Hand: The Man and the Judge* (New York: Knopf, 1994), p. 7.

34. Ibid., p. 578.

35. Ibid.

36. *Masses Pub. Co. v. Patten*, 244 F. 535 (S.D.N.Y. 1917).

37. Gunther, pp. 161–67.

38. Gunther, p. 579.

39. Ibid., pp. 579–86.

40. *United States v. Coplon*, 185 F.2d 629 (2d Cir. 1950).

41. *United States v. Dennis*, 183 F.2d 201 (2d Cir. 1950).

42. *Dennis et al v. United States*, 341 U.S. 494 (1951).

43. Gunther, p. 599.

44. *Dennis*, 183 F.2d at 212. Scholars have argued the issue of whether the Hand-*Masses* or the Holmes test is more protective of free expression. The Gunther biography favors Hand and his *Masses* test. Bernard Schwartz, an eminent scholar of the era, rejects this position as dangerous, arguing the contrary: that where the stress in Hand-*Masses* is on the words themselves, the Holmes test brings in the matter of the circumstances prevailing and requires a direct relation to those circumstances. Thus, he argues that under Hand those leaflets in *Abrams* would have triggered governmental power but would not had Holmes's position and analysis prevailed. See Bernard Schwartz, "Holmes Versus Hand: Clear and Present Danger or Advocacy of Unlawful Action?" *Sup. Ct. Rev.* pp. 209 (1994).

45. *Dennis v. United States*, 183 F.2d at 213 (2d Cir. 1950).

46. Gunther, pp. 603–4. The other Red Scare case Hand participated in was *United States v. Remington*, 208 F.2d 567 (2d Cir. 1953), involving a second appeal of a second perjury conviction by William W. Remington, a government economist, convicted of lying when he said he was not a member of the Communist Party. The first appeal, *United States v. Remington*, 191 F.2d 246 (2d Cir. 1951), had reversed the perjury conviction. Remington was reindicted and found guilty again. In the second appeal, Hand vigorously dissented from the majority, who this time affirmed the conviction. To the disappointment of Judge Hand, the Supreme Court refused review of the case. See 347 U.S. 913 (1954). Frankfurter told Hand confidentially that three justices (including himself), had voted to hear the case. Remington was murdered in prison in 1954 (Gunther, pp. 612–

25). See also Gary May, *Un-American Activities: The Trials of William Remington* (New York: Oxford University Press), 1994.

47. Linda C. Gugin and James E. St. Clair, *Sherman Minton: New Deal Senator, Cold War Justice* (Indianapolis: Indiana Historical Society, 1997), pp. 221, 225–26. Minton wrote to Vinson after *Dennis* that "the opinion of yours will come rapidly to be recognized as one of the Court's greatest. I am proud to have been with you all the way" (p. 226). As his biographers stated, "Of course Minton was wrong" (p. 226).

48. Richard Kirkendall, "Fred M. Vinson," in Leon Friedman and Fred L. Israel, eds., *The Justices of the United States Supreme Court 1789–1969: Their Lives and Major Opinions* (New York: Chelsea House, 1969), pp. 2639–49; James A. Thompson, "Frederick Moore Vinson," in Melvin I. Urofsky, ed., *The Supreme Court Justices: A Bibliographical Dictionary* (New York: Garland, 1994).

49. Thompson, p. 492.

50. Caute, pp. 144–45.

51. Bernard Schwartz, *A Book of Legal Lists: The Best and Worst in American Law* (New York: Oxford University Press, 1997), pp. 32–34.

52. Thomas E. Baker, "Vinson," in Kermit Hall, *Oxford Companion*, pp. 898–99.

53. Thompson in Urofsky, p. 490.

54. *Dennis*, 341 U.S. 494 at 509.

55. Ibid., p. 510.

56. Ibid. The explanation for the use of the Hand approach may also lie in the fact that between 1937 and 1948, the Court had applied the "clear and present danger" test in fourteen cases—all resulting in ruling against the government. Michal R. Belknap, *Cold War Political Justice: The Smith Act, the Communist Party, and American Civil Liberties* (Westport, Conn.: Greenwood Press, 1977), pp. 132–33.

57. *Dennis*, 341 U.S. 494 at 578–79.

58. Ibid. at 579.

59. Ibid. at 580.

60. Ibid. at 581.

61. Ibid.

62. Ibid. at 588.

63. Douglas Papers, Manuscript Division, Library of Congress, LC310; see also Howard Ball and Philip J. Cooper, *Of Power and Right: Hugo Black, William O. Douglas, and America's Constitutional Revolution* (New York: Oxford University Press, 1992), p. 143; for these same conference notes they cite December 9, 1950, Douglas Papers, box 206.

64. Douglas, *Autobiography*, pp. 92–93.

65. "A Clear and Present Danger," *Los Angeles Times*, June 6, 1951.

66. *Chicago Tribune*, June 6, 1951.

67. *New York Times*, June 15, 1951.

68. *Newsweek*, June 18, 1951.

69. *New York Times*, September 3, 1951; Rep. Roy O. Woodruff (R-Mich.) was the accuser in an article entitled "Aid to Foe Charged to Justice Douglas."

70. *Dennis v. United States* file, no. 205, Douglas Papers.

71. *Newsweek*, June 18, 1951.

72. *Christian Century*, July 11, 1951.

73. *New Republic*, June 18, 1951, p. 5.

74. Mark H. Woolsey, "The Supreme Court: 1951–52," *Fortune*, October 11, 1951.

75. *Garner et al. v. Board of Public Works of Los Angeles et al.*, 341 U.S. 716 (1951).

Two of the petitioners had taken the oath but refused to sign the affidavit; the rest refused both to sign the affidavit and to take the oath.

76. *New Republic,* June 18, 1951, pp. 5–6.

77. *Dennis v. United States,* 339 U.S. 162 (1950).

78. *Harisides v. Shaughnessy, District Director of Immigration and Naturalization,* 342 U.S. 580 (1952). The petitioner was a Party member but quit before the passage of the 1940 Smith Act (Alien Registration Act), under which he was deported; his arguments of due process, freedom of speech, and ex post facto were rebuffed by the majority.

79. *Sacher et al. v. United States,* 343 U.S. 1 (1952).

Chapter 6. "The Courts Were of No Help Whatsoever"

1. Victor Rabinowitz, *Unrepentant Leftist: A Lawyer's Memoir* (Urbana: University of Illinois Press, 1996), p. 130.

2. Cabell Phillips, in the *New York Times,* June 10, 1951. It should be noted that early in the twentieth century a number of states enacted "criminal syndicalist" laws. Thus, while a political party was not singled out, those laws did presumably prohibit any party from advocating certain doctrines.

3. Robert Mollan, "Smith Act Prosecutions: The Effect of the *Dennis* and *Yates* Decisions," *University of Pennsylvania Law Review* 26 (1965): 705–48.

4. Michal R. Belknap, *Cold War Political Justice: The Smith Act, the Communist Party, and American Civil Liberties* (Westport, Conn.: Greenwood Press, 1977), p. 152.

5. "This Week—Twenty-One More," *New Republic,* July 2, 1951.

6. *New York Times,* June 7, 1951.

7. A. L. Wirin and Sam Rosenwein, "The Smith Act Prosecutions," *Nation,* December 12, 1953, pp. 485–90.

8. Belknap, p. 159. Another scholar agreed that the government's case was generally repetitious but that defense arguments began to change as trials continued: Peter L. Steinberg, *The Great "Red Menace": United States Prosecution of American Communists, 1947–1952* (Westport, Conn.: Greenwood Press, 1984), p. 248.

9. *United States v. Flynn,* 216 F.2d 354, 367 (2d Cir. 1954). The Korean War had ended in an armistice in 1953 but was very "hot" during the trial of the case.

10. Ibid. at 366–67. The following are some of the cases involving post-*Dennis* convictions, all of which were affirmed. *United States v. Schneiderman,* 106 F.Supp. 906 (S.D. Cal. 1952); *Wellman v. United States,* 227 F.2d 757 (6th Cir. 1955); *United States v. Silverman,* 129 F.Supp. 496 (D. Conn. 1955); *Yates v. United States,* 225 F.2d 146 (9th Cir. 1955); *United States v. Mesarosh,* 13 F.R.D. 180 (W.D. Pa. 1952), 223 F.2d 449 (3d Cir. 1955); *Frankfeld v. United States,* 198 F.2d 679 (4th Cir. 1952).

11. *United States v. Mesarosh,* 13 F.R.D. 180 (W.D. Pa. 1952); 223 F.2d 449 (3rd Cir. 1955), quote in 223 F.2d at 464. There were no dissents in the post-*Dennis* cases involving *Schneiderman, Wellman, Flynn, Silverman, Yates,* or *Frankfeld* (cited above).

12. Belknap, pp. 171–73, on bail problems.

13. Ibid., p. 154.

14. Ibid., pp. 152–57; 68 Stat. 1146 (1954).

15. Belknap, p. 175; Steinberg, pp. 251–54.

16. Eric F. Goldman, *The Crucial Decade—And After: America, 1945–1960* (New York: Knopf, 1966), p. 214.

17. *Frankfeld v. United States*, 344 U.S. 922 (1953).

18. *International Workers Order, Inc. v. People of State of New York*, 346 U.S. 857 (1953), and *Seligson v. People of State of New York*, 346 U.S. 857 (1953).

19. *Flynn v. United States*, 348 U.S. 909 (1955).

20. *Carlson et al. v. Landon, District Director of Immigration and Naturalization Service*, 342 U.S. 524 (1952). Argued November 26, 1951; decided March 10, 1952. The Eighth Amendment states: "Excessive Bail shall not be required, nor excessive fines imposed, nor cruel and unusual punishment inflicted."

21. Ibid. at 534–35.

22. Ibid. at 547–69.

23. Douglas Papers, box 213.

24. "A Lone Voice for Freedom: The Dissenting Opinion of Mr. Justice Douglas," *Education Digest*, April 1952.

25. The quotation appeared in a number of letters, e.g., to Mrs. Ralph L. Northrup, March 8, 1952. Sherman Minton Papers, Harry S. Truman Library, Independence, Mo.

26. Local 555, UPW, signed by Rose V. Russell, December 30, 1952, box 213, Douglas Papers.

27. *Sacher v. United States*, 343 U.S. 1, at 12–14 (1952).

28. Ibid. at p. 19.

29. Ibid. at p. 28.

30. Ibid. at p. 35.

31. *Sacher v. Association of the Bar of the City of New York et al.*, 347 U.S. 388 (1954).

32. *Dorsey K. Offutt, an Attorney, Petitioner, v. United States of America*, 348 U.S. 11 (1954).

33. *Wieman et al. v. Updegraff et al.*, 344 U.S. 183 (1952).

34. Ibid. at 190–91.

35. Ibid. at 193.

36. *In re Disbarment of Isserman*, 345 U.S. 286 (1953).

37. Box 222, Douglas Papers.

38. *In re Disbarment of Isserman*, 348 U.S. 1 (1954).

39. Among the numerous cases involving these issues were *United States v. Rosenberg*, 108 F. Supp. 798 (S.D.N.Y. 1952); 195 F.2d 583 (2d Cir. 1952); certiorari denied by 73 S.Ct. 20 (1952); rehearing denied by 73 S.Ct. 134 (1952); certiorari further denied by 73 S.Ct. 21, 1952 and 73 S.Ct. 134, 1952; 200 F.2d 666 (2d Cir. 1952); certiorari denied by 73 S.Ct. 949 (1953); rehearing denied by 73 S.Ct. 951 (1953); further certiorari denied by 73 S.Ct. 951 (1953). A chronology of the *Rosenberg* case and appeals is found in William Cohen, "Justice Douglas and the Rosenberg Case: Setting the Record Straight," *Cornell Law Review* 70 (1985): n. 43. Several Confederate spies were arrested, tried, and executed in the North, but these were military trials rather than under civilian law.

40. Arthur J. Sabin, *Red Scare in Court: New York Versus the International Workers Order* (Philadelphia: University of Pennsylvania Press, 1993), pp. 213–15; Record of *Rosenberg* case recited with testimony of Julius Rosenberg as cross-examined by Saypol.

41. David Caute, *The Great Fear: The Anti-Communist Purge Under Truman and Eisenhower* (New York: Simon and Schuster, 1978), pp. 62–64; William K. Klingaman, ed., *Encyclopedia of the McCarthy Era* (New York: Facts on File, 1996), pp.

209–10. As judge, Saypol's handling of the case of *Joseph Julian v. American Business Consultants* for libel after Julian was blacklisted by this organization and saw his career ruined has been severely criticized; see this entry.

42. Joseph H. Sharlitt, *Fatal Error: The Miscarriage of Justice That Sealed the Rosenbergs' Fate* (New York: Scribner's, 1989) is an in-depth study of the Supreme Court and the *Rosenberg* case.

43. Melvin I. Urofsky, *Felix Frankfurter: Judicial Restraint and Individual Liberties* (Boston: Twayne, 1991), pp. 119–27. See also C. Herman Pritchett, *Civil Liberties and the Vinson Court* (Chicago: University of Chicago Press, 1966). The author characterizes Douglas's voting as "rather puzzling" on the matter of the stay (pp. 7–8).

44. William O. Douglas, *The Court Years 1939–1975: The Autobiography of William O. Douglas* (New York: Random House, 1980), pp. 79–89.

A sense of the continuing academic interest and struggle to understand who voted how and why can be gleaned from contrasting Michael Parrish, "Cold War Justice: The Supreme Court and The Rosenbergs," *American Historical Review* 82 (1977): 805, which places Douglas as the principal villain and the retort of William Cohen, where he concludes:

> Douglas's voting pattern was not erratic, mysterious, or self-serving. Quite simply, Douglas voted on the merits of the issues presented, without reference to the public clamor either to save the Rosenbergs, or to execute them. He followed that course to the end, when his vote to grant a stay of execution showed the courage and conviction for which he is best remembered. (p. 249)

Cohen's villain is Frankfurter for having allowed his dislike of Douglas to impede the latter's efforts for court review.

45. Cohen, pp. 80–82. The voting was complicated by those justices willing to hear oral arguments and to stay the execution (Black, Frankfurter, and Jackson), as against Douglas who voted to stay the execution but not to hear oral arguments, and Burton who was willing to hear oral arguments but not to stay the execution without argument. Thus, in no variation were five votes obtained.

46. Roger K. Newman, *Hugo Black: A Biography* (New York: Pantheon Books, 1994), p. 424.

47. Ibid., pp. 421–24.

48. Douglas, pp. 82–83. Douglas reported that his home town wired him "stating the mood of the country: If you grant the Rosenbergs a stay, there will be a lynching party waiting for you here" (p. 81), and that he "became temporarily a leper," subjected to social isolation. Even his old friend Lyndon Johnson refused to speak to him (pp. 85–86). He was denounced by Congressmen and an impeachment resolution was introduced (pp. 86–87).

49. James F. Simon, *The Antagonists: Hugo Black, Felix Frankfurter, and Civil Liberties in Modern America* (New York: Simon and Schuster, 1989), pp. 203–8; quotations on pp. 205 and 207.

50. George Anastaplo, "Speed Kills: The Rosenberg Case and the Perils of Indignation," *Chicago Lawyer*, July 1979. The author's conclusion about the speed of execution was this:

> Why, then, was there such unlawyerlike haste? In order, it would seem, to attempt to stop the agitation, in this country and abroad, of the question of what should be done with the Rosenbergs. I have yet to hear of any other ex-

planation that makes any sense at all. That is, the executions were rushed, in the spirit of impassioned partisanship, in order to deprive us of the opportunity, sorely needed, to think about what was being done in our name.

He blames the government attorneys for the unprecedented rush, labeling it misconduct. The two cases that were heard on appeal by the Court were *Burns v. Wilson*, 346 U.S. 137 (1953) (rape and murder) and *Stein v. New York*, 346 U.S. 156 (1953) (murder). This latter case was also heard by the Court in 1954 and 1955.

51. There was a "retrial" of the Rosenberg case in 1993 at the American Bar Association meeting in New York. Two juries of New York citizens were used in the reenactment with considerable pains taken to make it as realistic as possible. The basic unreality could not, however, be overcome. The times were too different for a jury to find the defendants guilty; they both returned not guilty verdicts within minutes of the close of the case.

Chapter 7. Transitions

1. Henry J. Abraham, *Justices and Presidents: A Political History of Appointments to the Supreme Court* (New York: Oxford University Press, 1985), pp. 241–42. Vinson was chief justice for some seven years. He was "an indifferent, even poor" opinion writer. The Court's work output (cases heard and decided), was "exceptionally low," and Vinson "demonstrated an astounding lack of leadership." There were more five-to-four opinions under his leadership than during any comparable period. He died "a disappointed and dissatisfied occupant of the center chair." Quotes from pp. 241–44.

2. G. Edward White, "Earl Warren's Influence on the Warren Court," in Mark Tushnet, ed., *The Warren Court in Historical and Political Perspective* (Charlottesville: University Press of Virginia, 1993).

3. Bernard Schwartz, ed., *The Warren Court: A Retrospective* (New York: Oxford University Press, 1996); G. Edward White, *Earl Warren: A Public Life* (New York: Oxford University Press, 1982); Bernard Schwartz, *Super Chief: Earl Warren and His Supreme Court, A Judicial Biography* (New York: New York University Press; 1983); Ed Cray, *Chief Justice: A Biography of Earl Warren* (New York: Simon and Schuster, 1997).

4. Schwartz, preface to *Warren Court*. He could have added that Warren and his Court accomplished this feat in about one-half the time: John Marshall was chief justice for thirty-four years, Warren for sixteen.

5. Daniel J. Boorstin, *The Americans: The Democratic Experience* (New York: Random House, 1973), p. 243.

6. Justice Charles E. Whittaker was nominated in March 1957 to replace Stanley Reed. He participated in only one of the four Red Monday cases of June 17, 1957, *Service v. Dulles*, in which he voted with the majority.

7. Justice Brennan did not participate in the *Yates v. United States* decision, but he was in the majority on the other three decisions.

8. After writing the decisions in the *Yates* and *Service* cases, Harlan rewarded Eisenhower with a move to the conservative side, taking over Frankfurter's role as the leader of and spokesman for judicial restraint after Frankfurter retired in 1962 (Abraham, p. 260). Eisenhower was asked whether he had made any mistakes while he was president. His response was: "Yes, two and they are both sitting on the Supreme Court." Eisenhower was referring to Warren and Brennan

(Abraham, p. 263, citing a quote in Elmo Richardson, *The Presidency of Dwight D. Eisenhower* (Lawrence: Regents Press of Kansas, 1979, p. 108).

9. A great deal has been written about how narrow a call it was that Warren got the nomination from Eisenhower. While Warren's political support had won a promise of the first vacancy on the Court, the seat that opened up was that of chief justice, so there was a question as to whether the commitment would encompass that post. Warren felt that it did, and the president finally agreed. G. Edward White characterized the matter by stating that "Warren's nomination to the Court, in sum, was a fortuitous and relatively prosaic process." White, *Earl Warren*, p. 151.

10. Ibid., p. 154. There appears to be little in Warren's public life that would have concretely predicted who and what he was to become as chief justice—first among equals on the most powerful court in the world. Reading accounts by biographers and commentators, one comes away with the feeling that Warren put legal formalities aside to reach the heart of what could simply be expressed as "what is fair" and was willing to use the powers of his office and personality to solve problems and right wrongs.

11. Cray, p. 268.

12. White comments that given Warren's experience and temperament, he was far better suited to be chief justice than an associate justice. *Earl Warren*, p. 152.

13. White, *Earl Warren*, pp. 159–61; Anthony Lewis, "Earl Warren" in Leon Friedman and Fred L. Israel, eds., *The Justices of the United States Supreme Court, 1789–1969: Their Lives and Major Opinions* (New York: Chelsea House, 1969), 4: 2721–22; Schwartz, *Super Chief*, pp. 17–28.

14. White, *Earl Warren*, pp. 152–53; see also Schwartz, *Super Chief*, pp. 17–18; Lewis, pp. 2728–29 and Schwartz, *Warren Court*, pp. 258–64.

15. *Plessy v. Ferguson*, 163 U.S. 537 (1896).

16. *Brown v. Board of Education*, 347 U.S. 483 (1954).

17. Cray, p. 277.

18. Schwartz, *Super Chief*, p. 78.

19. Schwartz, in ibid., reprints the questions and details the manifold moves that resulted in their adoption and use (pp. 78–82).

20. Ibid., pp. 85–86.

21. Linda C. Gugin and James E. St. Clair, *Sherman Minton: New Deal Senator, Cold War Justice* (Indianapolis: Indiana Historical Society, 1997), pp. 262–65. There is no question that Minton was dedicated to using the Court to end segregation and that he was a significant force in accomplishing this goal.

22. See Cray, pp. 276–87; and Schwartz, *Super Chief*, pp. 75–110.

23. Schwartz, *Super Chief*, p. 110.

24. *Bolling v. Sharpe*, 347 U.S. 497 (1954).

25. *Mayor v. Dawson*, 350 U.S. 877 (1955), and *Holmes v. Atlanta*, 350 U.S. 879 (1955).

26. *Gayle v. Browder*, 352 U.S. 903 (1956).

27. *Johnson v. Virginia*, 373 U.S. 610, 620 (1963).

28. Earl Warren, *The Memoirs of Earl Warren* (New York: Doubleday, 1977), p. 211. See also Cray, p. 296.

29. Warren, p. 5.

30. Derrick A. Bell, Jr., "Racial Remediation: An Historical Perspective on Current Conditions," *Notre Dame Lawyer* 52 (1976): 12, citing an amicus curiae brief for the United States.

31. Ibid.

32. See speech of Justice Thurgood Marshall in 1992 quoted in the *Supreme Court Historical Society Quarterly* 18, 3 (1997): 6.:

> . . . that the success we achieved in the civil rights movement came in part because ordinary people sought to vindicate their rights in court, because they knew that in the political climate, at the time, the court system—more than the executive or the legislature—offered the greatest opportunity for social change. They understood that in a racial climate where negroes got nothing unless they could prove a right to it, that progress would come only if Afro-Americans changed the very thing that kept them enslaved—the law.

33. Tony Freyer, "Hugo L. Black and the Warren Court in Retrospect," in Tushnet, pp. 91–92, citing Black to Hugo Black, Jr., January 18, 1945, Black Papers, box 3., Manuscript Division, Library of Congress; and Tony A. Freyer, *Hugo L. Black and the Liberal Dilemma of American Liberalism* (Glenview, Ill.: Scott, Foresman/Little Brown, 1990), p. 109.

34. "To All on Equal Terms," *Time*, May 24, 1954, p. 21.

35. Roscoe Drummond, "Un-Americanism Redefined," *Chicago Sun-Times*, May 19, 1954, p. 36.

36. "All God's Chillun," *New York Times*, May 18, 1954, editorial page.

37. "Editorial Excerpts from the Nation's Press on Segregation Ruling," as reported in *New York Times*, May 18, 1954. These excerpts, from small as well as large newspapers including black newspapers, underscored the importance of *Brown* in countering communist propaganda.

38. "'Voice' Speaks in 34 Languages to Flash Court Ruling to World," *New York Times*, May 18, 1954.

39. "British Applaud Segregation Ban"; "French Voice Approval"; "Pakistanis Impressed," *New York Times*, May 19, 1954.

40. "Segregation Decision Undercuts Propaganda," *Science News Letter*, May 29, 1954. See also "Historians Laud Court's Decision;" "Court Said to End 'a Sense of Guilt,'" *New York Times*, May 18, 1954.

41. Alex Comfort, "McCarthyism: The Impact on Europe," *Nation*, April 13, 1953, pp. 302–3.

42. Ibid.

43. "Why Is U.S. Prestige Declining?" *New Republic*, August 23, 1954, p. 8 (emphasis in original).

44. Jean R. Hills, "The British Press on the 'Yanks,'" *New Republic*, August 23, 1954, pp. 9–12.

45. Herbert Tingsten, *New Republic*, September 13, 1954, p. 9.

46. See reports in *Time*, April 20, 1953, p. 26, and June 22, 1953, pp. 34, 36.

47. Richard Pells, *Not like Us: How Europeans Have Loved, Hated, and Transformed American Culture Since World War II* (New York: Basic Books, 1997), p. 82. Pells emphasized on the changing international situation, giving as examples the death of Stalin and the end of the Korean War.

48. Ibid., p. 76. The changing relationship between the Soviet Union and the United States during the Eisenhower administrations, particularly after the death of Stalin is chronicled in Walter L. Hixon, *Parting the Curtain: Propaganda, Culture, and the Cold War, 1945–1961* (New York: St. Martin's Press, 1997). Particularly relevant was his discussion of Eisenhower's role in the thaw that followed

Stalin's death, allowing cultural exchanges between the Soviets and Americans (pp. 100–119).

49. Robert Goldstein, *The American Nightmare: Senator Joseph R. McCarthy and the Politics of Hate* (Indianapolis: Bobbs-Merrill, 1973), p. 173.

50. McCarthy had attacked Marshall in 1951 when Truman fired General Douglas MacArthur. Marshall was then secretary of defense and had recommended MacArthur's dismissal. Richard M. Fried, *Nightmare in Red: The McCarthy Era in Perspective* (New York: Oxford University Press, 1990), p. 331.

51. Allen Weinstein, *Perjury: The Hiss-Chambers Case* (New York: Knopf, 1978), p. 513.

52. Richard G. Powers, *Secrecy and Power: The Life of J. Edgar Hoover* (New York: Free Press, 1987), pp. 300–301.

53. Ibid., pp. 316–18; Athan G. Theoharis and John Stuart Cox, *The Boss: J. Edgar Hoover and the Great American Inquisition* (Philadelphia: Temple University Press, 1988), pp. 183–97. Theoharis and Cox state that Hoover flagrantly lied in denying the unauthorized dissemination of FBI file information to McCarthy, his staff, and his subcommittee (pp. 17–18).

54. Powers, pp. 321–22.

55. This cutoff is confirmed by a memorandum, FBI Executives' Conference to FBI Director, October 14, 1953, FBI 121–23278, wherein the pipeline that had supplied McCarthy was shut down in late summer 1953. Athan G. Theoharis, *From the Secret Files of J. Edgar Hoover* (Chicago: Ivan R. Dee, 1991), p. 264.

56. Theoharis, pp. 292–99.

57. Goldstein, p. 155.

58. Fried, pp. 137–39.

59. Ibid., pp. 137–43.

60. Ibid., p. 142.

61. Powers, p. 337. Powers's notes on pp. 565–66 contain extensive lists of titles of FBI papers on the Communist Party supplied to the Eisenhower administration from 1953 to 1960.

62. Ibid., pp. 174–76; Walter F. Murphy, *Congress and the Court: A Case Study in the American Political Process* (Chicago: University of Chicago Press, 1962), pp. 86–90. Many southerners became avid anti-communists after the *Brown* and other desegregation decisions. It bolstered their case to see a communist conspiracy behind civil rights agitation. Thus the NAACP was alleged to be part of the conspiracy, and "Impeach Earl Warren" became popular with the radical right in the South.

63. Fried, pp. 175–76, quotes Senator Eastland complaining of "one pro-communist decision after another," with McCarthy responding, "you are so right" and Eastland's speculation that "some secret, but very powerful Communist or pro-communist influence" infected the Court.

64. *International Workers Order, Inc. v. People of State of New York*, 346 U.S. 857 (1953).

65. *Barsky v. Board of Regents*, 347 U.S. 442 (1954).

66. *Galvan v. Press*, 347 U.S. 522 (1954).

67. Ibid. at 533.

68. Lewis, p. 2729.

69. Ibid., at p. 2731.

70. Murphy, p. 86. Warren's principal biographer, the late Bernard Schwartz, agrees in *Super Chief* on the change in Warren's position, noting that this meant his refusal to go along with Frankfurter's philosophy of judicial restraint.

Schwartz states that James Reston of *New York Times* recognized a "liberal nucleus" of the three (p. 200).

71. Lewis, p. 2731.

72. Ibid., pp. 2731–32.

73. Earl Warren, "The Law and the Future," *Fortune*, November 1955, p. 106. Warren wrote, "In all times and places he [man] has had a sense of justice and a desire for justice. Any child expresses this fact of nature [in] his first judgment that this or that 'isn't fair.' A legal system is simply a mature and sophisticated attempt . . . to institutionalize this sense of justice and to free men from the terror and unpredictability of arbitrary force."

74. Jack H. Pollack, *Earl Warren: The Judge Who Changed America* (Englewood Cliffs, N.J.: Prentice-Hall, 1979), pp. 178–79.

75. Leo Katcher, *Earl Warren: A Political Biography* (New York: McGraw-Hill, 1967), p. 336.

76. Warren, "Law and the Future," p. 107.

77. Ibid., p. 108.

78. Ibid., p. 109.

79. Ibid., p. 107.

80. *United States v. Flynn*, 216 F.2d 354 (2d Cir. 1954).

81. Tinsley E. Yarbrough, *John Marshall Harlan: Great Dissenter of the Warren Court* (New York: Oxford University Press, 1992), pp. 71–113.

82. *Quinn v. United States*, 349 U.S. 155 (1955).

83. *Emspak v. United States*, 349 U.S. 190 (1955); *Bart v. United States*, 349 U.S. 219 (1955).

84. Preliminary Statement by the Chief Justice; *Emspak v. United States*, April 11, 1955, no. 573, Warren Papers, Manuscript Division, Library of Congress.

85. Ibid., p. 2.

86. *Bart v. United States*, 349 U.S. 219 (1955); see also Warren's "Preliminary Statement," April 11, 1955, no. 572, Warren Papers, Manuscript Division, Library of Congress.

87. Harlan to Warren, no. 574, April 25, 1955, Warren Papers.

88. Douglas to Warren, no. 574, April 28, 1955, Warren Papers.

89. Black to Warren, April 28, 1955, no. 574, Warren Papers.

90. "The Court and the Cold War," *Nation*, June 4, 1953, p. 475. The editorial noted the implicit attack on the pejorative use of "Fifth Amendment Communist" contained in the majority's opinion.

91. "Supreme Court on Fifth Amendment," *America*, June 11, 1955, p. 283. See also "Defending the Fifth," *Commonweal*, June 17, 1955, p. 270.

92. *Yates v. United States*, 354 U.S. 298 (1957). Certiorari was granted October 17, 1955.

93. *Supplementary Detailed Staff Reports on Intelligence Activities and the Rights of Americans*, Book 3, *Final Report of Select Committee to Study Governmental Operations With Respect to Intelligence Activities/United States Senate*, April 23, 1976 (Washington, D.C.: GPO, 1976) p. 449.

94. *Pennsylvania v. Nelson*, 350 U.S. 497 (1956).

95. *Slochower v. Board of Education of New York City*, 350 U.S. 551 (1956).

96. Ibid. at 557.

97. *The Communist Party of the United States v. Subversive Activities Control Board*, 351 U.S. 115 (1956).

98. 64 Stat. 987.

99. *Communist Party v. SACB*, 351 U.S. at 125.

100. Peter Irons and Stephanie Guitton, eds., *May It Please the Court: The Most Significant Oral Arguments Made Before the Supreme Court Since 1955* (New York: New Press, 1993), pp. 137–46.

101. *Cole v. Young,* 351 U.S. 536 (1956).

102. Ibid. at 540. See also Frankfurter's review of the case and his position on the issues in the paper entitled *Cole v. Young,* no. 15/pt.2, Frankfurter Papers, Harvard University.

103. *Cole,* 351 U.S. at 566.

104. See Murphy, pp. 89–91. Murphy points out that the "ideological alliance" of business interests, segregationists, and ultraconservatives joined against the Court was motivated by the fear that the Court would interfere with the proliferation of right-to-work laws.

105. Warren, *Memoirs,* pp. 319–37; William O. Douglas, *The Court Years 1939–1975: The Autobiography of William O. Douglas* (New York: Random House, 1980), pp. 96–98.

106. Warren, Memoirs, p. 325.

107. Murphy, pp. 92–96.

108. Douglas, p. 97.

109. Murphy, p. 97.

110. *Congressional Record,* Senate, April 11, 1956, p. 6063.

111. *Congressional Record,* House, April 16, 1956, p. 6385.

112. *Congressional Record,* House, April 16, 1956, p. 6386.

113. *Congressional Record,* House, May 2, 1956, p. 7341.

114. *Congressional Record,* Senate, May 2, 1956, p. 10173.

115. "A Crime Against the Nation," *America,* April 14, 1956.

116. *New Republic,* April 16, 1956, p. 5.

117. *New York Times,* June 13, 1956, p. 36.

118. *Christian Century,* June 27, 1956, p. 765.

119. "News of Science," *Science,* June 29, 1956, p. 1165.

120. Research conducted by Philip Farb, research assistant to the author.

121. Peter H. Buckingham, *America Sees Red: Anti-Communism in America, 1870s to 1980s* (Claremont, Calif.: Regina Books, 1988), p. 102; Harvey Matusow, *False Witness* (New York: Cameron and Kahn, 1955). Matusow was one of the three perjurers involved in the *Subversive Activities Control Board* case.

122. Buckingham, p. 102.

123. "Why Top Russ Talked to Publisher and Aides," *Chicago Herald & Examiner,* February 18, 1955.

124. *New York Times,* May 8, 1956.

125. Cray, pp. 322–23; Warren, *Memoirs,* p. 374.

126. C. Hermann Pritchett, "The Warren Court: Turn Toward Liberalism," *Nation,* July 14, 1956, pp. 31–34.

Chapter 8. The Red Monday Cases

1. Stephen J. Friedman, "William J. Brennan," in Leon Friedman and Fred L. Israel, eds., *The Justices of the United States Supreme Court, 1789–1969: Their Lives and Major Opinions* (New York: Chelsea House, 1969), 4: 2849–52; Henry J. Abraham *Justices and Presidents: A Political History of Appointments to the Supreme Court* (New York: Oxford University Press, 1985), pp. 262–63.

2. Ed Cray, *Chief Justice: A Biography of Earl Warren* (New York: Simon and Schuster, 1997), pp. 323–24.

3. William O. Douglas, *The Court Years, 1939–1975: The Autobiography of William O. Douglas* (New York: Random House, 1980), p. 243.

4. Abraham, p. 379; Bernard Schwartz, *A Book of Legal Lists: The Best and Worst in American Law* (New York: Oxford University Press, 1997), pp. 30–62. Bernard Schwartz, *Super Chief: Earl Warren and His Supreme Court, A Judicial Biography* (New York: New York University Press, 1983), states that Whittaker "may have been the worst Justice of the century" (p. 216).

5. *Service v. Dulles*, 354 U.S. 363 (1957).

6. *Kent v. Dulles*, 357 U.S. 116 (1958).

7. *Beilan v. Board of Education*, 357 U.S. 399 (1958).

8. *Schware v. Board of Bar Examiners of New Mexico*, 353 U.S. 232 (May 6, 1957); *Konigsberg v. State Bar of California*, 353 U.S. 252 (May 6, 1957).

9. Stone, p. 196.

10. *Schware*, at 235.

11. Schwartz, *Super Chief*, p. 229.

12. Clark to Black, n.d., no. 330, *Schware*, Harold H. Burton Papers, Manuscript Division, Library of Congress.

13. Clark to Black, memorandum, 5/2/57, Burton Papers.

14. Stone, pp. 196–97.

15. *Konigsberg*, 353 U.S.

16. Ibid., pp. 268–69.

17. Stone, p. 197.

18. Ibid., pp. 196–97.

19. *Konigsberg*, 353 U.S. at 276–312.

20. Warren to Black, no. 329, *Konigsberg*, Hugo L. Black Papers, Manuscript Division, Library of Congress. In Justice Black's *Konigsberg* file is an undated article torn out of a newspaper entitled "800 Hungarian Lawyers Disbarred in Red Crackdown on Intellectuals." It discussed reports of the Hungarian Communist Party investigation of the "loyalty" of 3,000 lawyers. Its juxtaposition to these two American cases was apparently meaningful to Black.

21. Stone, p. 199.

22. "Schware, Konigsberg and Independence of the Bar: The Return to Reason," *Lawyers Guild Review* (Summer 1957): 48–52.

23. *Konigsberg*, 353 U.S. at 273–74.

24. *Konigsberg v. State Bar of California*, 366 U.S. 36 (1961). In his autobiography, Justice Douglas recalled his recognition that a "new majority" existed, and that it decided this second *Konigsberg* case (Douglas, p. 100).

25. *Jencks v. United States*, 353 U.S. 657, 667 (1957).

26. Ibid. at 672.

27. Ibid. at 681–82.

28. Walter F. Murphy, *Congress and the Court: A Case Study on the American Political Process* (Chicago: University of Chicago Press, 1962), p. 110.

29. Schwartz, *Super Chief*, pp. 226–28.

30. Michal R. Belknap, *Cold War Political Justice: The Smith Act, the Communist Party, and American Civil Liberties* (Westport, Conn.: Greenwood Press, 1977), p. 265.

31. Kenneth O'Reilly, *Hoover and the Un-Americans: The FBI, HUAC, and the Red Menace* (Philadelphia: Temple University Press, 1983), p. 240.

32. Alexander Charns, *Cloak and Gavel: FBI Wiretaps, Bugs, Informers and the Supreme Court* (Urbana: University of Illinois Press, 1992), p. 8.

33. Ibid., p. 198.

34. Robert Morris, "Time Is Running Out!" *American Mercury*, November 1957, p. 135 (reprint of a speech given some months earlier).

35. Raymond Moley, "Files on Parade," *Newsweek*, June 17, 1957.

36. Cited in Murphy, p. 128. Murphy quotes from a variety of newspapers throughout the country to demonstrate the knee-jerk reaction to the *Jencks* decision. See pp. 128–30.

37. "The Jencks Decision," *Commonweal*, June 2, 1957, p. 294.

38. Murphy, p. 128.

39. *Statement by the Honorable Herbert Brownell, Jr., Attorney General of the United States*, June 28, 1957, Brownell Papers, box 156, folder: speeches vol. 2, Dwight D. Eisenhower Library, Abeline, Kansas.

40. Brownell to Adams, June 24, 1957, box 371, folder: 100 Judiciary (2), Central Files: Official File of 99–2(12), Brownell Papers.

41. Murphy, p. 131. Murphy's work on tracing the history of the Jencks Bill is the standard resource and is relied on in this rendition.

42. Ibid., pp. 140–41.

43. Ibid., p. 149.

44. Pub. L. 85-269; 71 Stat. 595.

45. Murphy, pp. 152–53.

46. "Jencks Revised," *New Republic*, September 16, 1957.

47. Ibid., p. 153.

48. *Service v. Dulles et al.*, 54 U.S. 363 (1957).

49. Schwartz, *Super Chief*, pp. 231–32.

50. E. J. Kahn, Jr., *The China Hands: America's Foreign Service Officers and What Befell Them* (New York: Viking Press, 1975), pp. 267–76.

51. Cray, p. 335.

52. *Watkins v. United States*, 354 U.S. 178, 182 (1957).

53. Ibid. at 183.

54. Ibid. at 182.

55. Ibid. at 185; see also Walter Goodman, *The Committee: The Extraordinary Career of the House Committee on Un-American Activities* (New York: Farrar, Straus and Giroux, 1968), pp. 358–59.

56. Goodman, p. 358.

57. Schwartz, *Super Chief*, p. 235.

58. *Watkins*, at 214–15.

59. Tinsley E. Yarbrough, *John Marshall Harlan: Great Dissenter of the Warren Court* (New York: Oxford University Press, 1992), pp. 200–210.

60. *Sweezy v. New Hampshire, by Wyman, Attorney General*, 354 U.S. 234, 242 (1957). Justice Clark's dissent pointed out that there was no sanction beyond branding a person as subversive and that he had not been found to be subversive, only in contempt of Wyman as interrogator. Ibid. at 270.

61. Ibid. at 241–42. In 1948 the Democratic Party, with Truman seeking reelection, suffered two defections. One split-off was a left-wing independent party, the Progressive Party, with former Secretary of Agriculture Henry A. Wallace as its standard-bearer; the other the segregationist Dixiecrat Party, with Senator Strom Thurmond (D-S.C.) as its leader.

62. David Caute, *The Great Fear: The Anti-Communist Purge Under Truman and Eisenhower* (New York: Simon and Schuster, 1978), pp. 75–76.

63. "Remarks of Louis C. Wyman, Esq.," *Journal of the Bar Association of the District of Columbia* (November 1957): 597–602.

64. *Sweezy,* 354 U.S. at 250.

65. Frankfurter to Warren, memorandum, June 3, 1957, box 580, *Watkins* and *Sweezy,* Warren Papers, Library of Congress.

66. Ibid., p. 2.

67. Harlan to Warren, May 31, 1957. Unconvinced by further argument, Justice Harlan, in a letter to Warren, stated, "I still think *Sweezy,* being a state case, we are not concerned here with anything more than the 'free speech' issue." Harlan to Warren, June 6, 1957, Warren Papers.

68. Warren to Frankfurter, memorandum, June 5, 1957, Warren Papers.

69. *Sweezy,* 353 U.S. at 265. Wyman, in his speech, critically referred to these words of Frankfurter, expressing dismay that the justice just did not understand Communist activity and subversion. Wyman, p. 550.

70. *Sweezy,* 353 U.S. at 268.

71. Ibid. at 250.

72. Ibid. at 270.

73. Bernard Schwartz, *Inside the Warren Court* (New York: Doubleday, 1983), p. 120.

74. Stone, pp. 204–206.

75. *Dennis v. United States,* 341 U.S. 494 (1951).

76. *Flynn v. United States,* 216 F.2d 354 (2d Cir. 1954); (1955); rehearing denied 348 U.S. 909 (1955); petition for rehearing denied 348 U.S. 956 (1955).

77. Yarbrough, pp. 190–91.

78. One Warren biographer attributes Harlan's change to the influence of Warren. Jack H. Pollack, *Earl Warren: The Judge Who Changed America* (Englewood Cliffs, N.J.: Prentice-Hall, 1979), p. 189.

79. The argument can be made that it was the fear of opening the jail doors to those convicted under the Smith Act that militated a less dramatic position.

80. *Dennis,* 341 U.S. at 581 (Justice Black dissenting).

81. Caute, p. 140.

82. Ibid. pp. 200–201.

83. Belknap, p. 239. The "attempt" referred to was the "Spirit of Geneva," coming as a result of the meeting of President Eisenhower (and other Allied leaders) with Premier Nikolai A. Bulganin and First Secretary of the Communist Party Nikita Khrushchev in Geneva, Switzerland in the summer of 1955, generating hope for a thawing of the Cold War.

84. Schwartz, *Super Chief,* pp. 232–33.

85. Ibid., p. 233.

86. Yarbrough, pp. 191–92.

87. This analysis relies on research by Elizabeth Niendorf.

88. William K. Klingaman, *Encyclopedia of the McCarthy Era* (New York: Facts on File, 1996), pp. 43–44.

89. *Yates v. United States,* 354 U.S. 328, 310 (1957).

90. Ibid. at 318.

91. Ibid. at 320.

92. Ibid. at 321.

93. Ibid. at 325.

94. Ibid. at 326–27.

95. Lawrence M. Friedman, *A History of American Law* (New York: Simon and Schuster, 1985), pp. 150–51.

96. Rep. Davis (D-Ga.), House, remarks of, *Congressional Record*, June 20, 1957.
97. *Yates*, 354 U.S. at 327.
98. Ibid. at 328–9.
99. Ibid. at 331.
100. "Secret Khrushchev Talk on Stalin 'Phobia' Related," *New York Times*, March 16, 1956; "The Kremlin—The Truth of Today," *Time*, April 9, 1956; "Khrushchev," *Chicago Tribune*, March 20, 1956.
101. Herbert Block, *Herblock's Special for Today* (New York: Simon and Schuster, 1958), p. 210.
102. *Yates*, 354 U.S. at 339.
103. Ibid. at 340.
104. Ibid. at 341.
105. Ibid. at 344.
106. Ibid. at 349.

Chapter 9. Red Monday: The Aftermath

1. *New York Times*, June 18, 1957.
2. Others reported to have been suicide or heart attack victims of HUAC hearings included Canadian Ambassador E. Herbert Norman, Harry Dexter White, and actor John Garfield. *Chicago Sun-Times*, June 21, 1957.
3. "2 Down, 18 Felled by Heat," "High Court Upholds Silence on Reds," *Washington Post & Times Herald*, June 18, 1957; "90 Degree Forecast Again Today," "High Court Upsets Terms of 14 Reds," *Chicago Daily Tribune*, June 18, 1957; "97 Heat Due Today," "Supreme Court Frees 5 Cal. Reds, Orders New Trial for 9 Others," *Los Angeles Times*, June 18, 1957.
4. *New York Times*, June 18, 1957.
5. James Reston, *New York Times*, June 18, 1957.
6. *New York Times*, June 18, 1957.
7. *Daily Worker*, June 19, 1957.
8. Ibid.
9. For example, newspapers quoted from the *Daily Worker* to show the "enemy"'s glee. Typical was the *New York Journal-American*, whose editorial on June 19, 1957 quoted the *Daily Worker* and ended its comments, "That's what the Communist leaders think of the Supreme Court decisions."
10. *St. Louis Post-Dispatch*, June 18, 1957.
11. *Washington Post*, June 18, 1957.
12. *Atlanta Constitution*, June 20, 1957.
13. *New York Times*, June 18, 1957.
14. *New York Daily Mirror*, June 18, 1957.
15. *Chicago Tribune*, June 18, 1957.
16. *Cleveland Plain Dealer*, June 18, 1957.
17. *New York Journal-American*, June 19, 1957.
18. *Portland Oregonian*, June 18, 1957.
19. *New York World Telegram & Sun*, June 18, 1957.
20. James Reston, *New York Times*, June 22, 1957.
21. Walter Lippmann, *Washington Post & Times Herald*, June 25, 1957.
22. George Sokolsky, *Washington Post & Times Herald*, June 24, 1957.
23. Dorothy Thompson, *Washington Star*, June 27, 1957.
24. Richard L. Strout, *Christian Science Monitor*, September 29, 1957.

25. *Time,* July 1, 1957, pp. 1–17.

26. *Newsweek,* July 1, 1957, p. 20.

27. *Newsweek,* July 1, 1957, p. 21.

28. *Business Week,* July 6, 1957, pp. 33–36.

29. David Lawrence, *U.S. News & World Report,* June 28, 1957, pp. 150–52.

30. *Atlantic Monthly,* August 8, 1957, p. 16.

31. *Nation,* June 29, 1957, p. 558.

32. Alan Barth, *New Republic,* July 1, 1957.

33. David Reisman, "New Critics of the Court," *New Republic,* July 29, 1957.

34. Eric Sevareid, reprinted in the *Reporter,* July 11, 1957.

35. *Christian Science Monitor,* June 19, 1957, p. 22.

36. *Commonweal,* July 5, 1957, p. 340.

37. *Chicago Daily Tribune,* June 18, 1957, p. 14.

38. *Chattanooga News—Free Press,* July 1, 1957, p. 6.

39. *Washington Post & Times Herald,* June 22, 1957, p. A8.

40. Walter F. Murphy, *Congress and the Court: A Case Study in the American Political Process* (Chicago: University of Chicago Press, 1962), p. 111.

41. *Congressional Record,* 103 Cong., 1957, p. 9721.

42. *Congressional Record,* 103 Cong., 1957, p. 9725.

43. *Congressional Record,* 103 Cong., 1957, pp. 9890–91.

44. *Congressional Record,* 103 Cong., 1957, p. 9895.

45. *Congressional Record,* 103 Cong., 1957, pp. 10122–23.

46. *Congressional Record,* remarks of Clare E. Hoffman (R-Mich.), 103 Cong., 1957, p. 10123.

47. *Congressional Record,* remarks of Overton Brooks (D-La.), 103 Cong., 1957, p. 10187.

48. *Congressional Record,* 103 Cong., 1957, p. 10279.

49. Murphy, p. 116.

50. *Congressional Record,* 103 Cong., 1957, pp. 11928–29.

51. Murphy, p. 154.

52. Ibid., p. 156.

53. Ibid., p. 183.

54. No. 1, part 2, *Emspak* case, no. 67, Felix Frankfurter Papers, Harvard University.

55. Bernard Schwartz, *Super Chief: Earl Warren and His Supreme Court, a Judicial Biography* (New York: New York University Press, 1983), pp. 250–54.

56. G. Edward White, *Earl Warren: A Public Life* (New York: Oxford University Press, 1982), pp. 173–90.

57. Frankfurter's clashes with Black are detailed in Roger K. Newman, *Hugo Black: A Biography* (New York: Pantheon Books, 1994), pp. 480–87.

58. *Rowoldt v. Perfetto,* 355 U.S. 115 (1957).

59. *Galvan v. Press,* 374 U.S. 522 (1954).

60. *Kent v. Dulles,* 357 U.S. 116 (1958). Kent had stated under oath, when he testified at the IWO trial, that he was never a Party member, but he was sympathetic to socialist and communist causes and clearly affiliated himself with such causes.

61. Ibid. at 121.

62. Ibid. at 141.

63. Walter Goodman, *The Committee: The Extraordinary Career of the House Committee on Un-American Activities* (New York: Farrar, Straus and Giroux, 1968), p. 361.

64. Michal R. Belknap, *Cold War Political Justice: The Smith Act, the Communist Party, and American Civil Liberties* (Westport, Conn.: Greenwood Press, 1977), p. 259.

65. *Annual Report of the Attorney General of the United States for the Fiscal Year Ending June 30, 1958* (Washington, D.C.: Department of Justice), its prosecutions in December 1957.

66. The government dismissed its prosecutions in December 1957.

67. Attorney general's *Report*, fiscal 1958, p. 255. *United States v. Mesarosh*, 352 U.S. 862 (1957).

68. Belknap, pp. 259–60.

69. Ibid., p. 262; *Scales v. United States*, 360 U.S. 924 (1959); 361 U.S. 952; with *Noto*; 367 U.S. 203 (1961); *Noto v. United States*, 367 U.S. 290 (1961); *United States v. Blumberg*, 207 F. Supp. 28 (E.D. Pa. 1962); *United States v. Lightfoot*, 228 F. 2d 561 (7th Cir. 1956).

70. Belknap, p. 263.

71. Ibid., pp. 263–64.

72. Prior to the Court's ruling, the government admitted that, in the light of *Jencks*, both ought to be remanded (Belknap, p. 265). See also attorney general's *Report*, fiscal 1958, pp. 256–57.

73. Belknap, p. 267. This explanation was the result of a personal interview between Belknap and Justice Clark in 1976. This same point is made by Murphy at p. 229.

74. Murphy, p. 246; Belknap, p. 268.

75. *Scales*, at pp. 221–23.

76. Ibid. at p. 263.

77. *Noto v. United States*, 367 U.S. 290 (1961).

78. Ibid. at 298.

79. Clark to Harlan, box 47, no. 494, *Noto*, Harlan Papers, Manuscript Division, Library of Congress.

80. *Hellman v. United States*, 298 F.2d 810 (9th Cir. 1961). See Mack Rohr, "Communists and the First Amendment: The Shaping of Freedom of Advocacy in the Cold War Era," *San Diego Law Review* 28 (1991): 21 n. 143. See also Belknap, pp. 270–72 for commentaries on *Scales* and *Noto*, as well as subsequent developments in terms of further membership prosecutions. In the fiscal 1961 U.S. attorney general's *Report*, the Justice Department was reported as having undertaken a full scale review of membership cases (p. 257); the report also recounted the highlights of the *Scales* and *Noto* cases.

81. Belknap, p. 270.

82. President John F. Kennedy commuted Scales's sentence to time served, so his imprisonment lasted fifteen months. Tinsley E. Yarbrough, *John Marshall Harlan: Great Dissenter of the Warren Court* (New York: Oxford University Press, 1992), p. 196.

83. Belknap, p. 272.

84. Yarbrough, p. 179. The biographer also expresses the belief that Scales was innocent; that crucial evidence against him was false and thus that "he had been [wrongly] sent to prison with the Supreme Court's approval" (p. 179).

85. *Barenblatt v. U.S.*, 360 U.S. 109 (1959).

86. *Uphaus v. Wyman, Attorney General of New Hampshire*, 360 U.S. 72 (1959).

87. Ibid.

88. Schwartz, *Super Chief*, p. 324.

89. *Uphaus v. Wyman*, at pp. 93–94. Among the accusations in the report were those that accused citizens of having "signed open letters and petitions against deportations, to have criticized the Federal Bureau of Investigation, to have given free medical treatment to Communist Party officials, and the like" (p. 92).

90. *Barenblatt v. United States*, 360 U.S. 109, June 8, 1959.

91. Yarbrough, pp. 201–203.

92. *Barenblatt* 360 U.S. 109 at 166.

93. Goodman, *The Committee*, p. 363.

94. Frankfurter to Brennan, January 7, 1959, *Uphaus v. Wyman*, box 64, William J. Brennan, Jr. Papers, Library of Congress.

95. Murphy, pp. 246–51.

96. Murphy termed these cases a "tactical withdrawal," suggesting perhaps that this was a preconceived plan (pp. 246, 267).

97. Murphy, p. 266.

Chapter 10. In Retrospect

1. John E. Haynes and Harvet Klehr, "Outed from the Cold," *Weekly Standard*, April 15, 1996. See also Pavel A. Sodoplatov, Anatoli P. Sodoplatov, Jerrold Schecter, and Leona Schecter, *Special Tasks: The Memoirs of an Unwanted Witness* (New York: Little, Brown, 1994); John E. Haynes, *Red Scare or Red Menace? American Communism and Anticommunism in the Cold War Era* (Chicago: Ivan R. Dee, 1996); Harvey Klehr and Ronald Radosh, *The Amerasia Case: Prelude to McCarthyism* (Chapel Hill: University of North Carolina Press, 1996); Harvey Klehr, John Earl Haynes, and Fridrikh Igorevich Firsov, *The Secret World of American Communism* (New Haven, Conn.: Yale University Press, 1995); John E. Haynes and Harvey Klehr, "Messages from Moscow: What the Secret Cables Say," *Weekly Standard*, November 1995; and Haynes and Klehr, "Two Gentlemen of Venona," *Weekly Standard*, May 13, 1996.

2. Haynes, *Red Scare*, p. 200; Richard G. Powers, *Not Without Honor: The History of American Anticommunism* (New York: Free Press, 1995).

3. Courtney Leatherman, "New Fight About the Old Left," *Chronicle of Higher Education*, June 7, 1996; John B. Judis, "TRB from Washington: The Heretic," *New Republic*, June 17, 1996. The author concludes:

Radosh, as the historian Martin Sklar told me, is a victim of "left-wing McCarthyism." McCarthy attempted to discredit liberals by labeling them communists. He sometimes succeeded in getting them fired—not necessarily because their employers believed they were communists, but because they feared the publicity. It's an apt analogy but not one that would occur to the academic zealots of today's left, who, like their distant predecessors, are blinded by the light of their own self-righteousness.

4. Stanley I. Kutler, reviewing Klehr and Radosh's *Amerasia Spy Case*, in the *Chicago Tribune*, June 9, 1996. Another review was more favorable; see William L. O'Neill's review of this book in *New York Times Book Review*, March 3, 1996, which concluded, "People who want to believe all victims of McCarthyism were innocent will not care for this book. But anyone with an open mind and a taste for deception will find it valuable, even gripping."

5. Haynes and Klehr, "Outed from the Cold" p. 16.

6. William K. Klingaman, *Encyclopedia of the McCarthy Era* (New York: Facts on File, 1996), pp. 92–93.

7. Peter L. Steinberg, *The Great "Red Menace": United States Prosecution of Communists, 1947–1952* (Westport, Conn.: Greenwood Press, 1984), pp. 96–97.

8. David H. Bennett, *The Party of Fear: From Nativist Movements to the New Right in American History* (New York: Vintage Books, 1996), pp. 443–63.

9. *Chicago Tribune*, April 25, 1997, sec. 1, p. 27.

10. *Brandenburg v. Ohio*, 395 U.S. 444 (1969); see R. J. Larizza, "Paranoia, Patriotism, and the Citizen Militia Movement: Constitutional Right or Criminal Conduct?" *Mercer Law Review* 47 (1996): 581, which includes a discussion of the applicability of the *Brandenburg* standard. See also Joseph Grinstein, "Jihad and the Constitution: The First Amendment Implications of Combatting Religiously Motivated Terrorism." *Yale Law Journal* 105 (1996): 1347.

11. Larizza, p. 592.

12. *New York Times*, March 19, 1951.

13. Nicholas K. Geranios, "Jury Proves Hurdle in Domestic Terror Cases," *Chicago Daily Law Bulletin*, April 7, 1997. The author claims that federal charges against "homegrown terrorists end in dismissals, acquittals or mistrials more than 57 percent of the time." One source for these statistics came from Brent L. Smith and Gregory P. Orvis, "America's Response to Terrorism: An Empirical Analysis of Federal Intervention Strategies During the 1980s," *Justice Quarterly* (December 1993). Smith, in a letter to this author, dated April 29, 1997, challenged the appropriateness of the statistics contained in the news article but added that "the overall thrust of his summary of our work is correct: that prosecution rates are lower for crimes when political motive is mentioned or is a major aspect of the case." The opposite was true in the 1950s.

14. Not only is the antigovernment movement, in all its many manifestations, an indicator of changed attitudes, but it can also be seen in related attitudes. ·*Parade*, the Sunday newspaper magazine, has a column that is read by millions weekly, "Walter Scott's Personality Parade." The following question and answer were given in the June 1, 1997, issue:

Q: Why hasn't the public reacted more negatively to all the scandals involving the Clinton White House, especially given the fact that the President and his men have been caught in so many misstatements, untruths and prevarications?—J. S., Washington, D.C.

A: The public's apathy indicates that President Clinton has succeeded in convincing many Americans that, while his administration may be guilty of numerous misdeeds, so are his opponents in the Republican Party. This deliberate "everybody-does-it" strategy has worked because the public seems to believe that all politicians are bad. However, Mr. Clinton is concerned that this apathy could easily turn into outrage.

Another example is contained in an article by Francis X. Clines, "America's Jaded Eye on Sex in Public Life," *New York Times*, June 1, 1997, sec. E, p. 5.

15. *Brandenberg v. Ohio*, 395 U.S. 444 (1969).

Table of Cases

Index

Acknowledgments

Without the consistent support of the administration of The John Marshall Law School, this book could not have been written. Over a period of six years, the school showed its commitment in the form of summer research grants, a sabbatical leave, and funds for research assistants who worked with me at the school and at libraries and archives throughout the country.

Beyond these forms of assistance was the intangible but vital encouragement and support that did not flag. Special thanks go to Dean Robert G. Johnston, who always demonstrated interest and enthusiasm for the work. Other administrators who were helpful and sensitive to the needs involved in writing this book were Deans Susan L. Brody and John E. Corkery.

Special thanks also go to Professor Samuel R. Olkin, a legal historian colleague at The John Marshall Law School, who read and critiqued the manuscript. Dr. Duke Frederick, professor emeritus of history, Northeastern Illinois University, read and critiqued the entire manuscript, as he did my last book. Especially appreciated, once again, was his sharp eye for historical detail.

The John Marshall Law School library staff was always of assistance in obtaining source materials and searching out specific requests.

During the years of research, the work of law students as research assistants was invaluable. Thus, I owe a great debt to Hugh Balsam and Philip Farb for their contributions in undertaking major research projects related to the work. They not only provided superior leg work but also read and made valuable comments on the manuscript.

James Lasser, before commencing law studies at Vanderbilt University Law School, spent a summer working as a researcher and made many valuable contributions, one of which was his knowledge of the world of political cartoons. Other law student researchers included Susan Lasser, John O. Anderson, Eric C. Hoffman, and Donella McKinnon. Ms. Mc-

Kinnon did a superb job of organizing all of the research files and devising clever ways of accessing topics and materials.

A rare benefit was bestowed on this work by Elizabeth K. Niendorf, whose superb editing skills were so important and so generously given. Additionally, her optimism helped me over many difficult and taxing times.

The typing and constant retyping of the manuscript was ably handled under the overall supervision of Gwen Konigsfeld, who took over from others and completed the actual work of transcribing my handwritten manuscript into the computer. Yolanda Aparicio, Vanessa Saffold, and Diane Gordon contributed major typing efforts over the years of preparation, as did Elizabeth Niendorf.

I am especially indebted to Ms. Lucy S. Caswell of the Cartoon Research Library at Ohio State University for her assistance with the political cartoons found in this book.

My thanks and gratitude also go to Eric Halpern, director of the University of Pennsylvania Press, for his abiding belief in the worth of the book and for his sensitive guidance through the evaluation and production process.

Many other people, institutions, and archival sources provided material and expertise. To all, I am grateful. More than six years of research and writing make one realize the interdependence of academicians and academic institutions in the production of any work. It is a truism that has resounded through the ages: we all benefit from the paths trodden by those who have labored in these fields before we came to them.